A BOMB IN
EVERY ISSUE

A BOMB IN EVERY ISSUE

How the Short, Unruly Life of *Ramparts* Magazine Changed America

Peter Richardson

THE NEW PRESS

NEW YORK
LONDON

Published in the United States by The New Press, New York, 2009
Distributed by Perseus Distribution

978-1-59558-439-7 (hc.)
CIP data is available

The New Press was established in 1990 as a not-for-profit alternative to the large,
commercial publishing houses currently dominating the book publishing industry.
The New Press operates in the public interest rather than for private gain, and is
committed to publishing, in innovative ways, works of educational, cultural, and
community value that are often deemed insufficiently profitable.

www.thenewpress.com

Composition by dix!
This book was set in Bembo

Printed in the United States of America

10   9   8   7   6   5   4   3   2   1

CONTENTS

INTRODUCTION

In May 1962, a magazine was born. Published in suburban Menlo Park, California, it described itself as "a forum for the mature American Catholic" focusing on "those positive principles of Hellenic-Christian tradition which have shaped and sustained our civilization for the past two thousand years." Its first issues debated the moral shortcomings of J. D. Salinger and Tennessee Williams. According to one designer, it looked like the poetry annual of a midwestern girls school.

By 1968, the magazine had moved to the bohemian North Beach neighborhood of San Francisco, added generous doses of sex and humor, adopted a cutting-edge design, forged links to the Black Panther Party, exposed illegal CIA activities in America and Vietnam, published the diaries of Che Guevara and staff writer Eldridge Cleaver, and boosted its monthly circulation to almost 250,000. A *Time* magazine headline from that period—"A Bomb in Every Issue"—described its impact. Seven years later, it was out of business for good.

What happened?

This book recounts the short, unruly life of *Ramparts* magazine, the premier leftist publication of its era. It features the magazine's outsized characters and explosive stories, the political movements that transformed it, and the fractious energies that destroyed it. Although it places *Ramparts* in its Bay Area milieu—the student movements in Berkeley, the rise and fall of the Black Panthers in Oakland, and the acid-inflected Summer of Love in San Francisco—the story is by no means a local one. *Ramparts* changed national media and politics, not only with its stories on civil rights, Vietnam, black power, and the CIA, but also by demonstrating that mainstream media techniques could be used to advance leftist politics. That precedent would fuel progressive journalism for a generation.

As a publication, *Ramparts* was unique. Its combination of radical content, sophisticated design, and public relations savvy distinguished it from its stodgier East Coast counterparts and grittier underground ones. Its investigative stories helped revive the tradition of muckraking, earned it a Polk Award for excellence in magazine reporting, and influenced a generation of young journalists as well as national leaders. After Martin Luther King Jr. saw a *Ramparts* piece on napalmed children in Vietnam, for example, he decided to speak out against the war for the first time. That side of *Ramparts*, former contributor and sociologist Todd Gitlin remarked later, "walked on solid ground." In a recent interview, former *Ramparts* staff writer William Turner summed up the magazine's legacy this way: "When you look back on it, where else would those articles appear? The *Saturday Evening Post*?"

At its peak, *Ramparts* was both a platform and a seedbed for a generation of reporters, activists, and social critics. Its contributors included Noam Chomsky, Seymour Hersh, Bobby Seale, Tom Hayden, Angela Davis, Susan Sontag, William Greider, Jonathan Kozol, and a young Christopher Hitchens, who wrote for *Ramparts* under a pseudonym. More surprising, perhaps, was the magazine's Washington, DC, contributing editor—Brit Hume, the Fox News host and anchor. Two *Ramparts* writers left to create *Rolling Stone*, and three editors decamped to found *Mother Jones*. On the literary side, the magazine ran work by Kurt Vonnegut, Jorge Luis Borges, Gary Snyder, Lawrence Ferlinghetti, Ken Kesey, Erica Jong, and Gabriel García Márquez—seven years before Márquez was awarded the Nobel Prize for literature.

Ramparts also represented an ethic—a deeply irreverent one. Although it covered Vietnam, CIA torture, and other grave issues, *Ramparts* maintained a humorous, even playful tone. Over and above its youthful desire to challenge political authority, *Ramparts* called attention to the stupefying effects of that authority on the media itself. It famously critiqued the Warren Report and then reviewed a fake book on the Kennedy assassination—in the same issue. When the faux review generated an avalanche of media calls and citations in serious publications, the staff was delighted. Like all good satire, the review demonstrated a mastery of the target's methods; but the response also confirmed the flatfootedness of the mainstream media—the very reason the satire was required in the first place. In this sense, the magazine consistently worked at another, more reflexive level. In addition to breaking big stories, *Ramparts* entertained readers, mirrored the New Left's fascination with the media, and exemplified new possibilities for American journalism.

Certainly the magazine's short life and current obscurity should figure in any evaluation of its achievement. *Ramparts* wasn't the *Nation*, *Harper's*, or the *Atlantic*, whose histories stretch back to the days of Mark Twain and Henry James. At its flashpoint, *Ramparts* was something else altogether: the journalistic equivalent of a rock band, a mercurial confluence of raw talent, youthful energy, and high audacity. Its sheer incandescence blew minds, launched solo careers, and spawned imitators. It was born, lived, bred, and died. Because it was mortal, not monumental, genealogy may be more important than longevity in understanding its significance. If so, *Ramparts* should be judged not only by what it published, but also by the subsequent work it made possible. By this measure, it accomplished a great deal.

Ramparts figures regularly and sometimes prominently in other histories, but few books have focused on its own brief, turbulent life. The most sustained treatment is Warren Hinckle's *If You Have a Lemon, Make Lemonade: An Essential Memoir of a Lunatic Decade*. Having worked as *Ramparts'* promotions director, editor, and publisher, Hinckle was perfectly positioned to deliver the inside story, and his book offers a picaresque version of the magazine's early period. But Hinckle drops the narrative in 1969, the year he left *Ramparts*, and the book's 1974 publication date precluded a discussion of the magazine's long-term influence.

Perhaps the best-known portrait of *Ramparts* can be found in *Radical Son*, former editor David Horowitz's memoir. Thanks to that book, *Ramparts* is remembered mostly for its prodigious spending, high-handed editorial practices, chaotic management, and ideological zeal. More hauntingly, Horowitz also recounts the murder (purportedly by Black Panthers) of former *Ramparts* bookkeeper Betty Van Patter. After the police fished Van Patter's battered body out of the San Francisco Bay, Horowitz began his long march to his current position as right-wing polemicist.

Both in tone and coverage, Horowitz's depiction of *Ramparts* is a counterweight to Hinckle's. Where Hinckle is freewheeling and irreverent, Horowitz is confessional and anguished. But Horowitz's years at the magazine were only one part of his personal journey, and *Radical Son* was never meant to be a detailed portrait of *Ramparts*. Moreover, he joined the magazine in January 1968, almost halfway through its short life and after it had made most of its important journalistic contributions. Horowitz's perspective is valuable, but even when we read his memoir alongside Hinckle's, we can't see *Ramparts* steadily and whole.

A Bomb in Every Issue addresses that problem by following *Ramparts* from inception to final collapse, situating the magazine in its time and place, and mapping its influence on American politics and media. Because *Ramparts* folded in 1975, much of that influence must now be sought elsewhere: in scholarly histories of the CIA, in the nation's unending fascination with the Black Panthers, in the continuing success of *Rolling Stone* and *Mother Jones*, in the energetic repudiations of the New Left by some former staffers, and in the netroots and media reform movements of today. Although *Ramparts* published its last issue more than three decades ago, its influence lives on.

I've benefited enormously from previous work on *Ramparts*, but I should mention one theme I stumbled upon myself: the key contributions made by women to the magazine's success. These include notable articles by Jessica Mitford, Susan Sontag, Judy Stone, Susan Griffin, and others, but many important contributions occurred behind the scenes. The magazine never would have existed without Helen Keating and her financial support. Two of the magazine's principals—Warren Hinckle and Robert Scheer—never would have met if it weren't for the friendship of Denise Hinckle and Anne Weills. And those men never would have heard of an obscure prisoner named Leroy Eldridge Cleaver without the efforts of lawyer Beverly Axelrod. No one has held up *Ramparts* as a shining example of feminist consciousness; in fact, a women's magazine once named Hinckle "Male Chauvinist of the Month" in 1968. But women were an important part of *Ramparts'* success, and their insights supplemented and clarified what their (mostly male) colleagues, spouses, lovers, and friends have said in print over the years. Their stories are an indispensable part of the one I tell here.

My own interest in the *Ramparts* story began with a series of accidents. I knew nothing of the magazine until I began researching my biography of Carey McWilliams, the extraordinary California author, activist, and editor of the *Nation*. In the course of interviewing McWilliams's younger colleagues, I discovered that some of them had also written for *Ramparts*. After that book appeared, I began attending monthly talks on California topics at the University of California, Berkeley. One speaker was Gene Marine, a *Ramparts* veteran who discussed the history of KPFA, the Berkeley public radio station founded in 1949. During his talk, I realized I was aware of several books about KPFA but not a single one about *Ramparts*. When I quizzed the very knowledgeable people in the room after the talk, no one could recall reading such a book. I decided to get to work.

If Gene's talk was the proximate cause of this work, it didn't begin to explain my deeper interest in the topic. That interest, I quickly realized, was quite personal. I was born in Berkeley in 1959 and grew up in nearby El Cerrito, a few blocks from the home of University of California president Clark Kerr. As youngsters, my friends and I occasionally borrowed Kerr's expansive lawn to play tackle football. Our neighborhood was fully integrated, but my parents remember when East Bay real estate agents wouldn't show homes, especially in the hills, to black or Asian families. We read the entertaining *San Francisco Chronicle* each morning, and my brothers and I delivered the more conservative *Oakland Tribune* in the hills each afternoon. My grandmother lived next door to folk singer Malvina ("Little Boxes") Reynolds in Berkeley. Her husband was a union carpenter and Communist organizer, and FBI agents questioned my grandmother about their activities. When my grandmother fell and broke her hip in her front yard, Malvina tended to her until my father arrived.

Occasionally my family drove through Golden Gate Park to Haight-Ashbury, where we marveled at the neighborhood's outlandish street life. I went to the city of Berkeley's summer music camp, where the cool kids taught me the lyrics to "For What It's Worth" ("Stop, hey, what's that sound . . .") and Country Joe and the Fish's "I Feel Like I'm Fixin' to Die Rag" ("Gimme an F!"). My cabin counselor lent me his copy of *The Autobiography of Malcolm X*, which I ingested between band practices. At high school basketball games in El Cerrito, I watched black teenagers sit (or even recline) through the national anthem. OK, I noted to myself; that's another thing that happens in the world.

My childhood, in short, unfolded in the unique milieu that gave rise to *Ramparts*. That milieu included the university and its discontents, the counterculture, and efforts to promote racial integration and accommodation. But *Ramparts* didn't just grow out of this milieu; it also helped create it. By studying the magazine and its influence, I found I was also exploring the world I was born into. That world shaped my sensibility and even my sensorium, making some life paths seem possible or even natural and others virtually unimaginable. I would have been interested in *Ramparts* even if its impact was only a regional affair. Since it was much more than that, I take extra pleasure in telling its story, all the way through, for the first time.

A word on the chapter titles. Because many of the magazine's critics, including the late William F. Buckley, considered *Ramparts* un–American, it may seem ironic to use phrases from "The Star-Spangled Banner" to organize its story. Especially as the 1960s drew to a close, the magazine courted Buckley's charge; its April 1969 cover caption read, "Alienation is when your country is at war and you want the other side to win." But one reason founder Edward Keating liked *Ramparts* as a title was that his magazine would receive a plug every time the national anthem was sung. And I would argue that for all its critique and irreverence, *Ramparts* in its heyday was centrally concerned with American ideals—and especially the nation's collective failure to live up to them.

To make sense of that claim, consider the world into which *Ramparts* was born.

1

THE DAWN'S EARLY LIGHT

On a bright spring day in 1962, two months before Edward Keating published the first issue of *Ramparts* magazine, President John F. Kennedy stepped to the podium at Berkeley's Memorial Stadium to address 88,000 eager listeners. It was the largest live audience Kennedy ever addressed and the biggest event in the University of California's history. The occasion was the university's ninety-fourth anniversary, but Kennedy's presence had turned it into something else: a celebration of cold war liberalism at its peak.

Draped in a dark ceremonial gown, Kennedy began by thanking his many hosts. One was Clark Kerr, president of the University of California, whose career up to that point was an unbroken series of triumphs. A former Berkeley graduate student, he was a leading labor arbitrator before returning to Cal to direct a new institute after World War II. When the spirit of McCarthyism settled over the campus a few years later, Kerr supported a ban on Communist professors but opposed the dismissal of faculty who refused to sign a new and more specifically anticommunist loyalty oath. That compromise earned him the respect of some faculty and the suspicion of several university regents. After Kerr became Berkeley's head administrator in 1952, one regent referred to him openly as the "Red Chancellor."

Another Kennedy host on the dais that day was California governor Pat Brown. Only the second Democratic governor in the twentieth century, Brown was presiding over the state's explosive growth, and his first term produced an unprecedented expansion of the state's colleges, highways, and aqueducts. Some of that expansion was guided by the state's Master Plan for Higher Education,

crafted largely by Kerr and passed in 1960. The plan accommo-
dated a tidal wave of students born after World War II and was
hailed as a blend of bold vision and shrewd practicality. It landed
Kerr on the cover of *Time* magazine, but much of the credit also
went to Brown.

Like Kennedy, Brown was Catholic, but his background otherwise diverged sharply from JFK's privileged upbringing. As a
youngster, Brown went to public school in San Francisco, worked
in his father's cigar store, and later attended law school at night. He
never had to publicly subordinate his religious loyalties to his political ones, as Kennedy did, but his faith may have influenced his
position on the death penalty, which he regarded as a barbaric
practice inflicted on "the weak, the poor, the ignorant." His son
Jerry, who had spent four years in a Jesuit seminary before en-
rolling at Cal in 1960, encouraged that view. As governor, Brown
struggled with the issue, staying many executions while letting
others go forward. He managed to alienate both death penalty ad-
vocates and critics when he delayed the execution of convicted
rapist Caryl Chessman, only to allow it in 1960. When he appeared
with Richard Nixon and Jerry at a San Francisco Giants game, he
was booed so energetically that the three men left the stadium.

Brown and Kennedy had their own brief history. When Brown
decided to run as a favorite son candidate in the 1960 California
presidential primary, he and Kennedy struck a secret deal. Kennedy
would stay out of the California primary if Brown agreed not to
accept the vice presidential nomination. Kennedy's motive was
clear; two Catholics couldn't possibly appear on the presidential
ticket.

Kennedy's visit to Berkeley was meant to support Brown's reelection bid against Richard Nixon, Kennedy's rival in the 1960
presidential race. Nixon was a formidable politician, but most voters were happy with Brown and the state's booming growth.
Moreover, Nixon had his own problems. He was still reeling from
his narrow loss to Kennedy, struggling with the switch to state-
level politics, and hitting false notes with the press. Asked by the

New York Times about Kennedy's visit to California, Nixon called the president a carpetbagger. Kennedy laughed off the comment at a White House press conference and casually asserted his right to go where he pleased.

Using the same light touch at Memorial Stadium, Kennedy played to his massive audience. Many of his top advisors were Cal men, and he singled out his secretary of state, secretary of defense, CIA director, and Atomic Energy Commission chairman. "It is a disturbing fact to me, and it may be to some of you," Kennedy said, "that the New Frontier owes as much to Berkeley as it does to Harvard University." The crowd roared its approval. Kennedy didn't mention his attempt to recruit yet another Cal man, Clark Kerr, as secretary of labor. Kerr regretfully declined so he could finish his work on California's Master Plan for Higher Education.

The rest of Kennedy's speech that day focused on the role of science in America's national aspirations. He picked a good place to do it. As he noted, Cal had produced more Nobel laureates, all in science, than the entire Soviet Union. Kennedy celebrated "the happy pursuit of knowledge," but his itinerary revealed a more specific interest in scientific research. After the president landed at the Alameda Naval Air Station earlier that day, his motorcade made its way to Building 70-A at the Ernest O. Lawrence Berkeley Laboratory, otherwise known as the Rad Lab. Perched on the hill above the Greek Theater, an earlier gift to the university from media giant William Randolph Hearst, the lab offered a commanding view of San Francisco Bay and played a key role in the nation's nuclear weapons research. Overseen by the University of California, the Rad Lab and its sister facility in Livermore were part of what Kerr called the "multiversity," which he regarded as "a prime instrument of national purpose." During his Berkeley visit, Kennedy chatted with the the lab's directors and scientists and then left for Memorial Stadium to deliver his speech.

After his remarks, President Kennedy headed south for Palm Springs, where he stayed with Bing Crosby. The next day, he called on Dwight Eisenhower, his White House predecessor, and had sex with Marilyn Monroe, another Crosby houseguest. The following day, he attended mass.

Not everyone in Berkeley was charmed by Kennedy's visit. That month, local leftist groups seized on the occasion to protest a long list of U.S. policies. One such group was SLATE, a student organization formed in 1958 to promote progressive change both on and off campus. The next year, SLATE candidates took control of Cal's student government, replacing the more conservative candidates from the fraternities and sororities for the first time.

For the Kennedy visit, SLATE scheduled a vigil in front of Cal's administration building and drafted an open letter:

Mr. President:

When you took office there were many who expressed hope that your administration would use the vast power at its disposal towards ending the arms race, championing the cause of civil rights and civil liberties for all Americans, and support of the struggles of the underdeveloped and colonial nations for a more just and humane life. The events of the past fourteen months, however, can lead us to no other conclusion but that your administration's policies are not formulated with such objectives foremost in mind. Specifically, your administration has carried out the following policies to our great dismay.

You have increased military expenditures by $8 billion and have aped the Soviet Union in the resumption of nuclear testing, thereby seriously intensifying the arms race.

You have organized, equipped and transported a military invasion against a small neighboring state, Cuba, in violation of the laws of this nation and of the United Nations Charter.

You have failed to take the initiative to repeal the McCarran Act and restore the rights of free expression to members of the Communist Party.

You have failed to implement even such minimal steps toward full citizenship for the Negro people as signing an executive order desegregating federally assisted housing.

You have continued to give active support to the corrupt dictatorships of Taiwan, South Vietnam, South Korea, Portugal, Spain and Nicaragua.

You have provided the governments of France and Portugal with military equipment that is being used for the suppression of the Algerian and Angolan people.

We believe that a continuation of such policies can only lead this nation further and further from its professed democratic and humanitarian ideals and closer and closer to a garrison state and a nuclear holocaust. As Americans concerned both with our own future and with all the people of the world, we cannot in good conscience celebrate with you this Charter Day. We choose rather to use the occasion of your visit here to protest directly to you the course of action which your administration continues to follow. As we protest, we yet hope that you will reverse that course and truly lead this nation forward in a "peace race" towards those democratic and humane objectives of which you so often speak.

SLATE's list of concerns was ripped out of the headlines. The nuclear arms race was raging, and in the first months of his administration, Kennedy had authorized a CIA-sponsored invasion of Cuba. It failed after Kennedy withdrew critical air support at the last second, and many young leftists shed no tears when Cuban forces beat back the advance at the Bay of Pigs and humiliated the United States.

For SLATE, Kennedy's support for Ngo Dinh Diem's regime in South Vietnam was a less urgent matter. During the 1950s, Communist forces had taken control of North Vietnam, and the United States aided Diem as part of an effort to contain communism in Southeast Asia. To that point, U.S. support for Diem had been modest, but two months before Kennedy arrived in Berkeley, the United States undertook its first combat mission when helicopters ferried 1,000 South Vietnamese soldiers to sweep a Vietcong stronghold near Saigon.

Diem was Catholic, as were many of the refugees streaming from North to South Vietnam. For that reason, and for his ardent anticommunism, he enjoyed the support of many influential American Catholics, including the Kennedys and Cardinal Francis Spellman, archbishop of New York. For them, Diem was the antidote to leaders like Fidel Castro, whom the Pope excommunicated in January 1962, the same month Attorney General Robert Kennedy told CIA director John McCone that overthrowing Castro was "the top priority of the United States Government." But for Berkeley students pinning their socialist and anticolonial hopes to Castro's Cuba, U.S. support for Diem's regime was a step in the wrong direction.

SLATE's position on the mistreatment of American Communists was more pointed. In its view, the House Committee on Un-American Activities (HUAC) was a high-profile culprit, and in 1960, SLATE joined other Bay Area groups to protest HUAC hearings in San Francisco. On the third and last day of the hearings, 5,000 protestors gathered at City Hall. The committee investigator later explained that he excluded protestors from the hearing room because he "wanted to keep the commies from stacking the meeting. We wanted some decent people in here." Outside, some protestors taunted the police, and a few banged on the hearing room doors. Dozens of protestors were promptly drenched with fire hoses, dragged down the slick front steps of City Hall, beaten with nightsticks, and arrested. Later, protestors would describe the experience as a "political baptism that transformed fear into determination."

As Bay Area leftists resisted the legacy of McCarthyism, California Democrats were fumbling their way toward a position on radicals in their midst. At the state party convention in 1962, they considered a resolution requiring any group with the name "Democrat" in it to deny entry to members of the Communist Party, the far-right John Birch Society, "or any other totalitarian group." The resolution failed after an East Bay legislator argued that a witch hunt could destroy the party. Besides, he noted, the combined strength of Communists and Birchers "couldn't hit a loud foul in a Class D League."

That view didn't prevent a Marxist reading group at Cal from launching *Root and Branch: A Radical Quarterly* that same year. The editors included David Horowitz, a graduate student in English, and Robert Scheer, a graduate fellow at the Center for Chinese Studies. Both were from working-class Jewish families in New York's outer boroughs, both identified strongly with the Cuban revolution, and both were keen to recruit local black activists to write for *Root and Branch*. One of those activists, a Berkeley law student named Donald Warden, argued that liberal white Northerners were sadly mistaken if they thought crusading efforts in the South would solve the so-called Negro problem. In his view, a more systemic solution was required, something more like the Cuban revolution. At a campus rally, he declared, "I'm for Castro because Castro is for the black man." To provide security at his street rallies, he hired an Oakland City College student named Huey P. Newton.

Despite the Bay Area's reputation for radical activity, most of its major newspapers were conservative. Chief among them was the Hearst family's *San Francisco Examiner* and the Knowland family's *Oakland Tribune*.

The Hearst press began when silver magnate and senator George Hearst bought his son a San Francisco newspaper. Over his long and storied life, William Randolph Hearst built a vast national audience by mastering the conventions of yellow journalism. He also created the nation's first media conglomerate by extending his newspaper holdings into magazines, radio, newsreels, feature films, and wire services. In 1962, more than a decade after Hearst died in his Beverly Hills home, that empire was far-flung, but the family retained special clout in California.

Though less famous than the Hearsts, the Knowland family figured heavily in California politics. Joseph Knowland served five terms in Congress before buying the *Tribune* in 1915. Later, he backed Alameda County prosecutor Earl Warren, who became governor in 1942 and immediately named Joseph's son to an open U.S. Senate seat. Although William Knowland eventually became Senate majority leader, he failed to impress the head of his own party. In his diary, President Eisenhower noted that in Knowland's case, "there seems to be no final answer to the question, 'How stupid can you get?' " In 1958, Knowland resigned his Senate seat to run for governor, lost decisively to Pat Brown, and later took over the *Tribune*.

The other major Bay Area newspaper was the *San Francisco Chronicle*. Founded in 1865, it quickly became the highest-circulation paper on the West Coast. Hearst's *Examiner* eclipsed it, but in the years after his death, the *Chronicle* began to rally. It combined colorful columnists with an exuberant willingness to manufacture news, including a series of front-page stories about Zambian astronauts launched by giant rubber bands. After the *Chronicle* overtook the *Examiner* in the mid-1960s, it agreed to a joint-operating arrangement with its longtime rival.

Despite their relatively long histories and political influence, the Bay Area newspapers had no special journalistic aspirations. Local writers, especially younger ones, had few chances to learn and practice big-time journalism. If they wanted those opportunities, they would have to create them.

In Palo Alto, one hour south of San Francisco and home to Stanford University, a very different scene was unfolding. The valley once known for its fruit orchards was rapidly becoming a science and technology center. By the end of the century, its discoveries and products would transform the global economy and create new empires to match Hearst's.

As in Berkeley, the university was the valley's prime mover, but the differences between the two institutions were stark. Cal earned international fame as a public knowledge factory; Stanford was a private money farm sustained by real estate development and strategic relationships with local high-tech entrepreneurs. The year Kennedy visited Cal, Hewlett-Packard appeared on the Fortune 500 list for the first time. That same year, Stanford opened its linear accelerator, which quickly became one of the world's leading research laboratories.

The Cal-Stanford rivalry, which President Kennedy mentioned jocularly in his Berkeley address, would now be played out in the new arena of Big Science. The prize would be millions of federal research dollars, much of it related to high-tech weaponry, aircraft, and other defense projects. In and around Palo Alto, that money supported a community whose other flagship institution, *Sunset* magazine, had for many years instructed readers on tasteful suburban living in the West.

But even genteel Palo Alto was generating countercultural energy in 1962. Ironically, some of it sprang from an exotic form of defense spending. In the early 1950s, the CIA had begun experimenting with LSD as a mind control drug. Soon the U.S. Army was conducting its own experiments in the hope that the mass dissemination of LSD would revolutionize combat. One army officer justified those experiments in a 1959 magazine article.

I do not contend that driving people crazy—even for a few hours—is a pleasant prospect. But warfare is never pleasant. And to those who feel that *any* kind of chemical weapon is more horrible than conventional weapons, I put this question: Would you rather be temporarily deranged, blinded, or paralyzed by a chemical agent, or burned alive by a conventional fire bomb?

It was a difficult question to answer satisfactorily.

While studying at Stanford, a young Ken Kesey volunteered

for experiments at the local VA hospital. A few weeks after taking
LSD under clinical conditions, he became a night attendant in the
hospital's psychiatric ward. Soon after that, the LSD was flowing
freely among Kesey's friends, a group that included musician Jerry
Garcia.

The month before Kennedy spoke at Berkeley, Kesey's first
novel, *One Flew Over the Cuckoo's Nest*, appeared to immediate ac-
claim. Set in a mental hospital and narrated from the perspective of
a schizophrenic Indian, the novel depicts a symbolic rebellion
against a suffocating, authoritarian system embodied by the Big
Nurse. Kesey later claimed that he wrote the opening pages under
the influence of peyote. With his royalties, Kesey bought a woody
retreat in the nearby coastal mountains and began assembling the
acid-fueled Merry Pranksters, who were playfully preparing for
what they called "the great freak forward."

Not far from the VA hospital, Edward M. Keating published
the first issue of *Ramparts*, a Catholic literary quarterly. He couldn't
possibly know what a long, strange trip it would be.

2

WHEN OUR CAUSE IT IS JUST

It was an inauspicious beginning.

The premiere issue of *Ramparts* was austere, even plain. On the front cover, a lone tower, vaguely medieval and resembling a rook, was "knocked out" in white against a solid orange background. The title and date were the only text. On the back cover, a thin white cross spread against the same orange field.

If the design was severe, the mission statement, announced on page 3, was a clarion call. *Ramparts* would serve as a showcase for creative writers and Christian intellectuals "in an age grown increasingly secular, bewildered, and afraid." Besides possessing literary excellence, its pieces would reflect "the Christian vision of man, his world, his God." It would demand no "special slanting of thought" but only that its authors "preserve the intellectual integrity that is their most valued possession" and pass this integrity on to their audience. A full-page announcement reached out to those authors. The magazine's first annual awards carried a first prize of $700 for short stories and essays. Another announcement on the inside back cover offered the same prize for art and $300 for poetry.

The masthead listed Edward M. Keating as editor-in-chief. His path to that position was anything but direct. Born in the slums of New York in 1925, he spent the first four years of his life shuttling between New Jersey orphanages every six months. That routine was meant to prevent emotional attachments, and it worked; as an adult, he remembered nothing about those years. In 1929, he was adopted by millionaire George T. Keating, whom he later suspected was his biological father. The Keatings had bought a ninety-acre estate in New Jersey and were concerned that their son George would be lonely. They adopted Edward (his new name) and, according to family lore, gave him to George for Christmas.

Little Eddie was a hellcat given to tantrums and property damage. Even the best private schools couldn't defuse his temper. One summer, the rest of the family gave up and went to Europe without him. Eddie felt like a second-class member of the family, a sense that may have fed a lifelong propensity to question, challenge, and rebel.

In 1940, the Keatings moved to Menlo Park, California. Ed attended prep school there and then Stanford University in nearby Palo Alto. At the end of his freshman year, he joined the navy to serve in World War II. Only seventeen at the time, he needed his parents' permission to enlist. They consented but didn't allow him to see his birth certificate, which bore the names of his biological parents. After four years of fixing radar equipment in the South Pacific, he returned to Stanford. There he befriended Frank Church, an undergraduate from Idaho. He also met Helen English, a smart, pretty coed from Los Angeles. Crowded into a corner booth with their friends at the Stanford Cellar, Ed and Helen launched into an energetic argument about China. Helen noted later, "Ed's politics at twenty-one were still those of his conservative Republican parents."

Helen was the product of a posh girls school and heir to a large fortune built on gypsum and sheetrock. Although Helen and Ed were from opposite coasts, she considered their upbringings similar, consisting as they did of "big business, lots of money, the best private schools, exposure to art, literature, music, and knowledgeable talk." Her family lived on a five-acre country estate with horses, tennis courts, a pool, and towering oak trees. When she was twelve, her parents divorced, and she moved into the city with her mother and her new stepfather. It was a difficult time for her, and she was delighted to leave home to begin her liberal arts coursework at Stanford. There she became interested in Catholicism, her mother's dormant faith, and began attending mass.

In Ed Keating, Helen found a young man who shared her passionate idealism. When they met, she was engaged to a young army captain who had recently returned from his tank command in Germany. But the attraction to Ed was strong, and breaking her engagement was her first act of defiance against her controlling mother. Ed and Helen married, and they began what she later called an "extremely conventional life" consisting of law school at Stanford for him (his father's idea) along with friends, football games, and "hammering out our beliefs against the anvils of each other's opinions."

They started a family, and Ed converted to Catholicism in 1952. Never given to half measures, he threw himself into his adopted faith. He was a regular at Angeles, the Catholic bookstore in Menlo Park owned by Earl "Duke" Douglass. Keating also taught English at Santa Clara University, the local Jesuit college. He lost that job after flunking a football player and clashing with the administration, but his religious zeal was undiminished. His political ideas evolved against the backdrop of McCarthyism, which appalled him. He also became preoccupied with the depersonalization and conformity of the "organization man" of the 1950s.

While playing with his daughter one day on the living room floor, Keating heard Duke Douglass on the radio lamenting the dearth of Catholic intellectuals in the United States. According to Helen, her husband "was getting angrier and more frustrated by the moment. Here was his old friend talking on the radio, while he, with far more to say, was out of work, unpublished, playing with the baby." He started planning a magazine, a shoestring operation funded with the $15,000 remaining in his trust fund. In Helen's recollection, the idea was to "present the ancient truths of the Church with intelligence and sophistication and . . . stimulate the artists who had been stifled by the narrowmindedness of the

Church in America." Years earlier, Helen had given Ed a statue of St. George and the Dragon because it captured Ed's "basic emotional posture." As he planned the magazine, "his thoughts began to take on the shape of 'mounting the Ramparts.' "

In 1954, Helen inherited a large fortune. In their late twenties and with three small children, she and Ed no longer needed to earn an income. They bought a thousand-acre farm in Virginia with a large brick house; Thomas Jefferson had lived in it when the British occupied Monticello. She hated it, but Ed argued that it was the only place he could write. Virginia didn't work out, and after two years, Ed enrolled at Yale to study playwriting. His diabetes, which he had developed in Virginia, grew worse. While he was hospitalized in New York, a specialist recommended a psychoanalyst. Soon his health improved, and the family returned to the Bay Area. They bought a large home in Atherton, an upscale suburb near Palo Alto, and resumed their friendships there. Their two-acre lot at 54 Rosewood Drive was two doors down from football star Y. A. Tittle's home. Shirley Temple Black, the former child film star, also lived nearby.

Once back in California, Keating launched his magazine. He bought a building at 1182 Chestnut Street in Menlo Park and set up shop. The shoestring idea gave way to something more lavish. "Here his taste and background betrayed him," Helen recalled. "*Ramparts* was supposed to be a low-budget magazine without advertising supported by its subscriptions and Ed's own private funds. But Ed was constitutionally incapable of doing anything cheap."

The editorial staff included Helen (fiction) and Duke Douglass (book reviews). Harry Stiehl, a fellow Catholic convert and published author, signed on as poetry editor but quickly took on more general editorial duties. Fastidious, formal, and learned, Stiehl also taught at the University of San Francisco, that city's Jesuit college. There he had come to know Warren Hinckle III, editor of the student newspaper. On Stiehl's recommendation, Keating invited Hinckle to a party at his home. The other guests, Keating told

Hinckle, would include the new magazine's contributors and supporters. "There might even be a swinging nun there," Keating added.

Still in his early twenties, Warren Hinckle had already made a small mark on San Francisco journalism. While drinking downtown at the House of Shields, an *Examiner* watering hole, he picked up some dirt on *Chronicle* columnist Count Marco, who dispensed outrageous advice on the women's page. "When you unsnap your brassiere," Count Marco once asked his readers, "do you let out a loud 'whoosh' of relief and stand there grunting and scratching like some kind of happy sow, or do you have [your husband] help with the snaps, then gracefully cross your arms as you let it slip down?" A crime reporter told Hinckle that the faux aristocrat was actually a former hairdresser who had recently been arrested at a public bathroom on Union Square. Writing for the *Foghorn*, the USF student newspaper, Hinckle exposed the Count's plebeian background and created minor embarrassment at the *Chronicle*.

Despite the Count Marco scoop, or maybe because of it, the *Chronicle* hired Hinckle. At the time, he was working as a public relations specialist and running for the San Francisco County Board of Supervisors. His new girlfriend, Denise Libarle, encouraged him to take the job at the *Chronicle*. After meeting Hinckle at a downtown bar, Denise saw that he had more to offer than publicity advice. He was gregarious, bright, energetic, and ambitious. He rarely left San Francisco, but he was already looking beyond the city's laid-back, café-society lifestyle. A courtship ensued, and Warren and Denise married in October 1962, the same month the United States and Soviet Union squared off over nuclear missiles in Cuba.

Hinckle was attracted to the *Chronicle*'s spirit of showmanship under editor Scott Newhall. In his memoir, Hinckle encapsulated that spirit by quoting entertainer George M. Cohan, who once advised Spencer Tracy, "Whatever you do, kid, always serve it with a little dressing." Hinckle's style reflected that advice. His white linen, velvet, or three-piece suits and patent-leather dancing pumps earned him a reputation as a dandy. His most distinctive accessory was a black eye patch, which he wore after a childhood auto accident. Newhall, the product of an old-money family, was another colorful figure. His office was full of nautical equipment, old coins, and other knickknacks. "It was decorated like something out of *Vanity Fair*," Hinckle recalled. Newhall's adventures had taken him to Mexico, where an altercation with a donkey led to the amputation of his right leg, which he replaced with an artificial one. Between the two of them, *Chronicle* columnist Herb Caen later quipped, Newhall and Hinckle made a damn good pirate.

Hinckle's apprenticeship at the *Chronicle* began on the Oakland police beat, where he quickly learned the racial double standard that informed daily journalism.

> Whether a homicide would be reported at all depended largely upon the neighborhood in which it was committed. Ghetto murders, being regarded as natural black events, were rarely considered newsworthy. . . . Yet none of us questioned the professional proposition that the loss of a white life had more news value than the loss of a black life.

After a short stint in Oakland, Hinckle returned to San Francisco to work in the *Chronicle*'s city room, where he continued his sentimental education.

A fourth-generation San Franciscan and parochial school graduate, Hinckle was still attending mass regularly, but his youthful experiences with Catholic institutions had failed to produce much in the way of reverence. In the third grade, a nun's flatulence discouraged any fantasies of otherworldly perfection. In high school, he learned to drink for free by crashing Catholic wedding receptions in the fog-shrouded Sunset District.

Early on, he concluded that priests were often untrustworthy and vicious when challenged; that religious orders were stocked with "failed hedonists and sexual malcontents"; and that Jesuit higher education consisted of "learning what I was forced to learn to stay in the place, then unlearning it from the original sources." Rebellion was good sport, but the prospect of changing the Church "was no more real than changing the ocean." That outlook prevented illusions and therefore disillusionment. "I came to accept the Church for the tinsel, lazy, corrupt, and at the same time appealing thing that it was," he later wrote.

For Hinckle, Keating's party in Atherton underscored the idiosyncratic nature of the new magazine. The house was packed with off-duty priests and plainclothes nuns, a pride of lawyers and accountants, and Episcopalians from Stanford's humanities faculty. Many were liberal Catholics, but on the eve of Vatican II, that label might mean little more than an openness to folk masses. Keating's keen sense of justice attuned him to racial inequality and civil rights issues, but his other views could be conservative, even reactionary. If he were president, he declared at the party, he would jail novelist J. D. Salinger "because he's dirty."

That remark blossomed into a symposium in the premiere issue, published in May 1962. Hinckle contributed a largely descriptive essay on Salinger's fiction, and *Ramparts* associate editor Robert Bowen excoriated Salinger and his work. It was another day at the office for Bowen, who had been fired from Santa Clara University for his far-right views. He landed at the conservative University of Dallas, where he maintained contact with Keating and published the *Dallas Review*. Its editorial policy—"Fear God and nobody else"—was borrowed from General Edwin A. Walker, best known at the time for distributing John Birch Society literature to his troops and thereby losing command of his infantry division in Germany.

Keating's essay in the symposium followed Bowen's screed. Keating found Salinger irritating and pretentious, but his main complaint was directed at the civilization that produced him. The only way to place Salinger's work in history's attic, Keating concluded, was to begin "the spiritual explorations that will lead us to a rock on which to wage the eternal battle."

The second issue of *Ramparts*, published in November, included a similarly structured symposium on Tennessee Williams. Once again, Keating lowered the moral boom in his essay "Mildew on the Old Magnolia." Williams was a decadent writer, his characters "psychotic or merely wretched." He rendered human pain exquisitely, but that suffering was senseless and unredeemed, and no Christian could share his despondent view of life. A third symposium on painter and author Wyndham Lewis, whom poet W. H. Auden had called "that lonely old volcano of the Right," was more complimentary.

Keating's chief goal for *Ramparts* was to host serious discussions between Catholic clergy and laity. Hinckle, by then the magazine's promotions director, doubted that Catholic leaders would welcome those colloquies. The Jesuits in particular had little incentive to help *Ramparts*, which would compete with *America*, their own magazine. Nevertheless, Keating announced that back-to-back issues would feature an exchange between laity and clergy on Jesuit university education.

The first of these two issues came off as planned in March 1963. Keating, Bowen, and another *Ramparts* staffer contributed pieces, and a fourth essay came from a Stanford graduate student whose writing credits included an accounting textbook. A full-page announcement stated that the second half of the symposium would appear in the May issue. Hinckle learned that *Time* magazine was planning a story on the symposium, and a reporter was dispatched to interview Keating. But when *Time*'s story didn't appear, Hinckle learned that the magazine killed the story after the Jesuits told *Time* that Bowen was a Bircher. Keating fired Bowen, but the Jesuits withdrew from the symposium anyway, prompting an awkward editorial note in the May issue under the heading "A Pause in the Conversation."

After that disappointment, Keating's battles were more likely to be waged against the hidebound Church, not decadent American writers. "From now on, it's no more Mr. Nice Guy," Keating told Hinckle.

Despite the Jesuit unpleasantness, the magazine was moving forward. The second issue featured a poem by modernist Djuna Barnes, and the poetry prize went to John Berryman, part of whose signature work, 77 *Dream Poems*, appeared in the January 1963 issue. That same year, a symposium on Judaism included an article by Maxwell Geismar, a prominent literary critic based in New York. Geismar, who appeared on the masthead as associate editor, soon became an important mentor to Hinckle.

During this time, *Ramparts* also began to include the work of high-profile Catholic converts Thomas Merton and John Howard Griffin. Both had led extraordinary lives. Born in France to a New Zealand painter and American artist and Quaker, Merton had lived in Bermuda and England before entering Cambridge and then Columbia University, where he received a master's degree in English. He taught English at a Catholic college, but three days after the Japanese attack on Pearl Harbor, he entered a Trappist monastery in Kentucky. In 1948, he produced his bestselling spiritual autobiography, *The Seven Storey Mountain*.

By 1963, Merton had shifted some of his attention to civil rights and social justice, and the *Ramparts* Christmas issue included a piece by him called "The Black Revolution: Letters to a White Liberal." Proceeding cautiously, Merton worked around to the claim that "our actual decisions and choices, with regard to the Negro, show us that we are not in fact interested in the rights of several million persons." Recent civil rights legislation had merely allowed those citizens to sue for what should have been granted freely. "If every time I want a Coca Cola I have to sue the owner of the snack bar, I think I will probably keep going to the same old place in my ghetto," wrote Merton. An African American might reasonably conclude that the only way to get his rights was to fight for them. "But we deplore his demonstrations," Merton observed, "we urge him to go slow, we warn him against the consequences of violence (when, at least so far, most of the organized violence has been on our side and not his)." From his hermitage, Merton warned his white audience about this approach, claiming there was "a serious possibility of an eventual civil war which might wreck the fabric of American society." He praised Dr. Martin Luther King's radical challenge of black nonviolence, but he also warned "there might be a danger of Marxist elements 'capturing' the revolution."

Merton's contributions to *Ramparts* strengthened its standing in the liberal Catholic and peace communities. He distributed copies of the magazine to his far-flung network, and in November 1963, he sent Keating the addresses of Catholic peace activist Daniel Berrigan, Rabbi Abraham Heschel of the Jewish Theological Seminary, and others who might be interested in the magazine's mission.

Griffin's background was as exotic as Merton's. Born in Texas, Griffin served as a medic in the French Resistance before joining the Army Air Corps in the South Pacific. After the war, he was struck blind for a decade; meanwhile, he studied music, published two novels, and converted to Catholicism. After regaining his sight, he became a passionate advocate for racial equality and wrote the bestselling *Black Like Me* about his experiences in the South disguised as an African American. Although he lived in Texas, he became an associate editor at *Ramparts* and bent the magazine toward his interests. In November 1963, just before Kennedy's assassination, Griffin gave a series of talks in the Bay Area and stayed with the Keatings in Atherton. The talks made a deep impression on Ed Keating. "I listened to John talk many times during the week on the subject of racism in America," Keating wrote to Merton, "and never found my fascination decrease nor my concern falter."

Although *Ramparts* was successfully recruiting established authors, its audience remained tiny. That began to change with Judy Stone's 1964 profile of German playwright Rolf Hochhuth. His new play,

The Deputy, was arousing rough passions throughout Europe by accusing Pope Pius XII of failing to challenge the Nazis during the Holocaust. Stone, the drama editor at the *Chronicle* and younger sister of political journalist I. F. Stone, had landed an exclusive interview with Hochhuth. When she received a rejection from *Look* magazine, Hinckle heard her cursing in the *Chronicle* mailroom and persuaded her to publish her interview in *Ramparts*.

Catholic groups and the Hearst press decried *The Deputy*, but Hinckle suggested that Keating defend it—or at least the producer's right to stage it. They formed a committee, flew to New York, checked into the Waldorf Astoria, and began planning a press conference. Marc Stone, Judy's brother, helped with the publicity and began a long relationship with the magazine as its New York representative. When Keating and Hinckle arrived in New York, they began contacting local sympathizers, including Abraham Heschel and Maxwell Geismar.

From his suite at the Waldorf, Hinckle frantically cabled every conceivable media outlet hoping someone would show up at the press conference. According to Hinckle, the distribution list that day included *Bedside Nurse*, *Detergent Age*, *Professional Barber*, and the *Jewish Braille Review*. Hinckle sweetened the pot for the media by laying in Bloody Marys and Danishes. The excitable Keating feared the worst when, two minutes before the press conference was to begin, the room was empty. Five minutes later, a media horde swept in, set up their cameras, and slashed into the refreshments. Drawing on his college theater training, Keating passionately defended the social importance of *The Deputy*.

The press conference was a major success, and Keating was finally making the splash he envisioned when he founded *Ramparts*. It wasn't cheap; accountant Joe Ippolito recalled that Keating's business plan called for an investment of $100,000 to $200,000 of his own money, but the tab for promoting the Hochhuth story alone came to $50,000. Keating's earlier refusal to produce a budget for the magazine had led Ippolito to resign, but after Hinckle encouraged him to return, they laid out a budget using the latest technology—a digital computer programmed with punched cards. Despite their high-tech approach, revenues never exceeded expenses, and Wells Fargo covered the company's overdrafts by selling Helen's U.S. Gypsum stock.

Some *Ramparts* supporters didn't regard the Hochhuth controversy as a blessing. Thomas Merton, for example, offered mixed praise. "You have done well to speak out," he wrote to Keating, but he added that pugnacity wouldn't get him far with the Church hierarchy. "If at all possible, one should try to say things in such a way as not to be dismissed out of hand as a man spoiling for a fight and a born trouble maker."

Keating was undeterred. He and Hinckle courted more controversy with the next issue of *Ramparts*, which was devoted to the murders of three civil rights workers in Mississippi. In that issue, Hinckle explained to publicist Marc Stone, black journalist Louis Lomax would name the killers. Stone called reporters in New York and arranged for a press conference, interviews, and television appearances. But after the scheduled publication date came and went, Stone was embarrassed. He met with Hinckle in New York and learned that Lomax was in Los Angeles, hadn't finished the piece, and wasn't answering his telephone. When Hinckle tried to shift Stone's attention to other pieces in the issue, Stone realized he had a problem. After stalling the New York media for days, he was told that the printer was refusing to run the issue.

The Lomax piece, Stone suspected, had never contained the names of the killers. "So I had to figure out how to get off the spot with the press people in New York," he recalled later. Stone and Hinckle decided to announce that they knew the killers' names but wouldn't tell the authorities unless the FBI offered "lifetime protection" to the witnesses. As they temporized, a Mississippi grand jury handed down indictments in the case. "We went into the press conference with that kind of story," Stone recounted, "and, you know, we got away with it. We got all kinds of publicity, radio, television. . . . The *Times* gave us a good story. We were off and running. That's when the *Ramparts* bug bit."

Keating quickly promoted Hinckle to executive editor. Now in a position to put his mark on the magazine, Hinckle sought the advice of another key mentor, advertising executive Howard Gossage. "Gossage was the Socrates of San Francisco," Hinckle wrote, a maverick who was "forever stirring up the waters that his bread was cast upon." From his office, a magnificently restored firehouse on Pacific Avenue, Gossage connected Hinckle and *Ramparts* to the city's major players, including *Chronicle* columnist Herb Caen. He also helped Hinckle hatch publicity campaigns, recruit key staffers, and smooth over leadership snags.

Hinckle soon switched *Ramparts* to saddle-stitch binding, sold more advertising, and juiced up the magazine's look. The October 1964 cover touted a special report on a Harlem riot, "the untold story of the American Nightmare." It also listed stories and contributors for the first time and featured a poster with profane language under an image of Christ. The cross on the back cover was gone. Replacing it was a large photo of a black man with a nasty head wound holding a bloody handkerchief; a helmeted white policeman loomed over him. Inside, a full-page photo of a white man inside a car with a broken windshield was accompanied by a provocative reading line: "An extraordinary account of the Harlem Riots—told by the people who were there—in words few white men have ever heard." The lead editorial defended a Los Angeles priest who had publicly criticized Cardinal James McIntyre, a staunch conservative, for failing to promulgate Church teachings on racism.

Ramparts was now a slick, not a literary journal, and its stories would henceforth be served with plenty of dressing.

Shortly after Hinckle's promotion, *Ramparts* also became a monthly, making it possible to run news. (Its quarterly status had almost cost the magazine Judy Stone's Hochhuth piece.) Producing a monthly tripled the magazine's costs, but the goal was to offset those increases with higher circulation and advertising revenue. In fact, circulation had already increased—from a miniscule 2,200 copies to a paltry 4,000. But Keating and Hinckle were on a mission. The magazine had found its voice, identified its causes, and joined the battle.

The November cover, timed to coincide with the 1964 presidential election, featured a cartoon of Republican candidate Barry Goldwater as a rattlesnake. Inside, Maxwell Geismar analyzed Goldwater's bestselling books, including *The Conscience of a Conservative*, which Geismar pronounced horrifying. Keating continued to attack Cardinal McIntyre by linking him to Goldwater, especially on the issue of fair housing, the most controversial proposition on the California ballot that year. "These are two men who simply fail to recognize that the world of their fuzzy dreams bears no relation to reality," Keating thundered. "If both had their way, Church and State would be carried back to those tranquil days where six-guns and the Inquisition settled matters both quickly and unequivocally."

Letters to the editor poured in, subscriptions were cancelled, and some vendors refused to display the magazines. They were making progress.

Merton again urged caution, this time more directly. Noting that his colleagues had been protesting to him about the magazine and urging him to intercede, he offered both criticism and advice.

> My own feeling on the new line in the magazine is that in the long run it is not a really solid editorial policy. . . . It seems to me that you are hurting yourself a bit by sensationalism, and that the element of ripeness is lacking, so that in the end you may give the impression of being emotional and prejudiced in much the same way as the right wing people are. . . . I do think that in certain areas a judicious restraint would perhaps do the magazine much more good than harm.

That restraint, Merton thought, was "not just a cowardly 'prudence' but rather a breadth of view that is genuinely Catholic and does not lack charity." Having done his duty, Merton offered his apology to Keating. "I am sorry for the homily, but in the end I was rather forced to it. Best wishes and God bless your courage and zeal."

As Merton's letter made its way to Menlo Park, Keating had more urgent matters on his mind. While sharing a drink with Hinckle in New York's Algonquin Hotel, he revealed a terrible secret: he was broke. "If only you knew what hell I've been through, carrying this secret by myself," Keating confided to Hinckle. "You can't even imagine how exhausting it is."

Along with staffing and publishing the magazine, Keating had made expensive purchases, including a Heidelberg printing press. Keating hoped that its thirty-person staff would take in printing jobs between issues. That hadn't panned out, and a visibly upset Keating told Hinckle he was "down to his last shopping center." It was a medium-sized one in Santa Clara; Keating thought he could clear $100,000 after he resolved a pending lawsuit with one of the tenants.

A stunned Hinckle advised Keating to get some rest. When he called for the check and added a generous tip, Keating thanked him. Hinckle reminded him that he was only signing his room number; Keating would eventually receive the hotel bill.

Keating's bombshell called for a new strategy. The two men agreed to seek more readers by reaching out to Protestants and Jews as well as Catholics. The goal, announced in the July 1965 issue, was an ecumenical editorial policy that combined "that which is greatest in all of us: love of God and love of fellow man."

They also tried to cut back on expenses. Accountant Joe Ippolito frequently advised Denise Hinckle "to leave the meat out of the pasta this week," but Denise's husband was no belt-tightener. He spent lavishly on travel, salaries, food, and drink. Even the magazine's cost-cutting measures could be expensive. In an effort to lower the telephone bill between headquarters and the New York

office, for example, management installed a costly telex-type machine. But when the first message rattled into the home office, it
directed Hinckle to call New York immediately.

To generate revenue, Hinckle began to court new advertisers.
One was Pan American Airways, which took out a back-cover ad.
But when *Ramparts* began attacking Goldwater, Pan Am wanted
out. In the end, Hinckle claimed, he made the airline pay *Ramparts*
a premium to stop running its ad.

Another advertiser was Jessica Mitford, whose 1962 exposé of
the funeral industry, *The American Way of Death*, became a bestseller. Having moved to Oakland after the war with her husband,
labor lawyer Robert Treuhaft, Mitford became involved in civil
rights organizing, joined the Communist Party, and resigned in
1958 because she found it doctrinaire and ineffective. "Oh, dear,"
she wrote to a friend eight years later, "we *were* so rigid!" But she
was proud of her opposition to HUAC: so proud, in fact, that she
listed her subpoena in her resume under "Honors, Awards &
Prizes." Now she had something she wanted to sell: a desolate island she had inherited off the Scottish coast. According to
Hinckle, British Communists had already blocked her attempt to
donate the island to the party. Howard Gossage offered her ad
space if she allowed *Ramparts* to list her on its masthead.

In the meantime, *Ramparts* needed to raise some capital. Keating and Hinckle recruited Judson Clark Chrisney to fill the publisher's slot. Chrisney had been the chief fundraiser for the Atlantic
Community Council, which Hinckle later described as "another
High Protestant Eastern Establishment organization of vague purpose." Announcing that the magazine would "bring morality back
into the marketplace," Chrisney moved to San Francisco, started a
list of prospective investors, fired off letters to national publications, and bought a Jaguar.

Chrisney was soon let go, and raising money became a collective effort. Recruiting investors was an ongoing challenge. Many
older leftists balked at the magazine's splashy format; even affluent
ones were accustomed to less expensive operations like the *Nation*,

which used newsprint—"butcher paper," in Hinckle's description. Younger leftists didn't consider *Ramparts* a movement publication, and most of them were broke anyway. During one particularly desperate period, a prospective investor known as the Herring King declined to contribute any money but sent off his visitors with jars of his pickled product. The *Ramparts* team also pitched a leftist pants manufacturer, whose slogan was "I cover the asses of the masses." In Chicago, they waited days to meet *Playboy* publisher Hugh Hefner, who always seemed to be sleeping or swimming in his pool. Again, no dice.

When it came to fundraising disasters, however, a tall tale about the Eleanor Gimbel pitch took the prize. Gimbel had married into the department-store dynasty and was a longstanding supporter of leftist causes. She had backed *PM*, a short-lived national liberal daily of the late 1940s, and served as national chair of the Women for Wallace committee in 1948. Equipped with flip charts to emphasize *Ramparts'* imminent success, Hinckle began his presentation at her Park Avenue apartment. As he spoke, Gimbel's rare toy dogs scampered around the apartment. The purebreds were so tiny, one observer said later, they looked like "moving slippers." Deep into his pitch, Hinckle accidentally stepped on one and killed it. "I'll get you another one," he reportedly assured Gimbel, and slipped the dog into his pocket.

Despite these setbacks, Hinckle became an accomplished fundraiser. In the five years he ran the magazine, he claimed to raise about $2 million over and above Keating's investment. His presentations didn't stress the financial upside of the venture; in fact, investors had to sign a statement vouching for their mental fitness after receiving disclosures about the magazine's finances. Many were sophisticated businessmen with no illusions about the magazine's financial prospects. They almost certainly knew that few if any American political magazines, left or right, had consistently broken even, largely because their content—ideas and outrage— didn't help advertisers identify consumers of particular products like cars, skis, or jewelry. But Hinckle's success lay in creating the impression that supporting *Ramparts'* editorial mission was a unique opportunity. Given the magazine's success in generating high-profile stories, his proposition could be presented as a single question: in or out? His fundraising team's nonchalance masked an intense singleness of purpose. "Warren made it seem like he was doing you a favor," *Ramparts* accountant Joe Ippolito recalled. "But they were as ruthless as the people they were criticizing."

Among the willing investors Hinckle landed was Frederick Mitchell, a graduate student at Cal who had inherited a substantial fortune, and Louis "Bill" Honig, a partner in California's largest advertising firm. Irving Laucks, a multimillionaire who had invented plywood, also invested. "I like the way you spend my money," Laucks reportedly told Hinckle. Laucks had links to the Center for the Study of Democratic Institutions in Santa Barbara, a think tank founded by former University of Chicago president Robert Maynard Hutchins. Merton had mentioned the center frequently in his correspondence and urged Keating to contact several fellows and supporters.

Of the new investors, Mitchell would become the most actively involved in the magazine's daily operation. Raised in Erie, Pennsylvania, he prepped at Exeter and graduated from Yale, where the CIA recruited one of his roommates. Although the roommate never acknowledged that affiliation, Mitchell and his wife Margaretta began to see a pattern. "We always knew that wherever he went, something would happen later," Margaretta recalled.

The Mitchells moved to the Bay Area in 1961 to begin Fred's graduate studies in Latin American history. The following year, he inherited "a comfortable six figures of money" from his paternal grandfather, a lawyer, bank director, and investor. Mitchell's portfolio was growing as the stock and bond market expanded during the 1960s. "It's like a well," he explained to Margaretta. "You draw money out of the well and more seeps back in. Simple, really."

But Fred Mitchell—a handsome, charming, mild-mannered idealist—was foundering in graduate school and casting about for

a vocation. "I did try therapy with a silent uh-huh sort of thera-
pist," he wrote later, but he was deeply uncertain about his direction. Determined to do something, he responded to a full-page ad
in the *San Francisco Chronicle* about *Ramparts*. "So I called the magazine and someone answered, and I said that if they needed some
money, I had some money. 'Oh,' said the voice. 'Well, thank you.' "
A staff writer forwarded the message to Hinckle, who considered
it a long shot. He followed up only when the magazine's finances
became especially desperate.

Eventually Hinckle and Keating were invited to lunch at
Mitchell's home in the Berkeley hills. Hinckle discussed the goals
of the magazine, but Margaretta was wary. "My wife distrusted
him on sight, mostly because he did not eat," Mitchell recalled. "A
few days later, without consulting anyone, I sold some stock and
sent a check for $100,000 over to the magazine. . . . I did not
know what to ask for in return." Soon Mitchell was invited to a
Ramparts party at Gossage's San Francisco office. He took the bus,
walked to Pacific Avenue, trudged up the stairs, and noticed a
hand-lettered sign on the landing outside the office. "Welcome to
the Savior!" It didn't occur to Mitchell that the sign referred to
him. "I had apparently saved *Ramparts* from something dire," he
wrote later.

In 1966, Mitchell accepted a teaching position at the University of Kansas, but his interest in *Ramparts* continued. He told the
campus newspaper that he received all the manuscripts for approval and described the magazine's mission. "It's a dangerous
thing—and a marvelously dangerous thing—to try to change the
consensus," he said. "There's no telling what would happen then.
But *Ramparts* is doing what I as an individual would like to do and
do not have the courage to do." After a year in Kansas, Mitchell decided to return to the Bay Area and take a more active role in the
magazine. He told the campus paper that he had purchased stock
and lent the magazine money, which he was "damn well going to
recover . . . someday."

Decades later, Mitchell reflected on that decision.

I see little more than an earnest and naïve young man here, muddled in his identity, deeply worried about how this must appear to others, in a sort of crusader's trance of trying to do the right thing. . . . I knew that I had no plan. I knew that I looked lost in my dreamland. I was hooked up to a considerable amount of cash. I was headed for a point of life decision.

At the time, Margaretta had misgivings about the move. "He was riding this wave with all these crazy people to cloud cuckoo land," she recalled. "But I wanted him to protect his investment."

In the years to come, Fred Mitchell would serve as associate editor, senior editor, and publisher of *Ramparts*. His total investment in the magazine between 1966 and 1971, he wrote to a friend later, was "a frightening amount of money." He didn't discuss his cash infusions with Margaretta, but they probably came to between $700,000 and $800,000.

In that sense, Mitchell was indeed a kind of savior. Those who knew him well regarded him as a 1950s-vintage Clark Kent figure—personally modest but willing to use his gifts for the greater good. Others saw him as an easy mark with a reservoir of liberal guilt.

As new cash flowed in and out of the magazine's coffers, Keating's status at the magazine began to diminish. In the fall of 1965, Howard Gossage brokered a deal that kept Keating on as publisher but released one block of his stock to the staff and another to the new investors. But even as he struck the deal, Gossage was trying to engage Keating in other projects. During one meeting at Gossage's office, two *Ramparts* associates slipped out of the room and returned with signs that read "KEATING FOR CONGRESS" and "KEATING THE PEOPLE'S CHOICE." They began marching around the conference table with their signs and humming campaign tunes. To reinforce the message, Hinckle and Gossage joined the parade. "When it was all over," Earl Shorris wrote for the *Los Angeles Times* magazine, "Keating had decided to enter the primary and Hinckle was running the magazine."

In addition to handling Keating, Howard Gossage was recruiting new talent to improve the magazine's look. On a business trip to Houston, he met Dugald Stermer, who was working for a design shop there. Although Stermer had never worked on a magazine, Gossage arranged an interview for him at *Ramparts* in late 1964.

Like Hinckle, Stermer was a native Californian, but the similarities ended there. Born in Los Angeles, Stermer had a typical Lo-Cal upbringing. His father worked for McDonnell Douglas, the aerospace giant; his mother volunteered for the Children's Home Society and other causes. "I was a beach boy, your basic forties and fifties kid," he later said. "I liked playing cowboys and drawing pictures." As a teenager, he was something of a hood. "My image was surly, leather-jacketed, the white t-shirt with rolled up sleeves, the Levi's hanging low. A nasty little teenager. Who worked in a gas station, so I was greasy on top of all this." But a high school teacher noticed his talent as a cartoonist and encouraged him to attend college. He studied art at UCLA and worked for two years in a Los Angeles design shop before moving to Houston.

During his interview in Menlo Park, Stermer learned that the magazine had enough credit for two more issues. The principals seemed even less stable than the magazine's finances. Keating struck Stermer as eccentric, talking incessantly and naively about politics and conspiracy theories. Hinckle's sanity was also a question mark. But Stermer had no deep interest in designing corporate reports in Texas. When *Ramparts* offered him the art director's job, he packed his young family into his Volkswagen bus and headed for the Bay Area.

In his first week on the job, Stermer and Hinckle clashed over artistic control. According to Stermer, their exchange was brief and to the point.

Hinckle: What's this?
Stermer: It's the cover for the next issue.
Hinckle: Bullshit! . . . Where are you going?
Stermer: Back to Texas.

Hinckle yielded, and the exchange helped clarify Stermer's role as a key player at the magazine. "I was pretty intransigent about what I did, a 'my way or the highway' sort of thing," Stermer recalled. "I learned early that the person who gets there earliest and leaves latest makes all the decisions. Any territory you could defend was yours."

For Stermer, the fact that *Ramparts* was located in California was crucial. In part because the magazine wasn't based in New York, it was never expected to succeed. For this reason, Gossage said later, the *Ramparts* staff was like a troupe of dancing bears; their dancing ability was less impressive than the fact that they could dance at all. But these low expectations also allowed Stermer to innovate, and he made the most of his liberty.

Stermer didn't read magazines or the alternative press, so he had no preconceived notions of what *Ramparts* should look like. The *New York Herald Tribune*, whose Sunday supplement later morphed into *New York* magazine, was an influence, but mostly Stermer was guided by his UCLA professor's dictum that the best design is never noticed. To emphasize the magazine's message rather than its look, Stermer decided to set every line of type—the captions as well as the text—in Times Roman. That provided a frame and helped the other elements pop off the page. He also hired illustrators and photographers who read books; this, he believed, added an extra dimension to their work. Drawing on local styles, especially those developed by San Francisco printers Edwin and Robert Grabhorn, Stermer produced a bookish, elegant, and credible design.

In the office, Stermer usually roughed out the magazine in the morning with Hinckle, but because they were often on the road in search of fresh capital, they frequently planned issues on hotel room floors. As a result, staffers labored over the magazine back at the office while Stermer and Hinckle were deciding what would actually be printed. "It was high-handed," Stermer later admitted. Partly because of Hinckle's working style and personality, Stermer's arrival was a critical step forward for *Ramparts*. His easy-going manner and workhorse habits tempered Hinckle's extravagance and short attention span. Although Stermer also became part of the fundraising team, his unique contribution was creating a distinctive look that more established magazines would soon emulate. *Esquire* eventually went beyond emulation by trying to hire him. Stermer declined the offer, which would have matched his salary but diminished his artistic control.

With the addition of Hinckle and Stermer, *Ramparts* was beginning to resemble a major magazine. But the next addition to the staff would change the magazine's trajectory—and the nation's.

3

THE PERILOUS FIGHT

As *Ramparts* reinvented itself in late 1964, the nation was slowly turning its gaze to Vietnam. That obscure country had been a minor item in SLATE's 1962 litany of complaints about the Kennedy administration, but the situation there was changing rapidly. By the end of the following year, the Diem regime had lost support even in South Vietnam, where the Buddhist majority resented his pro-Catholic policies. When the Kennedy administration signaled that a coup would be welcome, South Vietnamese generals assassinated Diem and his brother. Three weeks later, President Kennedy himself was slain in Dallas.

In 1964, a U.S. spy ship captain reported that his vessel had been fired upon in the Gulf of Tonkin, and President Lyndon Johnson ordered a retaliatory air strike against two North Vietnamese naval bases. Three days later, and three months before the 1964 presidential election, Congress passed a resolution authorizing President Johnson to use whatever force was necessary to support freedom and to protect peace in Southeast Asia. Although Johnson declared that he sought no wider war, he also maintained that the United States would "continue to protect its national interests."

Ramparts rejected the official line. Its first cover photograph of 1965 was a dramatic close-up of a vulnerable Vietnamese woman and child. Inside was an interview with Frank Church, Keating's Stanford friend, who had become a U.S. Senator from Idaho. Church called the U.S. entry into Vietnam a mistake but insisted that the country was obliged to support the South Vietnamese effort. "The thing we must remember," he said, "is that there is no way for us to win their war for them." He called the South Vietnamese government "incompetent, to say the least," and warned that the United States must be prepared to withdraw if that government proved incapable of prevailing.

The issue also included a long article by Robert Scheer on naval medical officer Thomas Dooley and his bestselling book, *Deliver Us from Evil*. Although little remembered today, Dooley was a well-known figure with a remarkable personal history. Born into an affluent midwestern family, he attended Notre Dame University and squeaked through medical school before joining the navy in 1954. He volunteered for a mission called Passage to Freedom, whose purpose was to transport predominantly Catholic refugees to South Vietnam after Communists took control of the north. He administered a medical unit in Haiphong and successfully prevented major epidemics in the refugee camps. His efforts there drew the attention of journalists on the lookout for human-interest stories, and he soon decided to write a book about helping Vietnamese refugees. Published in 1956, *Deliver Us from Evil* presented the conflict in Vietnam as a morally simple one between godless Communists and freedom-loving Vietnamese. "We had come late to Vietnam, but we had come," Dooley wrote. "And we brought not bombs and guns, but help and love." The book sold briskly and was translated into more languages than any previous book except the Bible. One historian described it as "the *Uncle Tom's Cabin* of the Cold War."

In his piece for *Ramparts*, Scheer argued that the lack of historical context in *Deliver Us from Evil* made Dooley's book an unreliable guide to Vietnamese politics. In particular, Dooley neglected the effects of French colonialism and the popular uprising against it. For that reason, Scheer argued, the book "served to greatly confuse the American public on the true situation in Vietnam. It gave the delusion that we were simply helping a whole people along the path to *their* freedom when for better or worse they wanted to travel the other way."

•   •   •

Scheer's contribution marked another watershed in the magazine's development. The Keatings' passion and money had launched *Ramparts*, Hinckle's showmanship had transformed it, and Stermer had upgraded its look. But Scheer added political insight and deeper ideological commitments that grew out of his upbringing, studies, and activism.

Scheer was raised near the Allerton Avenue "Coops," the co-operative apartment complex in the Bronx built by Communists in the 1920s. Both of his parents were garment workers and labor activists. His father, a German immigrant, was an erstwhile Lutheran, Wobbly, and Communist who was kicked out of the party for refusing to settle a strike. Scheer lived with his mother, a Russian Jew who never applied for U.S. citizenship, in a building whose tenants were mostly Russian Jews or Russian Orthodox. A latchkey kid, Scheer delivered milk, scalped tickets, worked in a stencil factory, and did odd jobs around the neighborhood to sup-plement his mother's meager income.

Scheer struggled with learning disorders as a youth, but a sci-ence teacher encouraged him to study engineering, pointing out that it was his best chance to enter college. Once admitted to City College of New York, he switched his major to economics. He also learned to debate at City College, whose reputation for verbal conflict bordered on the gladiatorial. When his classes were over, Scheer worked at the post office before returning to his mother's apartment late in the evening.

After graduation, Scheer attended Syracuse University but soon transferred to Berkeley to study economics. Once there, he was offered a fellowship at the Center for Chinese Studies, but his interests weren't limited to Asia. "I couldn't go to China," he re-called later, "but I could go to Cuba." He made that trip in the summer of 1960. Back in Berkeley, he gave impassioned speeches about Cuba and American foreign policy on the Cal campus near Sather Gate. Maurice Zeitlin, a graduate student in sociology and a charismatic speaker, joined him in that effort. After one of their stem-winders, they were approached by Lawrence Ferlinghetti,

who suggested that they write a book for City Lights, the legendary San Francisco bookstore that he owned. Located in North
Beach, an Italian neighborhood stuffed with cafes, restaurants, and
Catholic churches, the bookstore added a bohemian accent to the
strip joints and taverns that festooned the corner of Broadway and
Columbus. Famous for publishing Allen Ginsberg's *Howl* and the
obscenity trial that followed, City Lights was a center of Beat literature and anarchist politics.

Scheer conducted some of his research for the book at the
Center for Chinese Studies, whose archives contained transcripts
of Cuban radio programs. Because of his dyslexia, he dictated
whole chapters of the manuscript. For editorial help, the authors
turned to their *Root and Branch* colleague, David Horowitz. In the
end, Scheer's work on the Cuba book didn't help his standing at
the Center for Chinese Studies. When a new director came on
board, Scheer was reprimanded for misusing the center's copier
and lost his fellowship. "They were pissed off that I was writing a
book and giving speeches," he said later. Scheer returned to the
economics department for financial support but came away
empty-handed.

When Scheer finished his master's thesis, he and Zeitlin celebrated in Berkeley before heading across the Bay Bridge on
Scheer's motor scooter. The plan was to show the thesis to Ferlinghetti at City Lights. While driving on the bridge, they noticed
that other drivers and passengers were gesturing at them, which
they construed as hostile reactions to their beards and long hair.
But when they turned around, they saw the pages of Scheer's thesis blowing off the back of the scooter, across the traffic lanes, and
into the bay. "In those days, it was very difficult to make a copy of
a large manuscript," Scheer recalled, "so I was out of luck." He
never completed his master's degree.

In 1961, Zeitlin accepted a position at Princeton University,
but that summer he traveled to Cuba with a press credential from
KPFA, the Berkeley public radio station. While staying in the Havana Libre, formerly the Hilton Hotel, he drank late into the night

with a man who turned out to be an economic advisor to Che Guevara, the Argentine physician turned Marxist guerrilla. The next day, Che's armed guards were at Zeitlin's door, telling him and his pregnant wife to climb into their jeep. They were driven to meet Che, who "looked like a movie star," Zeitlin said later. Che answered all of the couple's questions and offered medical advice to Zeitlin's wife about her pregnancy. Zeitlin also had a long unofficial interview with Che that started at 3 A.M. the day he and his wife left Cuba. The interview with Che appeared in the first issue of *Root and Branch*, and Zeitlin wrote three related articles for the *Nation*.

In the end, Ferlinghetti didn't wish to publish Scheer and Zeitlin's Cuba manuscript. Stuffed with charts and tables, it was too academic for City Lights. "I wanted a book like the speech you gave," he told them. The manuscript eventually landed at Grove Press after sixteen other publishers turned it down. In declining the project, publisher Alfred Knopf reportedly told a senior editor that he didn't want to kick his president when he was down. At the time, Kennedy was taking heavy criticism because of the Bay of Pigs fiasco.

Cuba: Tragedy in Our Hemisphere finally appeared in 1963. By that time, the missile crisis of October 1962 had raised U.S.-Cuba relations to fever pitch. That showdown, Zeitlin and Scheer argued, epitomized "the failure and dangers of much of our foreign policy." In the case of Cuba, that policy was based on "false assumptions, self-righteous moralizing, and considerable arrogance toward the Cuban Revolutionary Government." In their conclusion, Zeitlin and Scheer also described the state of affairs at the time of the book's publication.

> The revolutionaries have tried, while taking measures necessary to protect the revolution, to instill by example and precept a respect for dissent. It remains to be seen whether continued U.S. pressures will force them to severely limit civil liberties and other personal freedoms. We have, by our

determined hostility, impelled the development in Cuba of an atmosphere which cannot accept dissent. By attacking Cuba in the name of democracy, the United States has also damaged democracy's meaning, and is increasingly alienating the revolutionaries from what is valuable in the Western tradition.

Zeitlin and Scheer also called for relaxed travel and trade restrictions between the two countries. Finally, they recommended an agreement in which the United States would convert the Guantánamo naval base into an inter-American university, but only if Cuba sent all Soviet military personnel home and worked to make Latin America a nuclear-free zone.

After losing his fellowship, Scheer began working at City Lights, where he read widely and eventually came upon an article about Vietnam in *China Quarterly*. His interest piqued, Scheer learned that Madame Nhu, Diem's sister-in-law, would be visiting San Francisco in 1963. Scheer helped organize a protest outside her hotel, the luxurious Sheraton-Palace. The next year, he traveled to Vietnam as a freelance journalist. Paul Krassner, publisher of the *Realist* and editor of Lenny Bruce's *How to Talk Dirty and Influence People*, met Scheer in New York and was impressed by his interest in Vietnam, which Krassner knew little about. Using the proceeds from a popular poster he had produced, Krassner offered to buy Scheer's ticket to Vietnam. (The poster, which read "Fuck Communism," satirized both contemporary obscenity laws and the cold war mentality; Kurt Vonnegut later called it "a miracle of compressed intelligence.") In return for the airfare, Krassner, who later served as *Ramparts*' "society editor," asked Scheer for an article on American activities in Vietnam.

More than twenty publishers passed on Scheer's subsequent pamphlet, *How the United States Got Involved in Vietnam*, before the Center for the Study of Democratic Institutions published it in 1965. Former labor organizer and journalist Paul Jacobs, who was connected to both the center and *Ramparts*, helped Scheer place the pamphlet. Jacobs's friend Saul Landau, a former Ballantine editor who had met Scheer in Cuba, shaped the manuscript. Scheer complained to Krassner that the editing process was like having one of his balls cut off; Krassner told him to send the other one to him at the *Realist*.

The Vietnam pamphlet offered a similar conclusion to the one presented in the Cuba book: namely, that a flawed policy had grown out of an unchallenged American consensus about anticommunist efforts abroad. "The idea that Communist or Viet Minh rule under Ho Chi Minh might be better for the Vietnamese than any alternative political system has never really been examined in the United States because it is unthinkable," Scheer maintained.

Scheer's big break at *Ramparts* came only after Denise Hinckle and Scheer's girlfriend, Anne Weills, met while working at a downtown brokerage. The two couples began to socialize, and Warren Hinckle was soon touting Scheer at the office. When he mentioned Scheer's intellect, Keating reportedly replied, "Never hire anyone smarter than you. They'll try and take over." Scheer had his own doubts about Keating, whom he later described as "an odd duck." Their first lunch together was served by topless waitresses, which distracted Scheer. "It didn't seem safe to serve hot food that way," he said later.

Keating bridled at Scheer's Berkeley-style radicalism and brash manner, but Hinckle stressed his Vietnam expertise and argued that he could help recruit leftist investors. Scheer's Berkeley connections were also useful in raising Keating's profile. In May 1965, Scheer and Keating spoke at the Vietnam teach-in on the Berkeley campus along with Norman Mailer, I. F. Stone, and other notables.

Scheer's role at the magazine began to expand, and in July 1965, he coordinated a special report on Southeast Asia. The cover featured a cartoon of Ho Chi Minh in a pose resembling George Washington crossing the Potomac. The issue included two pieces

by Scheer along with his exclusive interview with Prince Si-
hanouk of Cambodia. One of the pieces, co-authored with
Hinckle, drew from Scheer's pamphlet. The article traced the ori-
gins of U.S. support for Diem to his 1950 conversation with
Michigan State University political scientist Wesley Fishel in a
Tokyo tea room.

The interview with Prince Sihanouk, who had declined U.S.
aid, warned of a humiliating defeat for the Americans in Vietnam.
Sihanouk predicted that a major confrontation would favor the
spread of Communism in Southeast Asia. "Your compatriots understand nothing of Asia," he told Scheer. "They are afraid of it!
They mistrust it! And they are astonished that they are not loved!"
The following month, Scheer was promoted to Southeast Asia
correspondent; by October, he was listed as foreign editor.

During this time, Scheer was also working on *Ramparts'* first
major investigative piece. Drawn from his research and published
in April 1966, it was a classic whistleblower story about U.S. policy
in Vietnam. While digging through government documents in the
Cal library, Scheer came upon the name of Stanley Sheinbaum, a
Michigan State University professor who became co-director of
MSU's Vietnam Project in 1957. In that position, Sheinbaum
worked knowingly with the CIA, but due to an administrative
oversight, he never signed a secrecy pledge. As part of his duties,
Sheinbaum recruited trainers to set up a police force in South
Vietnam. But on a trip to Saigon, Sheinbaum was denied access
to an entire floor of the building that was supposedly under
his authority. Later he also learned that some of the CIA officers
on his project staff were torturing Vietnamese prisoners during
interrogations.

After returning to the United States, Sheinbaum met with four
top South Vietnamese officials in San Francisco. "Within an hour
of their arrival," Sheinbaum later recalled, "the youngest, a nephew
of Ngo Dinh Diem, conspiratorially drew me aside and informed

me that one of the others was going to kill the eldest of the group."
Feeling that his original goals had been badly compromised,
Sheinbaum resigned from the project in 1959.

By the time Scheer contacted him, Sheinbaum was at the Center for the Study of Democratic Institutions in Santa Barbara. He
cooperated with Scheer on the *Ramparts* story and even wrote an
introduction to it. The article made it clear that the CIA secretly
used Michigan State University to train Saigon police, maintain a
stock of ammunition, and write the South Vietnamese constitution. When the article ran, the cover featured an illustration of a
busty Madame Nhu wearing an MSU cheerleadering outfit and
holding a college pennant. Inside, the story's other characters were
depicted in cheerleading, coaching, and football gear. Hinckle
took the byline along with staff writer Sol Stern and Scheer, whose
research was credited for the piece.

In addition to undermining official U.S. pronouncements
about Vietnam, the story startled the U.S. intelligence community.
On April 18, CIA director William Raborn ordered a "rundown"
on *Ramparts*, especially Sheinbaum and Scheer, "on a high-
priority basis." The order violated the National Security Act of
1947, which established the CIA and prohibited it from spying on
U.S. residents. That violation meant that a cover-up would also be
required.

The CIA rundown traced the development of the magazine
and identified two Communist Party members on its staff. It also
noted that the magazine's most outspoken CIA critic wasn't a
Communist but rather former Special Forces sergeant Donald
Duncan, an anticommunist Catholic whose first-person account
of his Vietnam experience became the February 1966 cover story.
In that piece, Duncan concluded that anticommunism "was a
lousy substitute for democracy." The cover photograph of Duncan
in uniform and the caption ("The Whole Thing Was a Lie!") became a *Ramparts* icon. Duncan soon joined the *Ramparts* staff and
later wrote that America "would continue to be in danger as long
as the CIA is deciding policy and manipulating nations."

Meanwhile, CIA officers spent two months identifying the magazine's investors. By linking *Ramparts* to foreign funding, they could justify their surveillance of a U.S. magazine. Although that effort failed, the *Ramparts*-CIA saga was far from over.

Scheer's arrival gave *Ramparts* a significant boost, but it also highlighted a growing schism at the magazine. Whereas Keating's original hires were mostly Catholic suburbanites, Hinckle's recruits were secular, more likely to live in San Francisco or Berkeley, and more attuned to the Bay Area's burgeoning youth culture. There were no pitched battles between the two groups, but the gap between them was uncomfortably wide.

The schism was given full expression one day in the Menlo Park office when managing editor James Colaianni, a self-described lay Catholic theologian with a large family, told contributing editor Ralph Gleason that he had driven his children to see the Beatles at the Cow Palace, the San Francisco venue that had also hosted the 1964 Republican convention. Gleason, a Berkeley resident in his forties, listened attentively. He was the *Chronicle's* jazz critic, one of the nation's first and finest, but he had also written perceptively and appreciatively about folk and pop music. When Colaianni added that he remained in his car during the concert, Gleason was flabbergasted. "You mean you *really* stayed outside listening to some tin on the car radio *when you could be seeing the Beatles*? Man, you're putting me on. *Nobody* could be that un-hip."

As a young Catholic with few political investments of his own, Hinckle managed to bridge the gap between the two groups. But once put in charge of the magazine, he moved the office to San Francisco, where the magazine's younger secularists began to flourish. Located at 301 Broadway, the new headquarters lay between two neighborhoods with distinctive cultures and histories. Up the hill lay North Beach, home of the Jazz Workshop and the hungry i, the legendary nightclub that hosted Lenny Bruce and other cutting-edge comedians. Another North Beach nightclub, the Condor, featured topless dancer Carol Doda. Down the hill lay the old Barbary Coast, famous for its port activity and raucous nightlife during the gold rush days. (Hinckle's grandmother had been a dance-hall girl there.) Ravaged by the 1906 earthquake, that neighborhood had long since been built out with landfill and topped with office buildings. By the mid-1960s, it had become a favorite address for television stations and advertising agencies, including Gossage's.

Keating was displeased with the move to San Francisco, but he adjusted in part by decorating his new office to his liking. While on assignment for *Ramparts*, he had interviewed *Playboy* publisher Hugh Hefner in Chicago. Appearing in September 1965, "Sex and the Single Playboy: The Gospel According to Hugh Hefner" was laid out to resemble a medieval manuscript, and the unsigned interview ranged over the subjects of St. Paul, medieval asceticism, modern psychology, sexual mores, and Hefner's "philosophy." When Hinckle moved the magazine's headquarters to San Francisco, Keating brought in his original office manager and told her he wanted "a pad—just like Hefner's." Although the rest of the office was painted in a riot of bright colors, Keating chose heavy curtains, a thick black rug, black imitation leather couches, and swivel-balloon chairs. "They're going to cut me up," Keating reportedly told her. "I've got to do something to retain my identity—this is my last chance."

The move to San Francisco coincided with a change in the magazine's tone. A hip, cavalier urbanity replaced the moral earnestness of the early issues. Hinckle's irreverence blended with Scheer's chutzpah and Stermer's visual imagination to create striking effects. The Hefner article, for example, included a foldout—not of a naked model, but of a pipe-smoking Hefner. The following month's foldout, which accompanied an article about the Beatles' *A Hard Day's Night*, featured a close-up of a black beetle.

The office routine also began to reflect Hinckle's personality and habits. Staffers rarely arrived at the office on time, but they often worked late, partly because Hinckle frequently made major last-minute changes to the forthcoming issue. Managing editor Larry Benksy often arrived in the morning to find that Hinckle had completely rearranged the forthcoming issue overnight. "Warren couldn't keep his paws off the magazine," recalled Bensky, who bowed out less than a year later, telling Hinckle that he "wasn't put on the planet to do this." Bensky landed at KPFA, where he would eventually serve as station manager and host of the Sunday morning public affairs program.

The big question in the office was whether or not Hinckle would appear that day. When he did, the energy level rose dramatically. But even when he was in town, Hinckle usually worked out of Cookie Picetti's, a North Beach bar located near the old Hall of Justice. It was a favorite spot for police officers and other law enforcement types, and some of Hinckle's left-wing colleagues were uneasy about drinking there. Hinckle typically silenced their protests by challenging them to name a decent left-wing bar. Scheer also objected to Hinckle's favorite spots, both in San Francisco and on the road, but not on ideological grounds; his main complaint was that there weren't enough women there.

The *Ramparts* staff also made good use of the neighborhood's restaurants and other bars. Vanessi's and Swiss Louie's were favorites for lunches in North Beach, and Andre's was the default watering hole. Occasionally the *Ramparts* crew took the ferry to Tiburon, the upscale Marin County town, for lunch on the marina; on one such trip, Hinckle tossed an inadequate manuscript into the bay.

The staff learned to function without Hinckle in the office, but occasionally a junior member was dispatched to find him. On his first day as a part-time office assistant, Reese Erlich was told to summon Hinckle to check final galleys. He found Hinckle lunching with Gossage at Enrico's, a North Beach bistro a few blocks away. When Erlich delivered his message, Hinckle replied, "Fuck you, kid." Erlich, who was awaiting trial for his antiwar protests in the East Bay, was unfazed; the Oakland police had been far scarier.

"May I quote you on that?" he asked. When Hinckle assented, Erlich cheerfully shot back, "Fuck you, too." He was promoted
shortly thereafter.

Hinckle's style was nothing if not kinetic. Staff writer Adam
Hochschild recalled it this way:

> He raced through each 18-hour day with dizzying speed.
> All action at the magazine swirled around him: a pet mon-
> key named Henry Luce would sit on his shoulder while he
> paced his office, drink in hand, shouting instructions into a
> speakerphone across the room to someone in New York
> about a vast promotional mailing; on his couch would be
> sitting, slightly dazed, a French television crew, or Malcolm
> X's widow (who arrived one day surrounded by a dozen
> bodyguards with loaded shotguns), or the private detective
> to whom Hinckle had given the title Criminology Editor.
> Then would follow an afternoon-long lunch where
> Hinckle would consume a dozen Scotches without show-
> ing the slightest effect and sketch dummies of the next
> issue's pages on the restaurant's placemats. Finally he'd be
> off on the night plane to see new backers in the East.

In New York, the maelstrom continued. James Ridgeway's
1969 profile of Hinckle in the *New York Times Magazine* described
his fantastical performances at the Algonquin Hotel.

> In the dining room Hinckle would be recounting his
> scheme for a publishing empire, expanding *Ramparts*, start-
> ing one, two, or three radio and television stations, starting
> an author's agency, setting up teams of reporters who
> would get the goods on LBJ, NATO, the Pope, etc. *Ram-
> parts* would publish books, set up book clubs, start a syndi-
> cate. . . . If one dared to ask where the money was really
> going to come from, Hinckle would fall back into his chair

and suck on a grasshopper while Scheer lunged forward. "What's the matter?" he'd say, "Got no guts?"

Hinckle's effect on his colleagues, especially younger ones, was dazzling. "Hinckle was amazing," said Michael Ansara, a Harvard SDS leader and *Ramparts* researcher. "As an undergraduate, I'd visit him at the Algonquin. He'd start talking in the shower, continue the conversation while putting on his tuxedo, and then we'd be off for oysters with Abby Rockefeller." The company Hinckle kept was part of the glamour. "I once had dinner with him and Oriana Fallaci," Ansara said. "I was about eighteen years old. I'd never seen a woman like her, much less had dinner with her. He was the most cosmopolitan, flamboyant, creative guy I'd ever seen." By most accounts, Hinckle was larger than life. So were some of his belongings; during one visit to his apartment, Maurice Zeitlin maneuvered around a stuffed pink elephant that was ten feet wide.

As some of these portraits make clear, Hinckle's prodigious drinking was well known and frequently on display. On one occasion, Hinckle asked Erlich and his girlfriend, a secretary at *Ramparts*, to drive him to the airport. Along the way, he invited his companions to join him for a drink. Both were underage, but Erlich accompanied Hinckle into the bar. Without prompting, the bartender set up fifteen screwdrivers for Hinckle, who polished them off and missed his flight. "Going up there to drink with him was like going to Vietnam," Joe Ippolito recalled.

None of this made for smooth sailing, but most of the magazine's major achievements took place in San Francisco during Hinckle's tenure. Part of that success is attributable to his enormous network and media savvy. "Hinckle was a train wreck," Erlich recalled later, "but a brilliant publicist." Some of *Ramparts'* most successful publicity efforts—for example, full-page ads in the *New York Times*—were Gossage's ideas, but Hinckle also had a great feeling for the sport. When Erlich had an idea for a story on the valuable job skills he would acquire through military service—

for example, shooting people and blowing them up—Hinckle worked up a press release. Herb Caen, the influential *Chronicle* columnist and friend of Gossage, picked up the story, and the *Los Angeles Times* interviewed Erlich while he stood in line at the draft board office.

Hinckle was completely at home in San Francisco, and though Herb Caen routinely referred to *Ramparts'* star editor as "Berkeley Bob Scheer," Scheer also felt that San Francisco as a whole was their territory. "The Village is like a separate city in New York," Scheer said later. "But in San Francisco, even the stockbrokers were into it." When the magazine's interns hitchhiked around the Bay Area, they found that motorists were often familiar with the magazine. If two staffers mentioned *Ramparts* on the bus, the driver might turn around and compliment an article from a recent issue. "We loved the town and everything that was happening there," Scheer recalled. "It seemed like the center of the world. We weren't the farm club for anyone. At that time, for those of us who cared about challenging the culture, it was exhilarating."

That exhilaration, however, was accompanied by a growing sense of anxiety in the office. As *Ramparts* dug into the less savory aspects of America's most powerful institutions, the staff suspected that the government was watching them. One of their colleagues, William Turner, confirmed that suspicion. Raised Catholic in Buffalo, Turner had joined the FBI, received training in wiretapping and burglary, and listened in on telephone conversations in the Bay Area. But he had run afoul of Hoover after objecting to the FBI director's characterization of Martin Luther King Jr. as "the most notorious liar in the country."

Turner left the FBI after ten years of service, settled in Marin County, and wrote a piece about the bureau's failure to obtain convictions on civil rights violations in the south. After stumbling upon an issue of *Ramparts* at his tennis club, he called Keating, who encouraged him to submit the article. It was accepted immediately, and soon Turner became a staff writer. After his *Ramparts* articles appeared, Hoover wrote about him in an internal memo, "It's a shame we can't nail this jackal."

Turner assured his *Ramparts* colleagues that the government was watching them. "Wiretaps are your tax dollars at work," he told Stermer. "If your phone isn't bugged, we're not doing our job." At one *Ramparts* cocktail party, Turner wrote in the magazine, he had the odd sensation of hearing a voice from the past that he couldn't quite place. He studied the speaker's face, which was totally unfamiliar. Then he solved the puzzle. The voice belonged to Robert Treuhaft, Jessica Mitford's husband. As a young FBI agent in the 1950s, Turner had listened to hours of his telephone conversations.

There were other indications, too, that the magazine's adversaries were trying to undermine its efforts. Stermer was audited in two consecutive years, and when Turner arrived at the office the morning after Easter 1967, he found shattered windows, fire extinguisher goo covering the furniture, and an IBM Selectric typewriter lying askew in the toilet. Turner suspected that the CIA had ransacked the office but saw no signs of forced entry. Years later, Hinckle telephoned Turner from Cookie Picetti's; a former law enforcement officer and GOP official had just confessed to burglarizing the *Ramparts* office in 1967. Hinckle asked Turner to question his new acquaintance about his burglary story. "But he couldn't have done it," Hinckle added, "because Gene Marine and I did it." Hinckle and Marine, a staff writer, had trashed the office after a drinking session at Tosca Cafe, another North Beach bar. But the burglar claimed that his caper had occurred two nights earlier, and he convinced Hinckle by producing the editor's bar receipts from Cookie Picetti's along with some *Ramparts* files. He told Turner that right-wing organizations had sponsored the burglaries, and that the findings were shared with CIA agents.

The staff coped with its surveillance anxiety in various ways. Some used pay telephones to elude wiretaps, and heavy drinking was an all-purpose form of self-medication—not only for Hinckle, but also for Scheer and Stermer. Other drugs were readily available but not tolerated in the office. While serving as assistant managing editor, Sol Stern ejected staff writer Jann Wenner from the building for smoking pot. Stern didn't disapprove of marijuana, and their peers at the *Village Voice*, for example, regularly lit up at the office. But Stern figured correctly that the government was watching them, and a drug arrest was the last thing *Ramparts* needed.

As whistle-blowing exposés became the magazine's trademark, staffers had more difficulty distinguishing healthy skepticism from garden-variety paranoia. Both Keating and Hinckle had a soft spot for conspiracy theories, but even Hinckle recognized that these tales frequently shaded into delusion or baseless distrust of the government. He also understood that such delusions made psychic demands on the muckraker and were unwelcome in polite society.

> Paranoia is a little like dog shit. Once you step in it, you can never be sure it is not still with you. . . . You pretend—or really believe—it matters not which, since the result is the same—that the dog doo isn't there, you press on, leaving tracks across people's rugs and hardwood floors, generally creating a stink, and giving the impression of being some sort of nut.

For working journalists, the main drawback of paranoia is a loss of perspective on the stories at hand. Even Hinckle's memoir, a valuable account of the magazine's history, tilts strongly toward tales of intrigue whose upshots are sometimes negligible. But *Ramparts'* best work during this time consistently combined passion, brass, and factual accuracy.

As *Ramparts* continued to develop, it also became a launching pad for other ventures. In 1966, three *Ramparts* principals ran for Congress as peace candidates. Keating and Stanley Sheinbaum lost in the San Mateo and Santa Barbara Democratic primaries, respectively, but both surprised experts by receiving more than 40 percent of the vote. During his campaign, Keating announced that he wouldn't accept donations over one dollar. He lost again the next year when the incumbent's death led to a special election; his neighbor, Shirley Temple Black, also ran unsuccessfully and was later made a United Nations delegate. Sheinbaum's second effort in 1968 was likewise unsuccessful.

In the end, Scheer's campaign was the most remarkable of them all. In 1966, he challenged incumbent Jeffery Cohelan in California's District 7, which included Oakland and Berkeley. Democrats outnumbered Republicans two to one in the district, so their primary was the key race. Cohelan, a mainstream liberal, was a former milkman and local union leader who had received a master's degree in economics at Cal and a Fulbright scholarship to study at Oxford and Leeds. He supported Johnson's Great Society legislation, decried racism in southern cities, and opposed the exploitation of farm workers closer to home. But he didn't speak out strongly against the Vietnam War, HUAC, or the poverty and racism in his own district.

Scheer's candidacy was the product of rising impatience with the party line. At twenty-nine, Scheer was unknown to most voters in the district, but in October 1965, he was invited to attend a Faculty Peace Committee meeting on campus. He came on strong, forcefully pushing an antiwar line and advocating legalized marijuana and abortion. Some committee members recoiled, but Scheer emerged as the party's peace candidate, and he tempered his image as the campaign progressed. He favored dark Brooks Brothers suits to go along with his black-framed glasses and trim goatee. From the outset, he considered his campaign an elaborate attempt to persuade Cohelan to oppose the war, and he told crowds he would drop out of the race if Cohelan did so. Years later, he summed up his position by quoting the SDS slogan, "Part of the Way with LBJ."

By that time, Scheer was married to his second wife, Anne Weills. The daughter of a telephone company executive, Weills grew up in affluent Marin County, across the Golden Gate Bridge from San Francisco. Her studies took her to Paris, where she met French leftists and steeped herself in that country's troubled history in Vietnam. Returning to the Bay Area in late 1963, she began working with Denise Hinckle at a San Francisco brokerage and threw herself into political activism. After attending a debate on Cuba between Scheer and Saul Landau, she met Scheer and declined his advances. But their paths crossed again when they both picketed the local Cadillac dealership for refusing to employ blacks. She was arrested for that action, and at her trial, the police camera showed the picketers making their rounds. "Every time the camera picked Bobby up," she recalled, "he was with a different woman."

But Weills and Scheer had a great deal in common, and a courtship ensued. Weills had no urge to marry, but his mother, who had never married Scheer's late father, was adamant. After scheduling and canceling a wedding, Weills and Scheer finally went through with a City Hall ceremony. Members of the San Francisco Mime Troupe, already famous for its political satire, were there; years later, Weills jokingly compared the wedding to performance art. From City Hall, the wedding party repaired to 263 Castro Street, where the Hinckles had purchased a Victorian house from radical lawyers Fay and Marvin Stender, who had recently divorced.

Not all of Scheer's friends approved of his congressional bid. Berkeley activist and former *Root and Branch* colleague Frank Bardacke distrusted electoral politics as a vehicle for radical change, and though he admired Scheer, he wondered about his magazine. "*Ramparts* seemed a little slick to me," recalled Bardacke, who wrote for the underground *San Francisco Express-Times* and was reading *Liberation* and the *New Left Review*. Others regarded any affiliation with the Democratic Party as a form of selling out. But Scheer had the support of the California Democratic Council (CDC) and many Cal professors. His supporters also included Robert Treuhaft, who ran unsuccessfully for Alameda County district attorney the same year and later hired Hillary Clinton as a summer intern.

According to Weills, Scheer was a reluctant candidate. He was an excellent speaker, but he was too private, insecure, and self-critical to be a natural politician. Spurning the usual campaign staples of handshaking and baby kissing, Scheer focused instead on rousing critiques of the country's liberal consensus.

Carl Bloice, a black reporter for *People's World*, the Communist Party newspaper based in San Francisco, served as Scheer's campaign coordinator. Describing his candidate's effect on local voters, Bloice said Scheer was "probably the first person that appeared in front of them that forced them to think. God knows how many people had appeared before to flatter them." Scheer's speeches, all extemporaneous, were clear and pointed. In one, he claimed that everyone in Vietnam instantly recognized the U.S. official line as gibberish. Likewise, the language of Johnson's war on poverty was nonsense to those whom the programs were intended to help. If it was unreasonable to call out those discrepancies, Scheer said, "then this is going to be a very unreasonable campaign."

For Bloice, the campaign was also transformational. He later noted that it led to "spiritual and psychological salvation—no, that may not be the right word—say, stability—for the people of my generation. The temptation to go mad while everybody else was going mad, or opt out for some kind of escape—it's there, it's all very tempting. A lot of people who were ready to give up got heart from the Scheer campaign." That effect was similar to the one *Ramparts* had on many readers. For example, SLATE member and Free Speech Movement activist Jeff Lustig recalled that reading *Ramparts* during that time was "reassurance that we weren't going nuts."

Scheer's campaign assembled a coalition of antiwar liberals, blacks, and radicals. Breaking with Democratic tradition, he accepted support from Communists and International Socialists, arguing that anticommunism among American liberals had produced the Vietnam War in the first place. The campaign also gathered substantial support from the "hill people"—more affluent residents of the leafy East Bay hills that separated the working-class flatlands of Berkeley and Oakland from the plusher, whiter, and more conservative suburbs to the east. Scheer received endorsements from local black leaders, Julian Bond, Dick Gregory, Oregon senator Wayne Morse, and television star Robert Vaughn. He also tapped the idealism of many young voters, including Alice Waters, who would later found Chez Panisse, the Berkeley restaurant and landmark.

Cohelan ran endorsements from prominent Cal faculty, President Johnson, Vice President Hubert Humphrey, Governor Brown, U.S. senators William Fulbright and Mike Mansfield, the AFL-CIO's George Meany, and House Speaker John McCormack. Another supporter was Alameda County judge and Berkeley school board member Spurgeon "Sparky" Avakian, whose son Bob studied English at Cal and was a researcher for *Ramparts*.

The race made good copy. Three national magazines covered it, as did the *New York Times* and *Washington Post*. Scheer called Cohelan an example of "middle of the road extremism." Cohelan's campaign manager called the radical left "a bunch of unmade beds." The *Chronicle* endorsed Cohelan, and the *Examiner* charged that Scheer had "come not to praise the Democratic Party but to bury it." In their *Washington Post* column, Rowland Evans and Robert Novak called Scheer a "bearded editor of the leftist *Ramparts* magazine and an articulate apologist for the Communist Vietcong." They also described him as part of a sinister "leftist wrecking crew." They implied that this crew included Representative Phil Burton, a liberal Democrat from San Francisco, but failed to note that Cohelan was Burton's brother-in-law.

As the race tightened, the *National Observer* quoted an exasperated Cohelan.

> This is no fun. I've lost my sense of humor. I'm disturbed about this campaign. No, not disturbed. I'm plain outraged. I've been a good Congressman for eight years. I've reached a point in the House where I have the respect of my peers.

I really have some influence. And now, comes an arrogant
kid saying I don't deserve to go back. It's outrageous!

Cohelan's campaign manager was more dismissive. "The typical primary voter is probably a civil-service job-holder or someone who has a stake in the party. He's going to spend thirty to forty
seconds looking over the sample ballot and maybe a minute in the
booth. . . . And when he sees Scheer's name, he's going to ask,
'Who's he?' " About Scheer's coalition, the campaign manager
said, "What they're really trying to do is make Cal the capital of the
new left. But can you really take these people seriously? Aren't
they really staging an exercise like eating goldfish?" He scoffed at
the notion that Cohelan was out of touch with Oakland's black
voters. Scheer's supporters, he said, were "trying to tell Jeff about
what's going on in West Oakland. Who the hell do they think they
are? Jeff drove a milk truck in West Oakland before these kids were
even born."

The vote was uncomfortably close for Cohelan. White House
press secretary Bill Moyers, who had already received secret intelligence on Scheer from the CIA, called the Alameda County clerk
three times on election night to check the results. In the end,
Scheer drew 45 percent of the vote. Reflecting on the effort
shortly after the primary, Scheer said, "I think the main achievement of the campaign was that it was bold. Left liberal politics during the Cold War was characterized by fear, and our stance was
arrogant." Later observers would see the Scheer campaign as a
turning point in East Bay politics. Four years later, Ron Dellums
unseated Cohelan and became one of the most outspoken congressional critics of American militarism.

Scheer's congressional bid was remarkable, but it didn't reflect the
general direction of California politics. In fact, the state was poised
for a significant conservative backlash after two terms of Pat
Brown's leadership.

That movement's leader was Ronald Reagan. *Ramparts* began tracking his political fortunes in November 1965, when Jessica Mitford reviewed his autobiography, *Where's the Rest of Me?* A Truman supporter in 1948, Reagan spent most of the 1950s as a spokesman for General Electric after his film career began to flag. But in 1952, he resumed his position as president of the Screen Actor's Guild and pushed through an antitrust waiver for his longtime agent and sponsor, MCA's Lew Wasserman. (Testifying before a grand jury ten years later, Reagan claimed that he couldn't recall the details of an apparent conflict of interest.) Reagan supported Nixon in 1960 and offered to register as a Republican, but GOP leaders decided he was more useful as a Democrat. Two years later, he switched parties, and his speech at the 1964 GOP convention in San Francisco made him a rising political star.

Mitford's article, which was accompanied by cutout costumes for each of Reagan's public roles, appeared before Reagan announced his intention to run for governor. He went on to win the Republican nomination in 1966 and attack Brown for his permissiveness. Reagan's key campaign promises were to "clean up the mess in Berkeley," where the Free Speech Movement and antiwar protests had made national headlines, and to "send the welfare bums back to work." In an unscripted aside, Reagan also derided labor leader César Chávez, who wrote about his organizing experiences in the June 1966 issue of *Ramparts*. When Chávez led a 25-day, 300-mile march to Sacramento that spring, Reagan called it an "Easter egg roll." Reagan's aides cringed, but Brown failed to capitalize on the gaffe. Instead of meeting with Chávez when his contingent arrived at the state capitol, Brown spent Easter weekend at Frank Sinatra's house in Palm Springs.

Reagan also questioned California's recently minted fair housing act. The bill was sponsored by W. Byron Rumford, a black assemblyman from the East Bay, where residential segregation was a longstanding fact of life. The legislature passed the Rumford Act in 1963, but a statewide ballot initiative to disable it passed by a two-to-one margin the following year. Although the matter would eventually be settled in court, the issue reverberated though the 1966 gubernatorial contest. Brown referred the question to a nonpartisan commission; Reagan decried racism but claimed "the right of an individual to the ownership and disposition of property is inseparable from the right of freedom itself." Delivered to an audience of real estate brokers, Reagan's declaration prompted a standing ovation.

From his perch at the *Nation*, longtime California observer Carey McWilliams parsed Reagan's message. "There will be more of this kind of demagogy as the campaign comes to a climax," McWilliams predicted, "with Reagan using code words and phrases to let the electorate know his right-wing stand on racial issues without his having to voice outright racist sentiments." McWilliams also prepared his readers for a Reagan victory. "Unless Governor Brown can find some potent issues to outweigh this obsessive fear of open housing, he is in grave danger."

Behind Reagan's declaration lay an event that made fair housing an even more volatile issue. In the summer of 1965, the predominantly black Los Angeles neighborhood of Watts had erupted in six days of rioting, looting, and arson after a routine traffic stop spun out of control. The mayhem left thirty-four residents dead, more than a thousand injured, and the neighborhood's business district in flames. White residents became even more anxious than usual about residential integration, while some African Americans regarded the confrontation with Los Angeles police as both necessary and worthy. A horrified Martin Luther King Jr. visited Watts after the rioting and was heckled by black militants. Vacationing in Greece, Governor Brown was unable to calm the city.

Ramparts didn't overlook the conservative backlash, but it didn't appreciate its full import, either. Scheer joined the Reagan campaign to interview the challenger, but he fell asleep in one of the campaign's hotel rooms and awoke to find Reagan, who hadn't noticed him, changing his trousers. After more conservative Democrats vanquished the *Ramparts* candidates in the primaries, the staff watched the Reagan–Brown match with bemused

resignation. The October 1966 cover featured a Disneyland photograph of a life-sized Mickey Mouse with the caption, "Golly
gee, California is a strange state!" (The interjection was a Brown
trademark.) The cover story didn't take a strong stand against Reagan, but it did include Hollywood studio head Jack Warner's take
on the election. Returning from a long European vacation,
Warner was asked what he thought about Ronald Reagan for governor. "No," Warner replied, "Jimmy Stewart for governor.
Ronald Reagan for best friend."

Instead of pressing Reagan, *Ramparts* asked whether Pat Brown
would "go with the real liberalism."

> If he doesn't, it won't make much difference to California if
> Brown does or does not squeak through. The right will
> win in any case, because it has already won. . . . And it is
> just as painfully clear that the triumph of the right is in-
> evitable because liberalism—not just unfortunate, well
> meaning Pat Brown—has failed California.

By this time, Hinckle had begun publishing a spinoff newspaper, the *Sunday Ramparts*, which was even more explicitly anti-
Brown. It accused Brown's campaign of "Birchbaiting" Reagan
and concluded that Brown's defeat, "while not particularly desirable, would not necessarily destroy our way of life." When staff
writer Bill Turner asked Hinckle and Scheer about the anti-
Brown spin, Hinckle explained their position: "Brown's so wishy-
washy he has to go. Reagan will make a fool of himself, and in four
years we'll be able to elect a real Democrat." By associating the
campaign with Disneyland, conflating the two candidates' approaches, and resigning itself to a conservative triumph, *Ramparts*
pounded one more nail into the coffin of American liberalism.
Years later, Scheer admitted that the New Left's key mistake was
exaggerating the strength of the liberal center.

Reagan easily defeated Brown the next month. Although he
governed more moderately than his campaign rhetoric suggested,

he kept his promise to crack down on Berkeley and moved quickly to dismiss Clark Kerr as president of the University of California. Caught in a whipsaw between radical students and a conservative governor, Kerr also had powerful enemies in Washington. Well before Reagan's victory, regent Edwin Pauley had contacted CIA director John McCone, a Cal alumnus, about removing Kerr from his leadership post. McCone referred him to J. Edgar Hoover, who supplied Pauley with confidential FBI information about Kerr, some of which the bureau knew to be false. President Johnson, who had planned to offer Kerr a cabinet position, scratched the nomination after receiving Kerr's background check. With Reagan's support, the regents dismissed Kerr in January 1967. Kerr would later say he "left the presidency just as I had entered it—fired with enthusiasm."

Reagan also clashed publicly with students, cut the university's budget, and instituted "educational fees" for the first time in UC history. (The euphemism evaded the university charter's ban on tuition.) Later, he made good on his pledge to tighten welfare requirements. His political career—and California's conservative backlash—was under way.

4

WHEN FREEMEN SHALL STAND

As Reagan dashed Pat Brown's bid for a third term, *Ramparts* was helping radical San Francisco lawyer Beverly Axelrod with a client, an inmate at California's San Quentin State Prison. At Axelrod's request, Keating visited him in prison, read his work, and helped arrange his parole. The following month, Axelrod's client was released, and *Ramparts* added his name to its masthead.

Eldridge Cleaver, thirty-one, had spent most of his adult life in prison. While still a teenager in Los Angeles, he was convicted of marijuana possession and sent to Soledad State Prison. There, he later wrote, "I fell in with a group of young blacks who, like myself, were in vociferous rebellion against what we perceived as continuation of slavery on a higher plane. We cursed everything American, including baseball and hot dogs." Three years later, Cleaver was convicted again, this time of assault with intent to murder. While incarcerated in San Quentin, a thirty-minute drive north of San Francisco in Marin County, he began writing as a way to attract the attention of an attorney. His own lawyer hadn't appealed his conviction, and he thought he could pay for new counsel with his earnings as a writer. Cleaver saw Axelrod's picture in a black newspaper and decided to contact her. Unlike most attorneys, she responded. When she visited him in San Quentin, he disguised his essays as legal correspondence and passed them to Axelrod, who showed them to Keating.

In August 1965, Keating passed along Cleaver's writings to Thomas Merton and asked for his opinion of them. "I draw your attention particularly to the letters he wrote to his attorney, Mrs. Beverly Axelrod," he wrote to Merton.

It was somewhere in the third letter, I believe, that I began to think of you: two men behind walls; I wondered then and I wonder now whether or not, cutting through all of the obvious things, there is a subtle underlying parallel between you.

Keating urged Merton to contact Cleaver: "Bev is really the only person he can communicate with, and I believe that you are the only other person in this country with whom he could communicate. . . . In brief, I feel he needs you and anything that you can say to him." Keating also sent Cleaver's essays to Maxwell Geismar, John Howard Griffin, Norman Mailer, and Fred Jordan of Grove Press.

Keating aided Cleaver's parole bid by publishing "Notes on a Native Son," which ran in June 1966. This time, Cleaver's rebellion wasn't directed at symbols of mainstream white America, but rather at James Baldwin, the black homosexual writer who built his reputation in part by critiquing the work of his mentor, novelist Richard Wright. Cleaver argued that Baldwin's work displayed "the most grueling, agonizing, total hatred of the blacks, particularly of himself, and the most shameful, fanatical, fawning, sycophantic love of the whites that one can find in the writings of any black American writer of note in our time." Cleaver also claimed that Baldwin despised Richard Wright's masculinity. Unable to "confront the stud in others," Baldwin could only "submit to it or destroy it."

Cleaver's "Letters from Prison" appeared in the August issue of *Ramparts*. He described the United States as "a very sick country—I am perhaps sicker than most." Reflecting on his life before prison, he made a startling admission: "I became a rapist. To refine my technique and *modus operandi*, I started out practicing on black girls in the ghetto . . . and when I considered myself smooth enough, I crossed the tracks and sought out white prey." He then presented that practice as political action: "Rape was an insurrectionary act. It delighted me that I was defying and trampling upon

the white man's law, upon his system of values, and that I was defil-
ing his women." In the public mind, Cleaver's admission swamped
his confession that he had "gone astray—astray not so much from
the white man's law as from being human, civilized." In the
process, Cleaver noted, he had also lost his self-respect. "My pride
as a man dissolved and my whole fragile moral structure seemed to
collapse, completely shattered. That is why I started to write. To
save myself."

Cleaver's essays in *Ramparts* coincided with rising black na-
tionalism in the Bay Area. In October 1966, the same month
Scheer was first listed as *Ramparts'* managing editor, Huey P. Newton and Bobby Seale founded the Black Panther Party for Self-
Defense in Oakland. Like Pat Brown before him, Newton was
taking classes at San Francisco Law School; one of his instructors
was Edwin Meese III, who would later serve as President Reagan's
attorney general. Inspired in part by Robert Williams's *Negroes
with Guns*, Newton learned that California law allowed residents
to carry loaded rifles and shotguns as long as they were publicly
displayed and pointed at no one. This provision informed the Panthers' tactics, especially in their patrols of West Oakland neighborhoods. Unlike the Community Alert Program in Watts, one of
Newton's organizational models, the Panthers both observed police actions and brought loaded weapons to the scene. They raised
money for their first shotguns and M-16s by buying copies of
Mao's "Little Red Book" in San Francisco's Chinatown and selling
them for a healthy profit on street corners in Berkeley.

Newton and Seale developed the Panther uniform—powder
blue shirts, black pants, black leather jackets, and black berets—
along with a ten-point program calling for full employment, housing, education, exemption from military service, an end to police
brutality, and freedom for all black men in prison and jail. Drawing
on Marxist and Maoist revolutionary language, Newton and Seale
declared that their major political objective was a plebiscite, supervised by the United Nations, to allow the black community to determine its national destiny. But their martial look and willingness

to take up arms, not their proposed plebiscite, were the keys to their public image.

As the Black Panthers launched their program, Cleaver was released from prison and joined the *Ramparts* staff. His colleagues there formed various impressions of him. Stermer described the six-foot, five-inch Cleaver as a huge presence, literally and figuratively. "I may be the house nigger," Cleaver told him, "but I'm going to *be* the house nigger." Scheer's assistant, Peter Collier, also registered Cleaver's impact.

> The first day Eldridge came into the office after being paroled, I could tell he was going to be an important figure. He walked with a cantilevered prison-yard strut; his hooded green eyes conveyed a sense of danger mitigated by an odd introspection and self-irony. Talking to him was like playing tennis against a wall: the ball always came back just as hard as you hit it.

Collier's simile may explain why others found Cleaver less threatening. At a *Ramparts* party thrown for Cleaver upon his release, Denise Hinckle had a quiet conversation with him away from the hubbub. He asked her about her children, and she later described him as sweet and vulnerable.

Scheer thought Keating's feelings about race and civil rights arose from white guilt and a desire for atonement. "I put the Cleaver stuff in that category," Scheer said later. Wary of being used by Cleaver, Scheer asked about his intentions. Was the *Ramparts* job simply a way to get out of prison, or did Cleaver want to do the work? Cleaver pushed back, asking if Scheer had a problem with his being there. "We had it out," Scheer recalled, but they worked well together after that. "I liked Cleaver. I never saw the ugly side of him, though I heard about it later. He was a naturally brilliant writer, and he took it seriously."

Cleaver relished the San Francisco scene, which his wife Kathleen later described as a "seductive mix of artists, musicians, labor organizers, free thinkers, black nationalists, communists, and pot heads." Axelrod introduced him to Berkeley radicals, including Jerry Rubin and Stew Albert. When he first met Albert's wife, Judy Clavir, Cleaver disapproved of the fact that she hadn't adopted her husband's surname and addressed her as "Mrs. Stew." When she disapproved of that, he renamed her "Mrs. Gumbo." For years after that, Berkeley radicals referred to her as Judy Gumbo.

Cleaver founded the Bay Area's Malcolm X Afro American Society and began to meet activists from other organizations, including the Student Nonviolent Coordinating Committee (SNCC) and the Black Panthers. His introduction to the Panthers occurred in a storefront meeting in San Francisco's Fillmore district in February 1967. The purpose of the meeting was to organize a memorial for Malcolm X and invite his widow, Betty Shabazz, to speak there. The Black Panther leaders arrived at the meeting bristling with arms: Newton with a riot pump shotgun, Seale with a .45 automatic, Bobby Hutton with a shotgun, and Sherwin Forte with an M-1 carbine with a banana clip. For Cleaver, it was love at first sight.

Cleaver forged a deeper connection to the Panthers later that month at the *Ramparts* office. It began when Cleaver heard a secretary's terrified announcement that twenty armed men were invading the office. "Don't worry," he told her, "they're friends." Huey Newton and a detachment of Black Panthers were providing security for Betty Shabazz, whom they met at the San Francisco airport and escorted to 301 Broadway for an interview with Cleaver. After wading through the office's hallways, which were clogged with curious staffers, Cleaver stepped onto the sidewalk and noticed that traffic was stopped, spectators had gathered, and police cars were approaching with sirens blaring.

Cleaver brought Shabazz back to his office and conducted a short interview. Meanwhile, Newton stood at the window with his shotgun, observing the scene on the street. By that time, a police captain and drinking buddy of Hinckle's had arrived. "We seem to have a tense situation," the captain told Hinckle. "What are we going to do?" Hinckle suggested that they urge everyone to relax and adjourn to Andre's for a drink. But the Panthers weren't in the mood for refreshments.

After Shabazz departed, Cleaver, Newton, and other Panthers lingered outside the office. One of the police officers directed the Panthers not to point their weapons at him. Newton stared at the officer, who undid the strap on his holster. "Huey, cool it, man. Let's split, man," Bobby Seale implored Newton, grabbing at Newton's jacket on his right arm. "Don't hold my hand, brother," Newton told him. "I let go of his hand right away," Seale wrote later, "because I know that's his shooting hand."

As Cleaver and others looked on, Newton approached the officer and said, "What's the matter, you got an itchy trigger finger?" The officer made no reply. "You want to draw your gun?" Newton asked. The officer remained silent while his colleagues counseled him to keep his cool. "OK, you big, fat, racist pig, draw your gun!" Newton said, loading a shell into his shotgun. "I'm waiting." The other officers stepped out of the line of fire, and Cleaver retreated into the doorway of the *Ramparts* office. His first thought, he later wrote, was "Goddam, that nigger is c-r-a-z-y!" After a tense moment, the officer sighed and lowered his head. The spell was broken. "Huey almost laughed in his face," Seale wrote later, "and we started backing up slowly." The Panthers returned to their cars and left the scene.

Meanwhile, the *Ramparts* office was buzzing with excitement. "Who was that?" Marianne Hinckle, Warren's younger sister, asked Cleaver. "That was Huey P. Newton," Cleaver answered, "Minister of Defense of the Black Panther Party." "Boy, is he gutsy," she said. "Yeah, he's out of sight!" Cleaver replied. Marianne later described Newton as a striking figure and jokingly compared him to Cleavon Little in *Blazing Saddles*, the Mel Brooks comedy. She also recalled Cleaver telling her not to come within two yards of Newton. "He's a very dangerous man," Cleaver said.

According to historian Peniel E. Joseph, the confrontation outside the *Ramparts* office was "a local story with national significance. For Newton and the Black Panther Party, the incident, if chiefly symbolic, was the first in a series of confrontations that, with help from *Ramparts*, transformed a small band of armed militants into internationally respected revolutionaries." In fact, the relationship worked both ways. *Ramparts* made celebrities of the Black Panthers, and their star power increased the magazine's cachet.

Newton's audacity also made an indelible impression on Cleaver. After years of jailhouse talk about revolution, he was witnessing the real thing: armed confrontation with the official order. In Cleaver's view, this was the natural extension of Malcolm X's teaching. Soon he was working with the Black Panthers as minister of information.

Weirdly, the showdown between Huey Newton and the San Francisco police wasn't the hottest story circulating through the *Ramparts* office at the time. That honor was reserved for an astounding follow-up story to Sheinbaum and Scheer's CIA exposé.

The story began in January 1967, when Hinckle entered the dining room of the Algonquin Hotel, where he split a piece of chocolate cake with a nervous twenty-four-year-old named Michael Wood. Wood was an SDS (Students for a Democratic Society) member and former fundraiser for the National Student Association (NSA), which represented American college students at various international meetings. After leaving NSA, Wood continued to work for leftist causes. When he met Marc Stone at a conference, he confided that he was wrestling with his conscience about whether or not to go public with a story about his experience at NSA. Stone asked that Wood consider contacting *Ramparts* if he decided to do so.

Wood's story proved to be a consequential one. While on the job at NSA, he learned that the CIA was funding his organization. The agency's goals were to counter similar groups under Soviet control abroad and to recruit foreign students. As the world would soon learn, the NSA wasn't the only organization receiving funding this way. During the 1950s and 1960s, a long list of cultural, labor, educational, religious, and media groups were on the CIA payroll. Recipients included the Congress for Cultural Freedom (Sidney Hook and Arthur Schlesinger Jr.), the AFL–CIO (George Meany), Harvard University's International Summer School (Henry Kissinger), political magazines (*Encounter* and *Partisan Review*), and the ironically named Independent Service for Information (Gloria Steinem).

The CIA divided these recipients into the witting and unwitting—those who did and didn't know about the CIA connection. The witting signed secrecy oaths that carried criminal penalties for violations. In the NSA's case, only the top leaders knew where the money was coming from. Many of these leaders went on to work for the CIA, and some of them would explain the arrangements to the next batch of NSA officers. Wood was one of the few NSA officers who hadn't signed a secrecy oath. After a year of fretting about the proper course of action, he decided to contact a dubious Hinckle.

During their meeting, Wood turned over copies of the NSA's financial records. While checking his story, *Ramparts* researchers found that a few years earlier, a Texas congressman had publicly identified eight foundations that the CIA used as financial conduits. When the researchers discovered that those foundations were also funding the NSA, they were amazed not only that Wood might be telling the truth, but also that the CIA was still using the same front organizations.

Those discoveries hinged on a stroke of luck. *Ramparts* staff writer Sol Stern tapped Michael Ansara, a Harvard SDS member whom Scheer had met at antiwar conferences, to conduct the research. One of Ansara's friends, a Democratic Party fundraiser, suggested that he start his research at the regional IRS office. When that office rebuffed Ansara, his friend called the regional manager. Chastened, the regional office turned over the entire file, not just the public form, to Ansara, who discovered that two foundations were funneling money to 110 organizations. Much of the money moved through law firms that had one thing in common: a partner with connections to the OSS, the CIA's precursor. Ansara mentioned these findings to his fundraiser friend, who called a former CIA contact of his. That contact confirmed Ansara's conclusion about CIA conduits.

By this time, the CIA's Directorate of Plans, the agency's clandestine counterintelligence section, had taken over the investigation of *Ramparts*. That section was headed by Desmond FitzGerald, whose background in many ways resembled Keating's and Mitchell's. Like many of his colleagues, FitzGerald had been recruited from an East Coast milieu that included prep schools, Ivy League colleges, military service, and Wall Street law firms. According to author Evan Thomas, that community was "secretive, insular, elitist, and secure in the rectitude of its purpose."

Many of this subculture's young men were intensely competitive and devoted to service, which included a duty to fight the nation's enemies ferociously. Their sense of duty was only heightened by the privileges they enjoyed and were prepared to defend. Beginning with prep school, their teachers and headmasters cast that duty in romantic, even chivalric terms. FitzGerald's daughter Frances, author of the acclaimed *Fire in the Lake* about the U.S. involvement in Vietnam, later noted, "He would have preferred to fight the Cold War by single combat. By jousts. Brave individuals fighting each other." But as the cold war wore on, chivalry and antique virtue gave way to less savory codes of conduct. By the 1960s, the CIA was illegally spying on American journalists and collaborating with American mobsters to assassinate Fidel Castro.

The same month Hinckle met with Wood, FitzGerald learned that *Ramparts* was preparing a story on the NSA's connection to the CIA. He put Richard Ober, a counterintelligence specialist, in charge of suppressing the story. After reviewing his legal options, Ober realized he couldn't prevent *Ramparts* from running its story and decided to focus instead on damage control. He planned to stage a press conference at which NSA leaders would admit to their CIA relationship and insist that it was over. The admission would make the *Ramparts* story look like old news when it appeared.

But Hinckle had his own informants in the NSA, and he discovered the CIA's plan before the press conference could be held. "I was damned if I was going to let the CIA scoop me," recalled Hinckle. "I bought full-page advertisements in the *New York Times* and *Washington Post* to scoop myself, which seemed the preferable alternative." On February 13, 1967, the day before the ads appeared, acting Secretary of State Nicholas Katzenbach wrote a secret memorandum to the White House suggesting that the State Department make a "bare bones" admission. Meanwhile, one of the student leaders confirmed the *Ramparts* story to Hinckle. A surprised Hinckle later wrote, "It is a rare thing in this business when you say bang and somebody says I'm dead."

Immediately after Hinckle's ads appeared, eight congressmen, including San Francisco Democrat Phil Burton, signed a letter of protest to President Johnson. "We were appalled to learn today that the Central Intelligence Agency has been subsidizing the National Student Association for more than a decade," the letter said. "It represents an unconscionable extension of power by an agency of government over institutions outside its jurisdiction. This disclosure leads us and many others here and abroad to believe that the CIA can be as much a threat to American as to foreign democratic institutions."

The story also sent shock waves through the New Left. David Weir, who later wrote for *Rolling Stone*, recalled its effect. He had just entered the Peace Corps and was flying to Kabul with forty colleagues.

On the plane, we were passing the magazine around hand-to-hand, discussing the story and arguing about it. We were so hungry for information, and there were so few credible sources. The old left publications didn't float our boat at all. The NSA story was like the Port Huron Statement. It had that kind of power.

That power wasn't lost on the CIA. The day after Hinckle's ads appeared, Ober received the magazine's tax returns from the IRS. It audited them along with Keating's personal returns from 1960 to 1964. A CIA officer reported that Keating had been writing off losses of about $450,000 per year, and that Helen's inheritance had evaporated by 1965. The agency found no foreign funding sources for *Ramparts*, the only legitimate justification for its investigation. But Ober wasn't ready to give up. The same day he received the IRS data, he circulated a memo discussing plans to discredit *Ramparts* with planted news stories.

Ten days later, a syndicated column by Carl Rowan, former director of the United States Information Agency, implied that the magazine's NSA exposé was part of a Communist plot.

A few days ago a brief, cryptic report out of Prague, Czechoslovakia, was passed among a handful of top officials in Washington. It said that an editor of *Ramparts* magazine had come to Prague and held a long, secret session with officers of the Communist-controlled International Union of Students. . . . The Prague report aroused deep suspicions here among officials who are privately shocked and dismayed at the damage to the CIA and to U.S. foreign policy interests caused by the needless series of busted intelligence "covers" that has resulted from the *Ramparts* exposé. . . . What, if any, relationship does *Ramparts* have to the IUS?

Rowan was right that Washington officials were dismayed by the *Ramparts* stories. The rest was disinformation from the CIA propaganda machine, which one agency official privately called the Mighty Wurlitzer—the famous organ that accompanied silent films and signaled how the audience should feel at any given moment.

Time magazine, whose press credentials had helped CIA agents with their covers, chipped in with some damage control by touting the agency's cold war victories and dedicated professionalism. The NSA story, *Time* claimed, "aroused the outrage of many in the academic community who—mistakenly—regard CIA as an evil manipulator of foreign policy." Fortunately, *Time* was on hand to put the whole thing in perspective. Admitting that the story was factually accurate, *Time* took aim at the messenger. *Ramparts* was "the sensation-seeking New Left-leaning monthly," and its article was predictably "larded with pejorative clichés." Those who were concerned about the story were captive to "the emotionalism of young Americans who worship honesty." *Time* also suggested that the *Ramparts* story wasn't really news in the first place: "The use of front foundations to handle CIA money is an old technique." According to *Time*, the only problem in this case was that the NSA president "broke his secrecy pledge to confess the CIA connection to one of his staff men—red-bearded New Leftist Michael Wood."

After plumping the CIA and its new director, Richard Helms, the *Time* article closed by clarifying the moral of the story:

> In an open society like the U.S., there will always be a degree of conflict between the public nature of policymaking and the secret, empirical processes by which decisions must be made and implemented. What is usually overlooked, when the CIA is the subject of controversy, is that it is only an arm—and a well-regulated one—of the U.S. Government. It does not, and cannot, manipulate American policies. It can only serve them.

The Mighty Wurlitzer was pitch perfect.

In the meantime, the CIA continued to investigate *Ramparts'* staff and associates. In March, two of Ober's men debriefed a CIA agent who was also a good friend of a *Ramparts* reporter. At the same time, Ober was trying to recruit five former *Ramparts* employees as informants. His team, which eventually grew to twelve officers, investigated 127 writers and researchers and 200 other Americans connected to the magazine. On April 4, Ober completed his status report. The next day, his task force offered its recommendations, which CIA officer Louis Dube later described as "heady shit."

Decades later, former CIA agent Edgar Applewhite recounted the *Ramparts* operation.

> I had all sorts of dirty tricks to hurt their circulation and financing. The people running *Ramparts* were vulnerable to blackmail. We had awful things in mind, some of which we carried off, though *Ramparts* fell of its own accord. We were not in the least inhibited by the fact that the CIA had no internal security role in the United States.

Applewhite refused to describe his dirty tricks, but when briefed on them at the time, Desmond FitzGerald was amused. "Eddie," he said, "you have a spot of blood on your pinafore."

The NSA story was a turning point in the magazine's development. Between October 1966 and January 1967, *Ramparts'* total circulation had doubled to 149,000. (Having recently celebrated its centennial, the *Nation* had about half that many subscribers.) After the March 1967 issue, however, *Ramparts'* circulation spiked to 229,000, more than half of it newsstand. The staff grew to six editors, eight staff writers, the same number of editorial assistants, and three administrators along with Hinckle, Scheer, and Stermer. Investors, directors, contributing editors, freelance writers, and part-time researchers swelled that number to the two hundred persons investigated by the CIA.

The NSA story was also a CIA benchmark. In the immediate aftermath of the *Ramparts* exposé, the agency expanded its domestic surveillance program, code-named Operation MHCHAOS and run by Ober. (Seymour Hersh, a *Ramparts* contributor turned *New York Times* reporter, would expose that program in 1974.) But the damage to the CIA was already done. The *New York Times* and other media outlets followed up with their own stories about CIA front organizations, all of which were compromised. Some recipients of CIA money denied the link, others disclaimed knowledge of it, and still others defended it.

In an effort to limit the damage, President Johnson assembled the Katzenbach Commission to review government dealings with the university community. Its members included HEW Secretary John Gardner and CIA director Richard Helms, who had already passed confidential information about *Ramparts* personnel to White House aide Bill Moyers. According to investigative writer Angus Mackenzie, the real purpose of the Katzenbach Commission "was to forestall further embarrassment and preclude any congressional investigation of CIA operations." But even without that congressional investigation, the exposure was one of the worst operational catastrophes in CIA history.

The NSA story led to further investigative work of CIA fronts, some of it conducted by *Ramparts*. Michael Ansara recruited fellow Harvard SDS member Jon Wiener to research the links between the CIA, its front foundations, and recipients of the agency's largesse. Wiener traveled to New York, reviewed foundation records, and discovered that CIA money had found its way to the *New Leader*, an anticommunist liberal magazine founded in 1924. After he reported his findings to *Ramparts*, Wiener was told to visit the magazine's editor and ask for a comment. It was an extraordinary assignment for a first-year graduate student in history. "First he yelled at me a little," Wiener recalled. "Then he got very quiet. 'Do they even pay you to do this?' he asked. And I told him, 'Well, I get air fare.' " The editor then issued what would become a standard defense: that the magazine had received funding from the CIA, but that its editorial mission wasn't affected in any way.

As the CIA story played out, the magazine's leadership was in an uproar. The issue was Keating, whose influence had been waning ever since his and Helen's cash stopped flowing into the magazine's coffers. Hinckle later maintained that other investors were eager to sack Keating altogether. That group included Fred Mitchell and Dick Russell, a wealthy Connecticut businessman. Hinckle rarely

fired anyone, preferring to ignore them until they quit. But his colleagues didn't regard his neglect as especially humane. Gossage told
him more than once, "You've got a trail of bodies behind you
stacked up like cordwood."

Keating still had some loyalists on the staff, especially in the
business office. Their positions made them keenly aware of the
magazine's shaky finances and Hinckle's improvidence. In his
memoir, Hinckle maintained that the magazine's survival in 1966
"depended on the simple proposition of not paying its printing
bill." He also acknowledged the effects of his extravagance on the
bean counters. "The business types were distressed over my apparent ability to play contradictory roles—those of raising the money
and planning the budgets, and spending the money and ignoring
the budgets."

By this time, Hinckle's reputation as a spendthrift was well established. James Ridgeway, who would later appear on the *Ramparts* masthead, detailed Hinckle's prodigious spending in a piece
for the *New York Times Magazine*. Playing to type, Hinckle supplied
Ridgeway with the relevant horror stories, but he was quick to
correct the record on one matter. He denied that he flew from
Chicago to Paris to get to New York during an airline strike. "In
fact," he explained, "I flew from San Francisco to Paris to get to
New York. If I had been in Chicago, I would have just taken a cab."

With the business department's support, Keating decided to
stage a showdown over control of the magazine. Hinckle heard
about Keating's move while quaffing cocktails at Jessica Mitford's.
"I say, Hink Three," Mitford announced, "there seems to be a bit of
a blackout call for you on the phone in the kitchen." It was Dick
Russell, who told Hinckle that Keating and the three-person business department were planning to fly out to meet with Russell the
next day. Their purpose was to document Hinckle's financial mis-
management and to present a new course for the magazine. Keating had asked Russell not to mention their plan to Hinckle.
Russell refused the request, advised Keating not to make the trip,

and called Hinckle. According to Hinckle's memoir, Russell pledged his support but also rebuked Hinckle for keeping Keating on in the first place.

Returning home, Hinckle called Keating, who declined to meet with him. "You'd better say your prayers, big boy," Keating said before hanging up.

Hinckle later referred to the subsequent clash as an "alley fight." Instead of rehearsing its details in his memoir, he included the full text of a letter from Jessica Mitford to Howard Gossage. In that letter, Mitford recounted the issues as they were presented to her and the other members of the editorial board. Their meeting, which had been called before the Keating affair had arisen, was supposed to address the resignations of Paul Jacobs and Ralph Gleason. Jacobs was fed up with the magazine's harum-scarum editorial practices, and Gleason was displeased with the magazine's coverage of the Haight-Ashbury scene. Gleason also condemned Hinckle's treatment of Keating. "Don't be surprised if you read in the paper one day that Keating has committed suicide," Gleason reportedly said. Adding to Gleason's fury was the fact that no one had acknowledged his resignation letter.

In her letter to Gossage, Mitford described Hinckle and Scheer ("Hink/Scheer" in her distinctive parlance) as "brilliant young bandits doing an extraordinary job." But Mitford acknowledged that their "ruthless handling of people" was creating problems, even if that approach might be "the necessary other-side-of-the-coin to their flair and forward thrust." In their editorial session, Mitford reported to Gossage, Hinckle recounted the events that took place at the recent directors meeting. He outlined the Keating challenge and opined that Keating was "clinically insane." By way of evidence, he noted that Keating kept saying "Point of order!" ("Just like in the McCarthy hearings," Mitford added.) Hinckle also said that Keating disrupted the proceedings by insisting on a tape-recording or transcript of the meeting. Mitford saw this detail as "some slight proof [Keating] might be clinically sane, because no-one in their right mind (speaking for *moi*) would go in to such a meeting *without* having the proceedings recorded! Don't you rather agree?"

Mitford then went to the heart of the matter:

> It seems obvious to me that if it had to come to a choice between Hink/Scheer and Keating—well, I mean there simply *is* no choice; Hink/Scheer *are* the mag, the creators of everything that's so splendid about it. . . . But one does wish they could be a trifle less Animal Farm-ish about it.

She added that she hadn't personally suffered at Hink/Scheer's hands. On the contrary, she found them "marvelously good company, clever, funny, all the things we like. Also they laugh at one's jokes which is always such a smashing quality." In her postscript to Gossage, she concluded, "Well, it's all fascinating and frightful; I only trust that *Ramparts* will survive it. Do be thinking of something clever to be done."

The directors meeting went poorly for Keating. In an attempt to avert a showdown, Bill Honig met with him beforehand. Honig offered to discuss Keating's grievances and noted that the new stockholders were united against him. But Keating was in no mood to negotiate. During the meeting, he warned that everyone who voted against him would be held financially responsible for that move. According to Hinckle, Keating looked directly at June Degnan, a wealthy Democratic Party fundraiser from San Francisco. "Move the question," she said coolly. Keating lost the vote 13–1.

Soon after the showdown, Scheer and Stermer visited Fred Mitchell in Kansas, where he had accepted an academic appointment. Mitchell agreed to step up his involvement with the magazine. "It certainly can be said that I bought my way into the magazine," Mitchell told his campus newspaper. "But they have tried to convince me—and I have allowed myself to be convinced—that the kind of understanding we have between each other is outside any financial interests." He expressed sympathy for Keating but noted that the founder had "lost touch with *Ramparts*." He also added that Keating didn't have "a sense of a story, in the modern way" and announced his own goals for the magazine. "I hope it will stay free of labels and resist being called the 'new left.' I want it to embrace those things in the so–called 'conservative movement' as well as the radical world when it sees a higher moral purpose served by it." Finally, he questioned the magazine's emphasis on muckraking. "I'm tired of muckraking. I think muckraking must go on, but it can't go on consistently because it's too wearing on the people doing the racking [*sic*]."

Both the *New York Times* and *Time* magazine covered the conflict over the magazine's control. In its story, "The Fall of the Archangel," *Time* couldn't conceal either its schadenfreude or its pro–Establishment bias. There were no ideological differences between Keating and Hinckle, the magazine reported: "Both are doctrinaire leftists with a passion for disparaging U.S. policies and institutions." The story noted *Ramparts'* impressive circulation, heavy losses, and efforts to recruit Hugh Hefner as an investor. It also mentioned a fantastical story idea, attributed to Keating, involving a slave camp in Louisiana for civil rights workers. Keating wanted to hire a detective and equip him with a hollow heel in his boot; the detective would store a compass there so he could find his way back to civilization. The *Time* story concluded with a Keating quote: "I put $860,000 into the magazine, and they threw me out like an old shoe."

Keating's investment and ouster had consequences for his entire family. Unlike her husband, Helen disliked the furor surrounding the magazine once it became a slick. The magazine's attacks on the Church were the most troubling. "All the children were in Catholic schools, and I was active in the Mothers Clubs," Helen noted privately. "It is a hard thing to go against the sensibilities of one's friends." Publicly, she remained philosophical. "It was never boring," she later told friends and family. But after the ouster, and with most of her fortune gone, the family felt the strain. Years later, one of her daughters crossed paths with Marianne Hinckle. "Your brother spent our inheritance," she told Marianne. "Well, it made an honest woman out of you," Marianne replied.

When combined with his electoral losses, the ouster was a devastating personal blow to Keating. Although the magazine never came close to turning a profit, it had been his most notable professional venture. He had written *The Scandal of Silence* for Random House in 1965, but his critique of the Catholic hierarchy disappeared quickly into oblivion. In addition to claiming his family's considerable resources, Keating's involvement with *Ramparts* had submitted him to IRS scrutiny and illegal surveillance by the CIA. Now he and the magazine would have to struggle on—separately.

5

THE HAVOC OF WAR

Shortly after Keating's departure, Scheer appeared on *Firing Line*, a television program that debuted in 1966 and featured debates with conservative host William F. Buckley. The episode's title ("Is *Ramparts* Magazine Un-American?") indicated that Buckley was leaving little to chance.

Buckley's interest in *Ramparts* was threefold. Like Keating, he was the founding publisher of a political magazine and was constantly battling the economic realities of that enterprise. Even a half century after its creation, with a circulation of almost 155,000 and a generation of conservative national leadership to support it, *National Review* was operating at a substantial deficit.

Another source of Buckley's interest in *Ramparts* was his Catholicism. His undergraduate experience at Yale had introduced him to the "nonchalant and cheeky secularism" that he targeted in his first book, *God and Man at Yale*. Buckley may have supported Keating's original urge to sponsor a Catholic literary quarterly, but he had every reason to deplore its transformation into a nonchalant, very cheeky, increasingly secular, and unabashedly left-wing publication under Hinckle and Scheer.

A third reason for Buckley's interest in *Ramparts* was his affiliation with the CIA. Four years before he founded his magazine, Buckley was recruited into the agency. After training in Washington, DC, he served in Mexico City as a deep cover agent. His supervisor was E. Howard Hunt, who gained more fame than a former CIA agent should when he was apprehended for the Watergate burglary in the 1970s. Buckley's CIA service was apparently short-lived; he lived in Mexico for less than year. In a 2005 *National Review* editorial, he referred to his government service.

> In 1980 I found myself seated next to the former president
> of Mexico at a ski-area restaurant. What, he asked amiably,
> had I done when I lived in Mexico? "I tried to undermine
> your regime, Mr. President." He thought this amusing, and
> that is all that it was, under the aspect of the heavens.

If subverting the Mexican government was amusing a half century later, Buckley was less diverted by Scheer's exposé of the CIA's activities in Vietnam while the conflict there was raging.

To prepare Scheer for the *Firing Line* taping, staff writer Bob Avakian assembled a packet of research material on Buckley and the show. Staffers also told Scheer that Buckley frequently interrupted his guests. They advised him not to tolerate that but rather to take the offensive, which Scheer proceeded to do. The result was an intellectual food fight at a time when such spectacles were rare on broadcast television.

The sharp words began with Buckley's backhanded introduction of Scheer, who emerged at *Ramparts* after the "liquidation" of its founder. Scheer had visited Asia several times, Buckley continued, "in his passion to find the United States responsible for all that goes wrong there." When his turn to speak came around, Scheer complimented Buckley's reading of his cue cards and then suggested a hypothetical and equally unfair introduction in which Buckley would be described as supporting white supremacist governments in Africa. "I think I see why you don't have your own show," Buckley quipped.

Most of the exchange centered on a story Scheer had written about British philosopher Bertrand Russell in May 1967. For that issue's cover, Stermer commissioned Norman Rockwell to draw Russell's portrait. Given Rockwell's reputation for all-American pictures, the cover was an ironic comment on Russell's criticism of U.S. foreign policy.

In an attempt to summarize his differences with Scheer, Buckley offered the following:

> Mr. Scheer, you seem to be extremely reluctant to accept what I consider to be the intellectual requirements of your analysis: namely, that sure, Bertrand Russell's anti-American, but he has a good right to be anti-American because during the 1960s we became a highly unlovely country and anybody in fact who is pro-American at this time has an addled wit, to say nothing of an unserviceable amoral sense. Now, why don't you say, Yes, I am anti-American?

Scheer refused to bite. If he accepted Buckley's invitation to endorse Russell's criticisms, Buckley would dub that position anti-American, then un-American, and then pin that label to *Ramparts* and its staff. The House Committee on Un-American Activities had ruined many lives and careers in the 1950s with similar tactics. HUAC was still active, but Berkeley activist Jerry Rubin had dramatized its waning authority when, describing himself as an American revolutionary, he appeared before the committee in full colonial garb.

The debate between Buckley and Scheer then took an even more personal turn. Buckley mocked Scheer's writing style, and Scheer made a crack about the faces Buckley made while speaking. As the program drew to a close, Scheer raised the moderator's hackles when he compared Buckley to a Stalinist or Maoist with an $11-million inheritance. "Mr. Chairman, don't get upset," Buckley told the moderator. "This is his syndrome."

Buckley closed as follows: "Here is a man who when he ran for election used as a campaign manager a Communist whose magazine defends a lot of positions that are uniquely defended by Communists. I don't think he understands the consequences of it." Scheer replied:

I mentioned Mr. Buckley's eleven million because I find it presumptuous that he could so accurately perceive the needs of people in underdeveloped countries who live on $50 a day [*sic*]. I also find him to be highly anti-American in that his contempt for freedom has supported the McCarthy Committee, the House Un-American Activities Committee, and his own red-baiting, and his own attacks on anyone that dissents in this society, and in fact his own attempts to make a person who is a Communist a non-person in much the same way as the Soviet Union has done.

The two spent most of the hour jousting rather than clarifying the underlying issues, which were matters of life and death for thousands of Vietnamese and Americans. When they touched on the original question, Scheer resisted but didn't refute Buckley's charge that *Ramparts* was un-American.

In fact, Buckley and the editors at *Time* weren't the only ones who considered the *Ramparts* crew unpatriotic. While relaxing at Elaine's in New York City, staff writer Peter Collier and Hinckle were approached by Willie Morris, the Mississippi native who became *Harper's* youngest editor in 1967. "The trouble with you all," Morris said, "is you didn't love America." Collier was struck by Morris's use of the past tense. Even if America had become unlovable (or, in Buckley's argot, *unlovely*), Morris implied that the *Ramparts* critique was diluted if they had *never* loved America.

Scheer saw it otherwise. For him, the main point of *Ramparts* was to apply what he had learned at City College about the American system, including the First Amendment, limited government, and checks and balances. "We weren't defending any ground," Scheer later said. "We weren't leading a movement. That was extremely liberating." As for foreign policy, Scheer's main point was that other countries, including Cuba and Vietnam, should be allowed to make their own histories without interference from the United States. In the context of the cold war, that position was widely regarded as procommunist, but it outlasted that conflict and eventually extended to nations like Iran, where, Scheer later wrote, U.S. mischief beginning in the 1950s had produced "a sorry history."

Although the *Firing Line* episode produced more heat than light, it showed that Scheer was becoming the magazine's face to the world. He was also recruiting more staff from his Berkeley circle. One such recruit was Peter Collier, a graduate student in English who dropped his dissertation on Jane Austen and joined the Free Speech Movement. The product of a Southern California suburb, Collier thought of Berkeley in the early 1960s as a vibrant, bohemian intellectual center. It was "an amazing time— Wordsworthian," he recalled, alluding to that poet's famous lyric on the French Revolution: "Bliss was it in that dawn to be alive, / But to be young was very heaven!"

After working on Scheer's campaign, Collier joined the staff at *Ramparts*, where his writing and editing skills were rewarded. He was skeptical of Hinckle, whom he later described as a "dime-store Citizen Hearst," but he appreciated Hinckle's fundamental insight that the New Left had broader appeal than the mainstream media suspected. During this time, Collier's three-year-old son became fascinated by Hinckle's eye patch and began referring to him as "that pirate guy." Collier later remarked that his son was closer to the truth than he could have known.

Collier's position at the magazine made him an eyewitness to some of its signature moments. One involved Hunter S. Thompson, a Haight-Ashbury veteran whose first bestseller, *Hell's Angels*, Collier had reviewed upon its publication in 1967. Later that year, Thompson stopped by the office for lunch with Hinckle. At the time, Hinckle was keeping a capuchin monkey there. He bought it for his daughter, but the family dog had gone after the monkey, which then bit Denise. Renaming the monkey Henry Luce after the founder of *Time* magazine, Hinckle decided to quarter him in the office. When he wasn't in his cage, Henry Luce frequently ran along the tops of the office dividers, screeching loudly. But after the office was burglarized overnight, the *San Francisco Chronicle* reported that Henry Luce was the only witness, and he wasn't talking.

In the end, Thompson's visit wasn't healthy for Henry Luce. When Thompson and Hinckle returned to the office after their lunch, they found Thompson's backpack open, pills of various colors strewn on the floor, and a deranged Henry Luce racing around the office. He was rushed to the veterinarian's to have his stomach pumped. An unsympathetic Thompson later wrote to Hinckle, "That fucking monkey should be killed—or at least arrested—on general principles." But Henry Luce remained at large until his penchant for self-interference became a distraction. "He kept jerking off, so he had to go," Hinckle said later. A sympathetic secretary took him home to Marin County.

Another Scheer recruit was Sol Stern. Born in Israel, Stern grew up on Vyse Avenue in the Bronx—Leon Trotsky's old address and the setting for *Marty*, the Oscar-winning film from 1955. Stern and Scheer knew each other from a leftist summer camp for Jewish children, and they attended City College together. In 1961, Stern began a doctoral program in political science at Berkeley, where he also worked with Scheer, David Horowitz, and Maurice Zeitlin on *Root and Branch*. Later, he became involved in the Free Speech Movement, dropped out of his graduate program, and joined *Ramparts*, where he wrote or contributed to many of the magazine's most memorable pieces, including the Michigan State and NSA stories.

Stern produced the first major press account of Huey Newton and the Black Panthers for the *New York Times Magazine* on August 6, 1967. In that piece, Stern described a street-corner meeting in San Francisco's Fillmore district where Newton said, "Every time you go to execute a white racist Gestapo cop, you are defending yourself." Stern asked Newton if he was truly prepared to kill a police officer; Newton replied that he was. He was also prepared to die, Newton said, a claim that presaged the title of his subsequent book, *Revolutionary Suicide*. Stern quoted Bobby Seale on the proper response to encountering a police officer on his coffee break: "shoot him down—boom, boom—with a 12-gauge shotgun." "To these young men," Stern concluded, "the execution of a police officer would be as natural and justifiable as the execution of a German soldier by a member of the French Resistance."

Stern followed up the next month with a piece in *Ramparts* called "America's Black Guerrillas." It featured a photograph of a regal Huey Newton in a wicker chair, shotgun in one hand and a spear in the other. The photograph, which was taken by Cleaver at Beverly Axelrod's house, later became a popular poster and counterculture icon.

Some months later, Stern was one of four *Ramparts* employees (along with Hinckle, Scheer, and Stermer) called before a New York grand jury for burning their draft cards. The cards were ignited for the December 1967 cover photograph, but the men were nowhere near the scene of the crime; the photographer had used hand models for the shoot. Once again, *Time* magazine provided free publicity by describing the four "holding aloft their burning draft cards in a kind of New Left salute." The photographer kept the burned cards and later turned them over to the FBI when asked. In the end, the grand jury issued no indictments, but that didn't stop *Esquire* from ribbing the Gang of Four. All had deferments, the *Esquire* piece pointed out, and were therefore undraftable. One of Stern's deferments was for a trick knee, and the illustration showed him on crutches with a bandage on his kneecap.

Like Stermer, Stern thought the magazine's Bay Area location was liberating. The main challenge, he recalled, was "working around Hinckle's madness." It wasn't only the missed issues, which would have been inconceivable at a mainstream eastern magazine. (Hinckle felt no overwhelming responsibility to put out twelve issues per year.) It was also that Hinckle himself was "a wild man." Stern recounted one incident after his return from a stint in New York. While moving items back into the San Francisco office, he briefly left the door of his rental car open. On an impulse, Hinckle intentionally ran his car into Stern's, taking off the door completely. "I don't have a lot of regard for private property," Hinckle said later.

Another Scheer associate, David Horowitz, was brought on to manage the recently formed book division of *Ramparts*, but he quickly assumed other writing and editing duties. Like Scheer, Horowitz grew up in New York City with radical parents. But Horowitz's parents were New York City schoolteachers, not garment workers, and he studied at Columbia, not CUNY, before beginning his graduate work at Berkeley. There he lived across the street from Scheer at the corner of Milvia and Francisco.

Following his work on *Root and Branch*, Horowitz established himself as a prolific writer. His book on Berkeley activism, *Student*, was edited by Saul Landau and published by Ballantine in 1962. *Student* sold briskly in paperback and reportedly inspired Mario Savio, a key leader in the Free Speech Movement, to move to Berkeley. But Horowitz's intellectual interests took him abroad, first to Sweden and then to London to work for Bertrand Russell's foundation. Scheer connected with him there while interviewing Russell and offered him a chance to join *Ramparts*.

In December 1967, Horowitz accepted the offer and moved back to Berkeley. He had reservations about Hink/Scheer's lavish style, but he had no ideological quarrels with the magazine's hard-hitting stories. He was also struck by changes in the Bay Area in the few years he had been away. "When we returned to Berkeley in January 1968," Horowitz wrote later, "the change was everywhere evident. People even looked different. Clothes were tie-dyed and bucolic, colors psychedelic, and hair long." Horowitz took his son to a nearby school to hear a local band called Purple Earthquake. It was the first time he had heard electric instruments in a live setting. "I looked around at the dreamy faces of the audience," he wrote later. "They were wearing the insignias and uniforms of the new counterculture that had blossomed from under the American surface while we were gone, and I experienced an unmistakable, strong kinship with them." Like his father, a Communist Party member who had visited the Soviet Union in the 1930s, Horowitz was beginning to feel that a new world was possible.

Although Scheer also brought on his brothers-in-law, Tuck and Christopher Weills, many of his recruits, and a significant proportion of the magazine's new investors, were Jewish. That pattern led I. F. Stone to remark, "There haven't been so many Jews involved in a Catholic operation since the twelve apostles." The shifting composition of the staff affected the magazine's tone and coverage, especially of the Middle East. Although Scheer grew up in a Jewish neighborhood and his family included Zionists, he hadn't thought seriously about the Middle East before the Six-Day War in June 1967. When that conflict flared, he turned to I. F. Stone for commentary and to Paul Jacobs for reporting. Through a *Ramparts* investor, Jacobs met Michael Ansara, whose father was active in the Arab League and arranged a trip to Egypt for Scheer and Jacobs. Upon their arrival, the three men were held at gunpoint due to a miscommunication between a commander and his troops. Eight hours later, a limousine arrived to whisk them away.

During his time in Egypt, Scheer developed what he called the Nasser thesis, which he published in two *Ramparts* articles. There he warned that the West should be careful with Egyptian president Gamal Abdel Nasser, noting that the likeliest alternative to his leadership was the Muslim Brotherhood and radical Islam.

Taken as a whole, *Ramparts'* coverage of the Middle East would now be considered balanced, perhaps even prescient. In the aftermath of the Six-Day War in 1967, for example, an editorial asserted:

> What is particularly outrageous about the new cold war consensus of the *New Republic* and the *National Review* [sic] is that it ignores the malicious and double-dealing role which U.S. foreign policy has played: supporting the most reactionary element in the Arab world, doing everything possible to keep the Arab world divided, and putting the

rights of American oil companies above the needs of the
Arab people. . . . There is no question that Arabs terror-
ized Israeli border communities, but it is also true that the
Israelis discriminated against their native Arab population.
It is also unfair to place the total responsibility for reconcil-
iation on the Jews. But now, especially in the flush of its
military triumph, Israel must take the initiative to forge a
progressive future for all the Mideast.

Two of the magazine's major shareholders, Martin Peretz and
Dick Russell, found that position intolerable. "To me, Nasser was
Hitler," Russell said. Peretz, an assistant professor at Harvard married to Singer Sewing Machine heiress Anne Farnsworth, argued
in *Commentary* magazine that the editorial provided "the most
carefully selective and skewed history of the conflict to come from
any source save possibly the propaganda machines of the respective
parties."

Some *Ramparts* readers agreed with Peretz. In the January 1968
issue, a letter to the editor maintained that the magazine's articles
"add up to a warm appreciation of the big-hearted Socialist,
Nasser, along with a thinly-veiled indictment of a fictional saber-
rattling Israel." The more immediate problem for the magazine,
however, was financial. When Scheer realized that Peretz and Russell would withdraw their money from *Ramparts*, he commissioned a pro-Israel article by Zeitlin, but it was too late. Hinckle
estimated that the editorial cost *Ramparts* $1 million.

As Scheer populated the office with his associates, Hinckle continued to recruit local newspaper writers. One was Adam
Hochschild, who started at *Ramparts* in September 1966 after two
years with the *Chronicle*. During his time at the San Francisco daily,
Hochschild profiled *Ramparts* for the last issue of the *New York
Herald Tribune Magazine*. That piece introduced him to Hinckle,
and he already knew Scheer from Berkeley, where Hochschild
also lived.

Like a growing number of his *Ramparts* colleagues, Hochschild was an easterner, but his background differed dramatically from theirs. His German-Jewish father headed AMAX, a multinational conglomerate whose interests included copper mines in Africa, and his mother's WASP background provided entry into elite social circles in New York and Princeton. Guests at the family's Adirondack summer estate included Adlai Stevenson, George Kennan, and the occasional CIA officer. One frequent visitor, Hochschild later discovered, was the agency's liaison with his father's company. When he and his parents traveled abroad, company representatives routinely greeted them. "I still half expect a smiling man to be there anytime I arrive in a new country," Hochschild wrote later. "Even if I were on a plane that had been hijacked, with all the passengers held at gunpoint, a hand would quietly take my bag, a voice would say, 'You don't have to stay with the others, Mr. Hochschild. Come right this way.' "

Before joining *Ramparts*, Hochschild worked the police beat in San Francisco and confronted the same racial double standard that Hinckle noted during his time in Oakland. Hochschild also heard older reporters recount stories that they couldn't get into the newspaper: a sweetheart deal for a public construction job, racist comments by a mayoral candidate that the paper was backing, and other tales of corruption and malfeasance. "If you wanted to be a journalist but cared about social issues," Hochschild recalled, "the alternatives looked bleak." The two main options were writing for low-circulation radical journals or for daily newspapers, where social concerns had to be smuggled into stories.

For Hochschild and others, *Ramparts* was the solution to that problem. In addition to doing real investigative work, the magazine had a knack for making larger outlets respond to its stories. The formula was simple, Hochschild noted later: "Find an exposé that major newspapers are afraid to touch, publish it with a big enough splash so they can't afford to ignore it . . . and then publicize it in a way that plays the press off against each other." Certainly investors appreciated the magazine's ability to break stories that the

New York Times and other mainstream publications would play for a week or more. Hochschild also admired the literary flair *Ramparts* brought to its major stories, which were "written with the liveliness of detective novels."

Hochschild described his time at *Ramparts* as "zany but exciting." In a 1986 memoir about his relationship with his father, he sketched the scene inside the *Ramparts* office.

> Assuming the office phones are tapped, we dash out to make key calls from pay phones. We junior staffers work in cubicles with partitions that do not come all the way to the ceiling; sometimes I look up from my typewriter and see the hairy underside of a small monkey flying from partition to partition above my head. It is the office mascot, named Henry Luce.

Hochschild's wide-ranging contributions to *Ramparts* included a profile of Clark Kerr after his dismissal from the University of California, but many of his pieces focused on black communities, both in South Africa, where he had written for an antigovernment newspaper one summer, and in the American South, where he worked as a civil rights worker in the summer of 1964. Hochschild downplayed his family background, but it popped up awkwardly from time to time. While he was writing a story about a complicated oil-lease scandal in Colorado, a source informed him that AMAX executives "had half the legislature in their pockets." A fellow *Ramparts* staffer researching American corporations in Africa came across Hochschild's father's name and asked, "Hey, Adam, are you related to this guy?" After a slew of CIA front operations were exposed in the wake of the NSA story, one such organization turned out to be the African-American Institute, where his father had been board chairman for a decade.

Hochschild's tenure at *Ramparts* coincided with a string of exceptionally strong issues. In September 1967, for example, he wrote a piece about Régis Debray, the twenty-six-year-old French intellectual whose contact with Che Guevara had landed him in a Bolivian prison. The other articles in that issue included Sol Stern on the Panthers and other black radicals; a Bill Turner piece on New Orleans district attorney Jim Garrison; Noam Chomsky on Vietnam and Howard Zinn's "logic of withdrawal"; Judy Stone on B. Traven, the mysterious author of *Treasure of the Sierra Madre*; Paul Goodman on the Diggers, the Haight–Ashbury anarchist troupe; Studs Terkel on Paul Goodman and American morality; and an article on Guatemalan guerrillas by Eduardo Galeano, the Uruguayan journalist who would later gain fame as the author of *The Open Veins of Latin America, Memory of Fire,* and *Soccer in Sun and Shadow.*

That sort of line-up was an extraordinary departure from mainstream American journalism, and in March 1967, *Ramparts* received the George Polk Memorial Award for excellence in magazine reporting. Ironically, the magazine shared its award with *Time*, its sharpest and most persistent critic.

Ramparts wasn't only a critical success. Its circulation was the envy of many more established magazines, and its impact was dramatic, especially among the nation's swelling ranks of college students. Jeff Cohen, who would later co-found Fairness and Accuracy in Reporting (FAIR), recalled the magazine's reception at the University of Michigan.

> I saw my first issue at seventeen and started reading it in '68 or '69. Each issue went around the dorm in Ann Arbor in 1969. It was dog-eared by the time I got it. It really was a radicalizing tool of its own. It ripped your head off. It helped us turn my cousin's fraternity into an SDS chapter.

Shaba Om, who would later stand trial in the New York Panther 21 case, was also radicalized by *Ramparts*:

> I was walking down the streets in midtown Manhattan and saw this magazine called *Ramparts*, and Black Panthers were

on the cover of the magazine. I'd heard about the Black Panther Party before, so I bought a copy of *Ramparts* and began reading it—and man these dudes are together and crazy as hell. The more I learned about the party, the more it excited me.

For the first time, a radical slick was reaching a broad audience—and blowing its mind.

Ramparts was also influencing national leaders, most notably Martin Luther King Jr. In January 1967, many were urging Dr. King to come out against the Vietnam War. Carey McWilliams invited him to a *Nation* forum the following month in Los Angeles, but many of King's advisors warned against commenting on foreign policy, and King was reluctant to shift his focus from civil rights.

That same January, *Ramparts* ran a photo-essay by human rights activist and political scientist William Pepper called "The Children of Vietnam." It showed in hideous detail the effects of U.S. bombing and protracted warfare on that country's children. The preface by pediatrician and bestselling author Dr. Benjamin Spock claimed that one million children "had been killed or wounded or burned in the war America is carrying on in Vietnam."

Predictably, *Time* magazine spun the story in a January 6 article called "A Bomb in Every Issue." It lambasted *Ramparts* for its sensationalism and denigrated it for various journalistic and moral shortcomings. *Time* maintained that the Michigan State story "had already been published in book form elsewhere" and noted that *Ramparts* had moved its office to "one of those topless streets in San Francisco's New Left bohemia." As usual, the article's last paragraph spelled out the moral for readers who might otherwise have missed it.

Ramparts is slick enough to lure the unwary and bedazzled reader into accepting flimflam as fact. After boasting that the January issue would "document" that a million Vietnamese children had been killed or wounded in the war, it produced a mere juggling of highly dubious statistics and a collection of very touching pictures, some of which could have been taken in any distressed country.

No story here, apparently, and no need for Americans to worry about the effects of bombing Vietnam's civilian population.

That month, Dr. King left for Jamaica for four weeks of solitude and writing. At the airport, he bought several magazines and met his friend, Bernard Lee, for lunch. Lee later recalled that King reacted strongly to the Vietnam story.

> When he came to *Ramparts* magazine, he stopped. He froze as he looked at the pictures from Vietnam. He saw a picture of a Vietnamese mother holding her dead baby, a baby killed by our military. Then Martin just pushed the plate of food away from him. I looked up and said, "Doesn't it taste any good?," and he answered, "Nothing will ever taste any good for me until I do everything I can to end that war."

King wasn't the only one moved by that piece; many staff members were in tears while working on the spread, and it gave art director Dugald Stermer nightmares. He later said it was "just about the nastiest job I've ever had."

When he returned from Jamaica, King spoke against the war in Los Angeles, but he saved his strongest comments for a speech at the Riverside Church on April 4, exactly one year before his assassination. King listed seven reasons for stopping the war and urged the U.S. government, which he called "the major purveyor of violence in the world," to end the bombing and set a date for troop withdrawal. "We must find new ways to speak for peace in Vietnam and justice throughout the developing world—a world that borders on our doors," he concluded. "If we do not act, we shall surely be dragged down the long, dark and shameful corridors of time reserved for those who possess power without compassion, might without morality, and strength without sight."

After the speech, King was buoyant. Although he was criticized in the mainstream media, he was satisfied with his position. In his study of King during this time, David Garrow noted that he "finally made the moral declaration he had felt obligated to deliver ever since that January day when he saw the photos in *Ramparts*." King offered *Ramparts* exclusive publication rights for the speech, which ran the following month with the title "Declaration of Independence from the War in Vietnam." At a Southern Leadership Christian Conference meeting that year, he told his colleagues, "I picked up an article entitled 'The Children of Vietnam,' and I read it, and after reading that article I said to myself, 'Never again will I be silent on an issue that is destroying the soul of our nation and destroying thousands and thousands of little children in Vietnam.' "

As *Ramparts'* national influence grew, its hometown was experiencing a historical transformation. In the spring and summer of 1967, roughly 75,000 young people flocked to San Francisco to create or sample the novel scene that was emerging there. Black musicians called the earliest arrivals "hipsters," but *Chronicle* columnist Herb Caen changed that to "hippies." After *Ramparts* picked up the term, the name stuck.

The scene's epicenter was Haight-Ashbury, originally an affluent neighborhood of ornate Victorian homes that had survived the 1906 earthquake. After World War II, many were divided into flats in response to an acute housing shortage, and their owners began moving out to newer suburbs. By the 1960s, the Haight had become a plentiful source of low-cost rental housing. It also offered easy access to Golden Gate Park's one thousand acres of woodlands, meadows, lakes, gardens, and recreation areas.

The Haight was to the hippies what North Beach was to the Beats, but its animating spirit differed from its precursor's. In their landmark work on the social history of LSD, Martin Lee and Bruce Shlain summarized that difference.

> More than anything the Haight was a unique state of mind, an arena of exploration and celebration. The new hipsters had cast aside the syndrome of alienation and despair that saddled many of the their beatnik forebears. The accent shifted from solitude to communion, from the individual to the interpersonal.

Ken Kesey and the Merry Pranksters reflected that change in spirit. They had generated a festive scene in and around Kesey's home in La Honda, a tiny community in the coastal mountains south of San Francisco. Their activities included wild parties with Hunter Thompson, Allen Ginsberg, and the Hell's Angels; a free-wheeling cross-country trip in a brightly painted school bus; and a series of "acid tests" in the Bay Area and Los Angeles, where revelers tripped on LSD. In January 1966, Kesey and the Pranksters also organized the Trips Festival, a three-day blowout in Golden Gate Park with music, guerrilla theater, mime exhibitions, trampolines, and plenty of acid. Jerry ("Captain Trips") Garcia performed with his band, the Grateful Dead, and later described the event as "thousands of people, man, all helplessly stoned. . . . It was magic, far-out beautiful magic." When LSD was outlawed in October 1966, Kesey and the Pranksters convened an Acid Test Graduation on Halloween; the event's theme, Kesey told television reporters, was "trip or treat."

In January 1967, the Diggers, a radical community-action group of improvisational actors, sponsored the Human Be-In, which drew more than twenty thousand people to Golden Gate Park. First announced in the *San Francisco Oracle*, an underground newspaper published in Haight-Ashbury, the event was described as "a gathering of tribes" to celebrate countercultural values. Speakers included Timothy Leary, Allen Ginsberg, and Gary

Snyder, and various San Francisco bands performed. But even by that time, some participants had misgivings about the Haight-Ashbury scene. Decades later, Grateful Dead singer Bob Weir recalled the warning signs.

> Even before the summer of '67, the strangers coming in were starting to outnumber the rest of us. We weren't quite getting the riffraff yet—people with missing teeth and stuff like that. But the folks who lived in our youth ghetto in Haight-Ashbury in '65 and '66 were of an artistic bent, almost all of them. Everyone brought something to the party. By the time of the Be-In, people were coming just to be at the party, not bringing anything. I could see the whole thing tilting.

Hunter Thompson had reached the same conclusion. He gloried in the early days of "Hashbury," which he later identified as his time and place.

> There was madness in any direction, at any hour. If not across the Bay, then up the Golden Gate or down 101 to Los Altos or La Honda. . . . You could strike sparks anywhere. There was a fantastic universal sense that whatever we were doing was right, that we were winning. . . . And that, I think, was the handle—that sense of inevitable victory over the forces of Old and Evil. Not in any mean or military sense; we didn't need that. Our energy would simply *prevail.*

Yet even before the Summer of Love rolled around, Thompson felt the magic slipping away. "By the end of '66," he wrote later, "the whole neighborhood had become a cop-magnet and a bad sideshow." The rest of the world was still fascinated, however, and Thompson advanced his budding career by describing the kaleidoscopic scene for the *New York Times Magazine.*

Theodore Roszak famously coined the term *counter culture* to describe this milieu, whose participants tended to share an interest in radical politics, psychedelic experience ("counterfeit infinity," in Roszak's parlance), sexual freedom, an aversion to technocracy, and an interest in Eastern religions, mysticism, and the occult. Roszak's study was by no means an uncritical celebration of this culture. He enjoyed puncturing its rhetorical excesses, including this passage from the *Oracle* on avoiding hepatitis.

> Doing your thing doesn't have to include dumping bad Karma on your soul-brothers. Don't touch food or drink or prepare it without first thoroughly washing your hands, especially if you've just been to the john. . . . You can even afford to get up tight about it, especially if your home is of the tribal kind.

"My pre-tribal father," Roszak noted, "used to phrase this piece of folk wisdom as: 'You wash up before you sit down at this table!' But I seem to remember being about five years old at the time."

Roszak also wondered about the politics of the counter-culture and its histrionic resistance to traditional values. The angriest dissenters, he observed, staged heroic confrontations that "opened themselves to the most obvious kinds of police and military violence."

> They quickly draw the conclusion that the status quo is supported by nothing more than bayonets, overlooking the fact that these bayonets enjoy the support of a vast consensus which has been won for the status quo by means far more subtle and enduring than armed force.

On balance, however, Roszak was sympathetic to the youthful revolt against technocracy and managerial liberalism. He was also receptive to Eastern spirituality. His conclusion cited Chuang Tzu and the virtues of government through nonaction; his source was a book by Thomas Merton.

Although Roszak was a Bay Area academic, he wrote his groundbreaking articles for Carey McWilliams at the *Nation* before producing his seminal book, *The Making of a Counter Culture*, in 1969. Likewise, McWilliams commissioned Hunter Thompson's articles on two Bay Area phenomena, the Hell's Angels and Free Speech Movement. Neither man wrote any signed pieces for *Ramparts*, though Thompson regarded the magazine highly and was listed as a contributing editor after he moved to Aspen. That esteem was evident in his later account of meeting Hinckle.

> I met [Hinckle] through his magazine, *Ramparts*. I met him before *Rolling Stone* ever existed. *Ramparts* was a cross-roads of my world in San Francisco, a slicker version of *The Nation*—with glossy covers and such. Warren had a genius for getting stories that could get placed on the front page of the *New York Times*. He had a beautiful eye for what story had a high, weird look to it. You know, busting the Defense Department—*Ramparts* was real left, radical. I paid a lot of attention to them and ended up being a columnist. *Ramparts* was the scene until some geek withdrew the funding and it collapsed. Jann Wenner, who founded *Rolling Stone*, actually worked there in the library—he was a copy boy or something.

Thompson also felt close enough to *Ramparts* to offer management pointers to Hinckle. After a visit to 301 Broadway, he struck off one of his famous letters.

> Again . . . it was a good show over there, and my advice to you is to give up all forms of booze and bookkeepers for the duration of the crisis. Moderation in all things. When you turn up a freak on the staff, don't just fire him/her—pursue him into the very bowels of the economy and queer

Founding publisher Edward Keating wanted to provide "a forum for the mature American Catholic." Within a few years, however, the magazine became the nation's premier muckraker. *(Photo courtesy of Steve Keating)*

Helen Keating's inheritance funded *Ramparts* through 1964. She shared her husband's passionate idealism but disliked the furor that later surrounded the magazine. *(Photo courtesy of Steve Keating)*

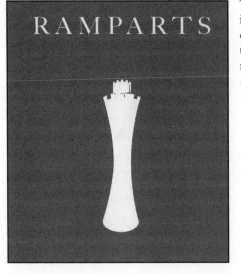

The cover of the first issue. One designer later compared the early issues to the poetry annuals of a midwestern girls' school. *(Photo courtesy of Guy and Gregory Stilson)*

John Howard Griffin (right), author of *Black Like Me,* was an early contributor and Keating hero. *(Photo courtesy of Steve Keating)*

Trappist monk and bestselling author Thomas Merton increased the magazine's cachet but privately warned Keating that the Church might dismiss him "as a man spoiling for a fight and a born trouble maker." *(Photo credit: AP Images / Matthew Lutts)*

Taking the editorial reins, a young Warren Hinckle courted controversy and transformed the Catholic literary quarterly into a monthly "slick." *(Photo courtesy of The Hunter S. Thompson Archives)*

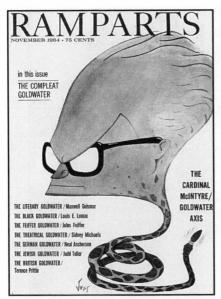

The November 1964 issue, timed to coincide with the presidential election, was pulled from many newsstands. They were making progress. *(Photo courtesy of Guy and Gregory Stilson)*

Advertising guru Howard Gossage was Hinckle's chief mentor. In addition to guiding the magazine's publicity strategy, he introduced its young staffers to key players in San Francisco and smoothed over leadership snags. *(Photo courtesy of the Estate of Jessica Mitford)*

Gossage recruited Dugald Stermer as art director. His innovations were a critical part of the magazine's rapid ascent. *(Photo credit: Bob Seidemann)*

Robert Scheer supercharged the magazine with his Vietnam coverage. In 1966, he also garnered 45 percent of the vote in the Democratic primary against East Bay incumbent Congressman Jeffery Cohelan. *(Photo credit: Michael Millman)*

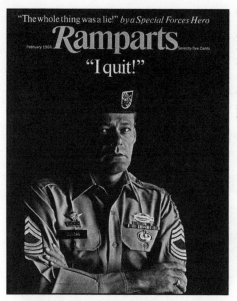

The February 1966 cover photograph of Donald Duncan became a *Ramparts* icon. Catholic and anti-communist, Duncan delivered a credible first-person account of the debacle in Vietnam. *(Photo courtesy of Guy and Gregory Stilson)*

Editorial board member Jessica Mitford applauded the magazine's achievements under Hinckle and Scheer but wished "they could be a trifle less Animal Farm–ish about it." *(Photo courtesy of the Estate of Jessica Mitford)*

After *Ramparts* exposed the link between Michigan State University and the CIA's covert activities, CIA director William Raborn ordered a rundown on the magazine and its principals. *(Photo courtesy of Guy and Gregory Stilson)*

Edward Sorel's "The Aviary [Hawkus Caucus Americanus]" exemplified the magazine's combination of visual sophistication and political irreverence. *(Photo courtesy of Guy and Gregory Stilson)*

Ramparts was the first major media outlet to question the Warren Report's account of President Kennedy's assassination. *(Photo courtesy of Guy and Gregory Stilson)*

After Ed Keating exhausted Helen's inheritance, he and Hinckle persuaded Fred Mitchell to underwrite the magazine. "I had apparently saved *Ramparts* from something dire," Mitchell wrote later. *(Photo courtesy of Margaretta Mitchell)*

Jann Wenner met his wife, Jane Schindelheim, at *Ramparts*. After the spinoff newspaper shut down in 1967, Wenner teamed with music critic Ralph Gleason, a contributing editor at the magazine, to co-found *Rolling Stone*. With Stermer's consent, Wenner based the new magazine's design on the *Sunday Ramparts*. *(Photo courtesy of Jann Wenner)*

Adam Hochschild did two tours of duty with *Ramparts* before co-founding *Mother Jones* in 1976. If *Ramparts'* wildness lived on in *Rolling Stone*, *Mother Jones* carried on its muckraking. *(Photo credit: Jeffrey Blankfort)*

The December 1967 cover showed the incineration of four draft cards, leading to a grand jury investigation. *Time* called the photo a "New Left salute." *(Photo courtesy of Guy and Gregory Stilson)*

The controversial "Women Power" issue led one women's group to conclude that *Ramparts* thought feminists had "two tits and no head." *(Photo courtesy of Guy and Gregory Stilson)*

Released from state prison with Keating's help, Eldridge Cleaver joined the *Ramparts* staff in December 1966 and began producing the bestselling *Soul on Ice*. After a 1968 shootout with the Oakland police, Cleaver was released on bail and ran for president that year on the Peace and Freedom Party ticket. *(Photo credit: Jeffrey Blankfort)*

Building on staffer Fred Gardner's suggestion, Hinckle published the *Ramparts Wall Poster* during the 1968 Democratic National Convention in Chicago. A single oversized sheet, the *Wall Poster* ran street news on the front and convention news on the back.

While *Ramparts* funding dwindled, Hinckle transported almost a dozen staffers to Chicago and installed them in the plush Ambassador Hotel. Out on the street, photographer Jeffrey Blankfort captured some of the violence for the magazine. *(Photo credit: Jeffrey Blankfort)*

A September 1968 cover featured North Beach stripper Carol Doda sporting the latest CIA recording device—a topic of great interest to staff members, who were convinced that the government was tapping their telephones. *(Photo courtesy of Guy and Gregory Stilson)*

Hunter S. Thompson described *Ramparts* as "a crossroads of my world in San Francisco." After *Ramparts* declared bankruptcy in 1969, Hinckle teamed him with artist Ralph Steadman at *Scanlan's* and thereby helped launch Gonzo journalism. Thompson borrowed the wall poster concept when he ran for sheriff in Colorado the following year. He also shaved his head so he could refer to the incumbent as "my longhaired opponent." *(Photo by David Hiser/Still Media)*

After reorganizing under Chapter 11, *Ramparts* came out swinging in April 1969. The cover caption read, "Alienation is when your country is at war and you want the other side to win." Later that year, David Horowitz and Peter Collier engineered Scheer's ouster. *(Photo courtesy of Guy and Gregory Stilson)*

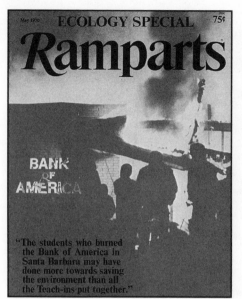

The "Ecology Special" cover featured the incineration of a Bank of America in Santa Barbara. Some longtime supporters began to distance themselves from the magazine. *(Photo courtesy of Guy and Gregory Stilson)*

Former *Ramparts* bookkeeper Betty Van Patter was murdered, purportedly by Black Panthers, after she began working for the Black Panther Party. David Horowitz cited her death as the beginning of his long march to the political right. *(Photo courtesy of Tamara Baltar)*

his act for all time. And get that nigger off the premises.
You've got to get a grip on yourself. Otherwise . . . they'll
cut your throat.

Closer in every way to the San Francisco counterculture than
the *Nation* would ever be, *Ramparts* did surprisingly little original
reporting on it. The radicals on the staff were unimpressed by the
flower children's fantasies about transcending politics, and Hinckle
viewed the city's newest residents skeptically. "The hippies grew
up in my backyard," he noted in his memoir. "I did not find them
good neighbors."

Yet it was Hinckle who wrote the magazine's major article on
the phenomenon, "A Social History of the Hippies." In that
March 1967 piece, Hinckle described the scene and its main players, but he also argued that the Beats, the hippies' immediate precursors, personified two dissonant political strains: fascism (as
embodied by Jack Kerouac) and resistance (as embodied by Allen
Ginsberg). That analysis led to a surprising conclusion.

The danger in the hippie movement is more than over-
crowded streets and possible hunger riots this summer. If
more and more youngsters begin to share the hippie posture of unrelenting quietism, the future of activist, serious
politics is bound to be affected. The hippies have shown
that it can be pleasant to drop out of the arduous task of at-
tempting to steer a difficult, unrewarding society. But when
that is done, you leave the driving to the Hell's Angels.

Hinckle's article so enraged Ralph Gleason that he promptly
resigned from the magazine. In a letter to Gossage, Mitford noted
Gleason's displeasure, which he aired at a meeting of the editorial
board.

He was not consulted about the Hippie article, which was
full of inaccuracies. He was originally supposed to write

this article, but Hink III went ahead without his knowledge, first thing he knew about it was when it was in print.
In February, he wrote a furious letter of resignation and demanded that this letter should be printed in the mag. He
got no acknowledgment, nobody contacted him at all, it
was never printed. . . . There was much more along this
line, and a good deal of son-of-a-bitching etc. I asked
Ralph if he would come to a meeting with Hink/Scheer,
he wasn't sure but certainly *not* if it were held at *Ramparts'*
office, he'd never set foot in that place again. He was, in a
word, simply *furious* with the lot of them.

Wiping his hands of *Ramparts*, Gleason turned his attention to
another venture. While attending a concert in Longshoreman's
Hall featuring Jefferson Airplane, Gleason met Jann Wenner, a
nineteen-year-old rock columnist for the Cal newspaper. After
leaving Berkeley, Wenner traveled to London and was living in a
New York suburb when Gleason wrote to him about a position at
the *Sunday Ramparts*, the spin-off newspaper Hinckle started in
1966. Wenner returned to the Bay Area and worked on the paper's
entertainment section. There he met his future wife, Jane Schindelheim, a receptionist at *Ramparts*.

Wenner tried to interest Hinckle in the Bay Area's burgeoning
counterculture, but his efforts were fruitless. "They were oblivious
to the cultural changes in San Francisco," Wenner recalled. "Warren ridiculed it, and Scheer had no use for it. Dugald got it. He respected the artists and musicians. But I didn't have much to do
with Warren, and I didn't get along with Scheer, who asked me to
get his coffee."

In 1967, Hinckle shut down the *Sunday Ramparts*, leaving
Wenner out of work. (Hinckle would briefly revive the paper as a
daily during the San Francisco newspaper strike of 1968.) Within
months, Wenner and Gleason conceived a new magazine, and after
borrowing the seed money from Schindelheim, Wenner began assembling the first issue in a spare room at 301 Broadway. Later, he

moved to a loft on Brannan Street over Garrett Press, which also printed *Ramparts*. At Gleason's suggestion, Wenner named his magazine after a Bob Dylan song, and with Stermer's permission, he lifted his design directly from the *Sunday Ramparts*. "I only had *Ramparts* and my high school yearbook as a model for the magazine," Wenner said later. "We still use some of the elements from *Ramparts*."

The first issue of *Rolling Stone* appeared in November 1967, and the magazine's success became an important if largely unacknowledged part of *Ramparts'* legacy. In his memoir, Hinckle disavowed Wenner and *Rolling Stone*.

> What I found objectionable about the hippies—or rather about some hippie promoters—was the attempt to make a serious political stance out of goofing off. . . . One of the leading merchandisers of this counterculture bullshit was *Rolling Stone*, the rock culture tabloid that was started by two disgruntled *Ramparts* types. One of them was Jann Wenner, then a fat and pudgy kid hanging around the office. . . . The truth of the matter is that I hardly knew the kid; and the only thing that *Ramparts* gave him to help start his paper was a bottle of rubber cement to paste up the first issue, and I screamed about *that*.

Hinckle was more deferential to Gleason, a key factor in *Rolling Stone's* success. Hinckle later claimed that he was sorry he "dumped on [Gleason's] flower children without giving him a chance to defend the little fascists." But for Hinckle, the bloodshed at the Altamont rock concert in 1969, when the Hell's Angels killed a spectator in front of the stage, was vindication of his theory that the "hippie cultists" aided the forces of fascism.

Ramparts may have held the hippies at arm's length, but Hinckle's article spread their story. Moreover, the magazine's pages increasingly reflected the counterculture's influence in and around San Francisco. Psychedelic art, nudity, drug references, and sexual

content became commonplace, especially but not only in the advertisements. One long-running full-page ad for *Avant-Garde*
magazine featured a close-up of a woman climaxing. (The marketing copy claimed that she had "just finished reading her latest issue
and, as usual, she's satisfied.") In many ways, however, *Ramparts'*
treatment of sex resembled *Esquire's*, and the earlier article on
Hugh Hefner was a thinly veiled appeal to *Playboy's* ethos and
readership. Gene Marine's "A Male Guide to Women's Liberation," which Marine spun into a book, would have been equally
at home in those magazines. Nor was the cover tease for that
piece especially sensitive to its homosexual audience. The November 1968 banner read, "Breaking the Faggot Barrier in Men's
Clothes."

Gratuitous appeals to sex produced other jarring results. One
cover story, "A Paranoid's Guide to Bugging," explored surveillance technology, a subject of great interest in the *Ramparts* office.
The cover photo featured Carol Doda, the busty blonde stripper
from a North Beach nightclub, in a black brassiere looking directly
into the camera; a recording device peeked out of her waistband,
and cords ran to two attachments on the bra near her nipples. Although brazen, the cover concept wasn't radical so much as business as usual. If it demonstrated the staff's explicit strategy—using
mainstream techniques to advance leftist ideas—it also reflected
that strategy's limitations.

When the magazine addressed feminist concerns, it frequently
fell short. Warren and Marianne Hinckle's generally laudatory
"Women Power" cover story of February 1968 was criticized for
its reference to "narrow-minded bitches," and the cover photograph caused a minor furor. The shot featured a female model's
cleavage, but her head was cropped out of the picture. The irony
wasn't lost on the female staff or readers, many of whom were organizing the first women's groups. In awarding Warren Hinckle
the "Male Chauvinist of the Month Award," the March issue of
Voice of the Women's Liberation Movement maintained that he "depicted 'political women' as having two tits and no head."

• • •

As the NSA and Haight-Ashbury stories found large audiences, Eldridge Cleaver was assembling the *Soul on Ice* manuscript for McGraw-Hill and becoming deeply involved in the Black Panther Party's activities. In May 1967, Cleaver accompanied Seale and seventeen other Panthers in full regalia to the state capitol in Sacramento. Their purpose was to protest a new gun control bill, which was widely regarded as a response to the Panthers' armed patrols.

Predominantly white, sleepy, and surrounded by farmland, Sacramento was an unlikely venue for eighteen armed black militants. Brandishing their shotguns and M-16s, the Panthers were met by reporters before entering the capitol and striding into the legislative chamber. As cameras flashed, police officers confiscated the weapons and led the Panthers off the floor of the assembly with minimal resistance. Outside the building, Bobby Seale read Executive Mandate Number One to the press.

> The Black Panther Party calls upon American people in general and black people in particular to take full note of the racist California legislature which is now considering legislation aimed at keeping the black people disarmed and powerless, at the very same time that racist police agencies throughout the country are intensifying the terror, brutality, murder and repression of black people.

When they returned to their cars, Cleaver told Seale, "Brother, we did it. We did it, man. We put it over." Seale replied, "That's right, brother, we did." Then Seale gave the order to leave. "Let's go. We gonna go eat all this fried chicken that we got here, 'cause I'm hungry and it's hot in this town."

On their way out of town, the Panthers were arrested at a gas station. The arresting officer approached Seale's car with his gun out. Seale directed him to holster his weapon. "And the next thing I heard was brothers jacking rounds, jacking shells off into the chambers of their guns," he recalled. The officer holstered his gun, and the Panthers were arrested without further incident. The news coverage made them instant celebrities. Six Panthers, including Seale, were eventually convicted on misdemeanor charges. Cleaver, who was represented by Beverly Axelrod, was released the next day because he was unarmed and covering the event for *Ramparts*.

Meanwhile, relations between the Panthers and the largely white Oakland police force continued to worsen. The party's literature featured images of heroic black men and women overcoming authority figures, especially the police, who were drawn as swine. One of the party's chants included the verse,

> The revolution has come.
> Off the pig!
> Time to pick up the gun.
> Off the pig!

At a Panther wedding, a group of children performed a variation on that theme: "We want a pork chop, off the pig!"

A few months after the Sacramento protest, Newton converted these words into action. On October 28, 1967, a young police officer named John Frey stopped Newton's car near the corner of Seventh and Willow streets in West Oakland. Newton and a friend named Gene McKinney had been celebrating the end of Newton's probation, which followed a conviction for stabbing a man at a party with a steak knife. Realizing he had stopped Newton, Frey called for backup. When officer Herbert Heanes arrived, Frey ordered Newton out of the car and led him toward the patrol cars. The two men scuffled, and Frey received a fatal gunshot wound. Heanes shot Newton in the stomach and was wounded himself before Newton and McKinney fled.

Newton and McKinney approached a passing car and told the driver to take them to a nearby address. According to the motorist, one of them had a gun, and Newton said, "I just shot two dudes." Newton made it to the home of a fellow Panther, who took him to

Kaiser Hospital, where Newton was arrested. A photograph of Newton handcuffed to an emergency room gurney, writhing in agony, went out to the rest of the nation.

With Seale in jail on the Sacramento misdemeanor, Cleaver was no longer an ordinary journalist—if he had ever been one. Instead, he was the acting leader of the Black Panther Party, America's premier revolutionary organization. The following year, he would lead the effort to free Newton and electrify the nation.

6

BOMBS BURSTING IN AIR

If 1968 was the year America had a nervous breakdown, *Ramparts* was its most reliable fever chart. The national crisis had complex and interlocking causes, including policy failures, mounting frustrations, social ruptures, and political violence. Most of these developments were reflected—and in some cases, aggravated—by *Ramparts* and its coverage that year. As the nation plunged into crisis, so did the magazine. *Ramparts* began 1968 in the coils of conspiracy theories, became embroiled in the nation's most controversial and violent domestic conflicts, and finished the year in fractious, chaotic collapse.

The political crisis had been brewing for years. Emotionally, the country was still recovering from the shock of the Kennedy assassination, which for many Americans had never been explained satisfactorily. In its aftermath, President Johnson signed sweeping civil rights and Great Society legislation, but he also escalated the conflict in Vietnam and thereby made violence a staple in the national media diet. As American soldiers decimated Vietnam and perished by the thousands, the major parties mulishly refused to acknowledge what administration insiders already knew—that military victory was impossible. Opinion polls showed that more and more Americans opposed the war, but even in liberal San Francisco, most residents still supported the effort despite mounting evidence that the Johnson administration hadn't been truthful about the war's origins or prospects.

Ramparts had exposed the official mendacity as forcefully as any media outlet, but the New Left had made little significant progress on its primary issue, and it blamed Johnson and mainstream liberals for that failure. After several years of organizing and protest, some movement leaders concluded that they had exhausted the opportunities provided by conventional politics. Radical leftists, who had never held out hope for electoral politics, redoubled their efforts to promote direct action. *Ramparts* fell somewhere between these two positions. Scheer's 1966 campaign had targeted major flaws in America's liberal consensus, but by 1968, the magazine had recoded those flaws as crimes, and liberalism itself became a key target. Although postwar America provided opportunity and prosperity to many, it also withheld them from those who needed them most. Moreover, its leaders lied about the true aims of the nation's foreign policy, and many young people were paying the ultimate price for that deception.

From *Ramparts*' perspective, liberals looked even worse than conservatives. "Cold War liberalism," a December 1967 editorial argued, "lost even the pretense of vitality in the pursuit of truth and change, and instead came to acquire the stench of decay." Grassroots liberals had become "reluctant revolutionaries," and a younger generation raised on the principles of liberalism was "outraged by the crimes committed ostensibly in their name."

In the February 1968 issue, Carl Oglesby extended the argument:

> We who are radicals have a task much different than the salvation of liberalism—to champion the values which made us radicals to begin with. . . . This is no time for taking cover on behalf of somebody else's disagreeable vision for the good-enough society.

Instead, Oglesby argued, it was time to "transform every attack upon ourselves into a still happier and more piercing attack upon those whose crimes created us." This was both a call to arms and an origin myth for young radicals. Oglesby stopped short of the more sensational pronouncements advanced by his peers. "Number One on the Yippie program," Jerry Rubin famously told one

student group, "is kill your parents." But Oglesby's analysis assumed a backdrop of intergenerational conflict.

What to do now? On this point, *Ramparts* joined an emerging
New Left consensus: turn up the militancy. That consensus moved
young radicals even further away from liberals, many of whom had
misgivings about the New Left's penchant for protest and distrust
of power. Old-school liberals like Clark Kerr and Pat Brown had
come of age during the New Deal, when the federal government
was an engine for progressive change. For them, power wasn't
something that you only spoke the truth to; it was something you
accrued and deployed to build new institutions and enact progressive reforms. Although Johnson and others had abused that power,
liberals were uneager to hand it over to Republicans like Ronald
Reagan or Richard Nixon, who had launched their political careers by attacking or persecuting leftists. And after years of cob-
bling together an unstable coalition of blue-collar workers, ethnic
minorities, intellectuals, and conservative southern Democrats,
many liberals had learned that throwing bombs was easier than
catching them.

But with body counts rising and millions of young men facing
conscription in a dubious war, frustration among antiwar activists
reached a boiling point. When students returned to Berkeley in
the fall of 1967, they were ready to act. Bay Area radicals organized
a street action to blockade the Oakland Induction Center for
draftees. A nonviolent sit-in on Monday would be followed by
more militant action the following days. The actions were announced in a telegram to Governor Reagan asking him to shut
down the induction center. "If you don't, we will," the telegram
read. In a later article for *Ramparts*, Reese Erlich and Terence Cannon described their telegram's tone as "good New Left arrogance." As the event's organizers finalized their plans, they learned
that Che Guevara, the revolutionary icon, had been captured and
executed in Bolivia.

The first day of Stop the Draft Week came off as planned. The
sit-in resulted in the arrest of 124 protestors, including Joan Baez,

all of whom walked peacefully into the paddy wagons. The second day, known afterward as Bloody Tuesday, featured a clash between 2,500 protestors and club-swinging cops, and street confrontations continued throughout the week. The action managed to delay busloads of inductees only by a few hours, but organizer Frank Bardacke counted it a success: "We blocked traffic and changed the streets from thoroughfares of business into a place for people to walk, talk, argue, and even dance. We felt liberated and we called our barricaded streets liberated territory." Such was the shift from protest to resistance.

In January 1968, Alameda County authorities indicted some protest leaders, who became known as the Oakland 7. In retrospect, the charges against them sound largely symbolic: conspiracy to trespass, to commit a public nuisance, and to resist, delay, and obstruct police officers. The defendants included Erlich, who began working for *Ramparts* after his suspension from Cal. The Oakland 7 were eventually acquitted, but the protests were just getting started.

Ramparts began 1968 in typical fashion; the January issue featured a story on the Kennedy assassination, a piece by Maurice Zeitlin on the Israeli left, and passages from Che's memoir. But letters to the editor indicated that some readers felt the magazine had crossed a line or two. One complained about the magazine's position on Israel, and two objected to the magazine's language, which, in the aftermath of the Lenny Bruce obscenity trial in San Francisco, had become increasingly earthy. One reader claimed that a recent issue contained "one 'motherfucker' too many."

Long before 1968, the JFK assassination had become a favorite subject for Hinckle. Regarding the Warren Report as soporific, he plunged the magazine into a dense thicket of conspiracy theories. The *Ramparts* office, he wrote later, "soon became a library, research center, information retrieval system, office, and all-night hot dog stand for free-lance assassination buffs." One intrepid investigator made an especially strong impression on him.

> One of the most horrific experiences of my life was when a dogged female sleuth trapped me in the men's room, where I was sitting in the morning after a long evening of drinking. She lounged against the urinal, lecturing me for half an hour through the stall door about the conspiratorial significance of Oswald's having shaved off all his pubic hair.

Scheer eventually banished the conspiracy theorists from the building, but Hinckle's appetite for sensation meant the stories would continue.

Led by Bill Turner, a team of *Ramparts* writers and researchers sorted through dozens of fantastical scenarios. In November 1966, the third anniversary of the assassination, *Ramparts* featured the work of small-town Texas editor Penn Jones. Hinckle described Jones as "a wash-and-wear version of Burgess Meredith," but he accepted John Howard Griffin's assessment of Jones as scrappy and reliable. Jones's work called attention to a string of mysterious deaths of Lee Harvey Oswald and Jack Ruby associates, but few other outlets credited his conclusions.

For the cover of that issue, Stermer asked a local manufacturer to make a jigsaw puzzle out of Kennedy's photograph. Stermer removed some of the pieces, photographed the puzzle, and ran the image on what would become one of the magazine's most memorable covers. Keating suggested that they pluck out the pieces where the bullets had actually entered Kennedy's head, but Stermer refused.

That issue's contents further distinguished *Ramparts* from other national outlets. The book review section included a notice on a four-volume opus called *Time of Assassins* by Ulov G. K. LeBoeuf. According to the reviewers, *New Yorker* writer Jacob Brackman and co-author Faye Levine, only LeBoeuf "had the courage not only to fly aggressively in the face of official arguments, but also to offer a recognizably new theory of his own." With that compliment paid, Brackman and Levine offered some cavils.

Where he falls short (as in the thinly veiled suggestion that Aldous Huxley, also dying on November 22, was in fact poisoned by a female FBI agent working as a servant in the Huxley household as part of a scheduled psyche-delic purge), one has the feeling that he has not had time to amass sufficient evidence and has decided, perhaps unwisely, to commit himself in print on the basis of intuition—as yet unproven, but not irrevocably so!

From there, Brackman and Levine went on to list a string of in-creasingly nonsensical bits of evidence purportedly catalogued in the book. ("Exhibit 226, III: 581: a James Beard cookbook from the pantry of Peggy Goldwater with a recipe for cinnamon rolls circled in red.")

The day after the magazine appeared on the newsstands, orders for the nonexistent book began flowing in to retailers, and over three hundred readers sent checks to *Ramparts* in the vain hope of acquiring the four-volume set. Some fellow writers fell for the hoax, too; Gene Marine received an urgent call from one reporter asking for LeBoeuf's contact information, and references to the work began to appear in other media accounts and bibliographies, including one published by the *Boston Globe*.

In January 1967, David Welsh and David Lifton's "The Case for Three Assassins," added to the burgeoning assassination litera-ture, and in two consecutive issues that spring, Bill Turner profiled New Orleans district attorney Jim Garrison and advanced his ar-gument that Lee Harvey Oswald was a CIA agent and fall guy. Re-turning to Garrison and his team in January 1968, Turner concluded that there was "no question that they have uncovered a conspiracy," though the nature of that conspiracy remained un-clear. Turner's reconstruction was as shaggy as Castro's beard and begging for an application of Occam's Razor. But the assassination story resisted any efforts to tame it, and thanks in part to *Ramparts*, it had taken on a self-propelled media life of its own. Just as the

New Left had helped take down liberalism without replacing it with anything stronger, *Ramparts* undermined the Warren Report without establishing a broadly acceptable counternarrative.

Hinckle was an ideal audience for Garrison, whom he described as "cool, sharp, informed, confident, convincing." His last contact with Garrison was a telephone call in November 1968. Directing Hinckle to take the call from the mailroom telephone, which was less likely to be tapped, Garrison explained that three aerospace firms had put up the money to assassinate Kennedy. Hinckle dutifully pulled out his pencil and wrote down the three culprits—Lockheed, Boeing, and General Dynamics—as well as the employees who set up the murder.

After hanging up, Hinckle went through his top-secret routine.

> I typed up a brief memorandum of the facts as Garrison had relayed them and burned my notes in an oversized ashtray I used for such purposes. I Xeroxed one copy of the memo, which I mailed to myself in care of a post office box in the name of Walter Snelling, a friendly, non-political bartender in the far-removed country town of Cotati, California, where I routinely sent copies of all supersecret Ramparts documents. That night I hand delivered the original to Bill Turner, the former FBI agent in charge of the magazine's investigation of the Warren Commission. Turner had drilled me in a little G–Man security lingo. According to our code, I called him at home and said something about a new vacuum cleaner. He replied that he'd be right over, and said he would meet me at the bar at Trader Vic's, which meant that I was to actually meet him at Blanco's, a dimly lit Filipino bar on the fringe of Chinatown, where we often held secret meetings.

"That was the way we did things in those days," Hinckle recalled.

·   ·   ·

As Hinckle indulged his appetite for conspiracies, McGraw-Hill was preparing to publish Cleaver's *Soul on Ice* for Ramparts Books, its new imprint. The volume was a collection of prison writings, most of which had appeared in the magazine. Cleaver thanked Keating, whom he described as the first professional to pay any attention to his writing; Maxwell Geismar, who contributed the book's introduction; and *Ramparts* staffer David Welsh for his editorial assistance. But he dedicated the book to Beverly Axelrod, with whom he had become romantically involved, and he included some of their emotionally charged correspondence in the book. Cleaver's dedication read, "To Beverly, with whom I share the ultimate of love."

Cleaver's romance with Axelrod was short-lived. In spring 1967, just as *Soul on Ice* appeared, Cleaver met Kathleen Neal at a conference in Nashville sponsored by SNCC. Kathleen, a Barnard student who had moved to Atlanta to work for SNCC, knew about Cleaver from his writings in *Ramparts*, which her boyfriend's roommate had brought to her attention. When she met Cleaver in person, she thought he was intimidating. "He filled up the doorframe and had no expression on his face," she recalled. "He had only been out of prison for three months, and he hadn't thawed out yet."

But Cleaver was smitten and decided to stay on after the conference. He was writing a story on Stokely Carmichael, who was scheduled to speak at Vanderbilt University the following week, but he also wanted to spend more time with Kathleen and offered to drive her and her colleagues back to Atlanta. When it was time to leave, Kathleen saw Cleaver strolling across the campus lawn with a white woman in a sundress and sandals. It was Axelrod, who seemed annoyed when Cleaver introduced her as his lawyer; in fact, they were engaged.

After Cleaver returned to San Francisco, he and Kathleen began to exchange letters. Axelrod discovered some of their correspondence when Sacramento authorities returned Cleaver's briefcase to her after his arrest. His parole restricted Cleaver's travel, but

Kathleen caught a ride to Los Angeles and flew to San Francisco on a $12 ticket. She stayed at Cleaver's apartment, a walk-up studio at 42 Castro Street that he had recently leased. (When first released from prison, he was officially living with Axelrod's brother; unofficially, he was living at Beverly's house in San Francisco.) On the first or second night of Kathleen's visit, she and Cleaver heard a ruckus outside; someone was trying to break in to his apartment. It turned out to be an irate Beverly. More than once, Cleaver pointed out Axelrod's Volvo parked outside his studio; apparently she was keeping an eye on them. Nevertheless, Cleaver proposed to Kathleen during her first visit to San Francisco, and they married later that year.

As that courtship unfolded, *Soul on Ice* drew reviews from the *New Republic* ("painful, aggressive, and undaunted"), the *New York Times Book Review* ("brilliant and revealing"), and other high-profile outlets. Most reviewers praised its originality and power. Some hedged their compliments; the *Saturday Review*, for example, claimed that Cleaver "can be a mature, perhaps even a great writer," implying that he was not yet either. Other reviews were overgenerous, a response that Geismar's introduction invited. He applauded Cleaver's essay on the Beatles, for example, which included this muddle of a paragraph:

Before we toss the Beatles a homosexual kiss—saying, "If a man be ass enough to reach for the bitch in them, that man will kiss a man, and if a woman reaches for the stud in them, that woman will kiss a woman"—let us marvel at the genius of their image, which comforts the owls and ostriches in the one spot where Elvis Presley bummed their kick: Elvis, with his unfunky (yet mechanical, alienated) bumpgrinding, was still too much Body (too soon) for the strained collapsing psyches of the Omnipotent Administrators and Ultrafeminines; whereas the Beatles, affecting the caucasoid crown of femininity and ignoring the Body on the visual plane (while their music on the contrary being full of Body), assuaged the doubts of the owls and ostriches by presenting an incorporeal, cerebral image.

A blurb from the *Nation* review ("beautifully written") was consistent with Geismar's hyperbolic assessment that Cleaver was "simply one of the best cultural critics writing today."

Taken together, the accolades supported Ishmael Reed's retrospective claim that the "New York Old Left and its branches in Northern California and Los Angeles" had "given up on the worker . . . and in his place substituted the black prisoner as a proxy in their fight against capitalism." But even more than their precursors, the New Left radicals regarded black prisoners as the vanguard of the revolution. In Panther David Hilliard's pithier formulation, white radicals wanted to "get a nigger to pull the trigger." A pungent whiff of danger accompanied *Soul on Ice* and its promotion, and Cleaver's attack on Baldwin was considered newsworthy. For all these reasons and others, *Soul on Ice* became an international publishing event.

Cleaver had little time to relish his status as a celebrity author. Less than a month after the book went on sale, Martin Luther King Jr. was assassinated in Memphis. Although the Black Panthers had mocked King's nonviolent tactics, they were outraged by his murder. Two days later, Cleaver sat in his *Ramparts* office and dictated his response to King's assassination.

It is hard to put words on this tape because words are no longer relevant. Action is all that counts now. And maybe America will understand that. I doubt it. I think that America is incapable of understanding *anything* relevant to human rights. I think that America has already committed suicide, and we who now thrash within its dead body are also dead and part and parcel of the corpse. America is truly a disgusting burden upon the planet. A burden upon all humanity. And if we here in America . . .

A telephone call interrupted Cleaver's dictation; when he hung up, he left the office for Oakland.

That night, Cleaver organized four carloads of Panthers for an outing in Oakland. Cleaver would later claim, perhaps jocularly, that they were preparing for a picnic, but their ostensible goal was to attack the Oakland police. When they encountered officers on a routine patrol, gunfire broke out. Two officers were wounded, and Cleaver and seventeen-year-old Bobby Hutton fled to the basement of a nearby house on 28th Street. Police surrounded the house, and a gun battle ensued. Cleaver was wounded in the foot by a ricocheting bullet and hit in the shoulder with a tear gas canister. He shouted to the police that he was coming out of the house. To ensure that his surrender was unambiguous, the prison-seasoned Cleaver emerged from the house naked with his hands in the air. A clothed Hutton also emerged and was apprehended. Accounts of what happened next vary; arresting officers claimed that Hutton tried to run after stumbling. Beyond dispute is the fact that the police shot and killed him.

After the shootout, Cleaver was taken to Highland Hospital, where Scheer and Marine tried to visit him. They were denied access but watched as Cleaver—surrounded by police, his eyes still swollen from the tear gas, and handcuffed to his gurney—was loaded into another ambulance for a transfer. "I thought they would kill him," Scheer said later. Officials booked Cleaver in Alameda County, revoked his parole, and sent him to the San Quentin prison hospital in nearby San Rafael. Later, he was transferred to the prison hospital in Vacaville, a short drive from Sacramento.

James Baldwin, Norman Mailer, Susan Sontag, and other prominent writers and intellectuals signed a letter decrying the violence against the Black Panthers. "We find little fundamental difference between the assassin's bullet which killed Dr. King on April 4, and the police barrage which killed Bobby James Hutton two days later," it read. A more modulated letter in the *New York*

Review of Books the following month condemned the Oakland police response as "acts of violent white racism."

In the May issue of *Ramparts*, Gene Marine covered the shootout in an article titled "Getting Eldridge Cleaver." He also published a Ramparts book, *The Black Panthers*, the following year. Supported by Bob Avakian's research, that book described Oakland's city government as "not only racist but Mesozoic." Yet Marine denied allegations that he was an apologist for the Black Panther Party. "I am frightened by them, and I am fascinated by them," he wrote. "I find myself stirred to admiration and stricken with apprehension. . . . In short, I am white and not particularly revolutionary. . . . I am, indeed, afraid of the Black Panther Party. I hope you are, too." The book's back cover copy appealed directly to that emotion. "Uniformed, Armed Black Men in America! Black Men Who Talk Back—and Shoot Back!"

From Vacaville, Cleaver smuggled out an article that ran in *Ramparts* with a brief introduction by David Welsh, who wrote that Cleaver "was imprisoned for the political crime of organizing black people for their own liberation." Cleaver's article, "A Letter from Jail," recounted his first encounters with the party's leaders and positioned Newton as the "ideological descendant, heir and successor of Malcolm X." Cleaver wrote that Newton "lifted the golden lid off the pot and blindly, trusting Malcolm, stuck his hand inside and grasped the tool."

> When he withdrew his hand and looked to see what he held, he saw the gun, cold in its metal and implacable in its message. . . . Huey P. Newton picked up the gun and pulled the trigger, freeing the genie of black revolutionary violence in Babylon.

Cleaver settled in for a lengthy prison spell, but a Superior Court judge unexpectedly released him on $50,000 bail the following month. Back on the streets, Cleaver began an extraordinary campaign.

Cleaver's disgust for America after the King assassination had a corollary in the antiwar movement. As the New Left turned from protest to resistance, its disdain for politics as usual—and for American culture more generally—began to grow. "Little by little," Todd Gitlin wrote later, "alienation from American life—contempt, even, for the conventions of flag, home, religion, suburbs, shopping, plain homely Norman Rockwell order—had become a rock-bottom prerequisite for membership in the movement core." As their disaffection deepened, some of these core members began to look abroad for their heroes, who came to include Mao, Algerian revolutionary Frantz Fanon, and Ho Chi Minh. If America had betrayed the young militants, perhaps their international comrades would not.

Chief among the revolutionary heroes was Che Guevara. After playing a pivotal role in the Cuban revolution, Che served in Castro's government, tried unsuccessfully to incite a revolution in the Congo, and eventually landed in Bolivia, where he ran a small training camp for Communist insurgents. Bolivian Special Forces led by a CIA operative captured and executed him there in October 1967. *Ramparts* ran several stories on his execution, which rattled the confidence of his American admirers. "If Che could be killed," Gitlin wrote later, "then 'the revolution' was more vulnerable than the Left wanted to think."

The Bolivian generals began selling Che's personal effects to the highest bidders, and his Bolivian diary immediately became a hot publishing property. Although *Ramparts* had a fledgling book division, it had no plans to bid on the English-language rights to Che's diaries. But Scheer had established a personal connection that other American publishers lacked. In early 1968, he traveled to Cuba with the understanding that he would be allowed to interview Castro. Scheer cooled his heels at the Havana Libre for a month, waiting for the still unscheduled appointment. Finally, he told the Cubans he needed to return to the United States to run his magazine. The night before his departure, armed men arrived at his room and took him through a series of houses and buildings. After midnight, Scheer said he needed to relieve himself. While he was in the men's room, Castro walked in. He had been playing basketball. Castro was willing to conduct the interview right then, but only on background. Scheer protested, but Castro assured him that their exchange would be better than an on-the-record interview. They talked until daybreak.

Although Scheer couldn't use that material for a story, his Castro connection allowed *Ramparts* to enter the publishers' sweepstakes. When Scheer returned from another trip to Cuba in April 1968, he told Hinckle that Castro had a copy of Che's diary, that he wanted *Ramparts* to publish an English translation, and that he would write the introduction. Scheer and Hinckle agreed to maintain strict silence about the matter. In general, the *Ramparts* staff "leaked like a bad kidney," Hinckle wrote later, but this time they weren't taking any chances.

As the months rolled by without any sign of the manuscript, Hinckle and Scheer grew uneasy. During that time, they were in touch with the editor-in-chief of McGraw-Hill's trade book division, with which *Ramparts* had an arrangement. "This is extremely confidential," the editor told Hinckle, "but we're getting the Che Diary. . . . It's the publishing coup of the year, and I think I may be able to work it so you can print some excerpts." Hinckle held his tongue.

When Hinckle finally received the manuscript in a cloak-and-dagger operation in New York, he discovered that Castro had arranged for the publication of a Spanish-language edition in a matter of days. (Castro had also lined up French, Italian, and German editions.) Hinckle concluded that the best option was to sell the rights. With the help of Cleaver's literary agent, he arranged a deal with Bantam, which was already in negotiations with McGraw-Hill for the paperback rights. Copyright issues clouded the deal, but those dissolved when Hinckle learned that Che's widow had granted rights to the Cuban state publishing house, which in turn authorized the *Ramparts* English-language edition.

In the meantime, *Ramparts* built the buzz. The March issue included an article by French journalist Michèle Ray, who had traveled to Bolivia to obtain the diaries. *Time* helped the publicity effort by impugning Ray in its March 15 issue. It described her as "a comely French journaliste" who "views the world as a vast fairy tale. There are cruel oppressors, who are mainly American. And there are the cruelly oppressed, who range from the Viet Cong to Castro's Cubans to Bolivian peasants." Referring to Ray's conclusion that two CIA operatives supervised Che's murder, the article closed by repeating the fairy-tale trope.

> [Ray's article] makes gripping reading, but it was apparently too much of a fairy tale for *New York Times* correspondent Juan de Onis, who claimed there was no evidence linking the CIA to Che's death. It was a fact, reported De Onis, that Che talked freely to a CIA agent shortly before he died. But when Che was finally gunned down by a Bolivian sergeant, the CIA man had gone.

It was a curious dismissal of Ray's conclusion. Evidently, the CIA couldn't have supervised Che's killing because one of its agents wasn't present at his execution. But whatever it lacked in logic, the *Time* story fit the pattern the magazine had developed for covering its left-wing doppelganger. *Ramparts'* tales were the misbegotten issue of a dubious ideological agenda, while *Time* was the levelheaded supplier of empirical fact.

When the English translation of Che's diary appeared, *Time* weighed in again. Its July 12 issue described the book as a "propaganda coup" for Castro and questioned the integrity of the text, which one writer who tried to acquire the rights described as "hasty, doctored and bowdlerized." Designed to downplay the story, the *Time* article closed by characterizing Che's efforts as a "sad crusade."

Two weeks later, *Ramparts* devoted an entire issue to excerpts from Che's diaries and included Castro's introduction. Castro described Che as a man of deep conviction, selfless courage, iron will, stoicism, and an irreproachable fighting spirit. His critics and adversaries were stupid, ridiculous, cowardly, reactionary chauvinists. Americans, Castro noted in passing, were "increasingly subjected to the moral barbarism of an irrational, alienating, dehumanized, and brutal system." They suffered from that system's "wars of aggression, its political crimes, its racial aberrations, the miserable hierarchy it has created among human beings, its repugnant waste of economic, scientific, and human resources on its enormous, reactionary, and repressive military apparatus—in the midst of a world where three-quarters of humanity lives in underdevelopment and hunger."

Che's legend didn't require *Ramparts* for its growth and dissemination, but the magazine's role in the diary saga reflected its rising position in American journalism. Five years earlier, *Ramparts* had failed to deliver its latest bombshell, a colloquy on Jesuit higher education. Now it was the one American outlet to which Fidel Castro entrusted Che's personal writings.

The book reportedly sold 500,000 copies, but it also produced security concerns for Scheer. He learned that Alpha 66, an anti-Castro paramilitary group, had placed him on its death list and would execute him by a certain time that week. Such threats couldn't be ignored; in July 1968, a different right-wing Cuban group launched a grenade through the window of Grove Press's New York office to protest the *Evergreen Review*'s celebration of Che.

Scheer called the FBI office in San Francisco, which downplayed the threat. He replied that if anything happened to him, *Ramparts* would release whatever information it had on the FBI's connections to right-wing groups. Later that day, Scheer received a call from the FBI instructing him to look out the window. When he did, he noticed an agent in front of the building. Still uncertain about his safety, Scheer visited the home of San Francisco private investigator Hal Lipset, a *Ramparts* contributing editor who later served as a technical consultant for Francis Ford Coppola's *The Conversation*. Lipset and Scheer broke out the vodka, and Scheer later reported that he "slept through the appointed hour of my death."

As the drama surrounding what Michèle Ray called "the relics of St. Che" unfolded, a different back story was making its way though the *Ramparts* office. According to David Horowitz, "the office was abuzz about an affair Scheer had while in Cuba with Michelle [*sic*] Ray, the journalist who secured the Guevara diaries for publication." When Scheer called a meeting to discuss the February 1968 "Women Power" issue, he reportedly snapped at Anne Weills, who was featured in the lead article. "What I didn't realize," Horowitz recalled, "was that Scheer's anger was provoked by his discovery that Anne was having a retaliatory affair with [Tom] Hayden. She had even trumped him politically: While his tryst with Michelle Ray had taken place in Cuba, hers had been consummated on a trip to Hanoi."

It's difficult to reconcile Horowitz's timeline with the one Hayden lays out in his memoir, but even if Horowitz's chronology is faulty, he was right that the bunking arrangements in the *Ramparts* community had become complicated. When Scheer returned from his Cuba trip, he learned that Weills wanted a separation. By that time, they had a son, Christopher. Soon after that, Hayden moved to Oakland, perhaps to be closer to Weills, but according to Hayden, she was unwilling to "enter a stable relationship so close to her own separation." Their romance was a prime example of what *Ramparts* writer Michael Lerner dubbed "armed snuggle."

That summer, *Ramparts* once again revised its publishing schedule. Now subscribers would receive twenty-four issues each year for $15 instead of $8.50 for twelve issues. Hinckle announced the plan in the June 15 issue and took the occasion to discuss the magazine's methods.

There is no secret about what *Ramparts* has done. It has used the same tools as, say, *Time*—color, professionalism, slickness, large distribution—to achieve essentially the opposite results, challenging rather than reinforcing stereotyped ideas, promoting dissent rather than putting it down.

Hinckle's point was valid, but the new schedule masked a grim financial picture. *Ramparts* was teetering on the brink of collapse.

7

THE BATTLE'S CONFUSION

As the nation lurched into the summer of 1968, the Democratic Party wasn't doing any better than the magazine. Antiwar activists were thrilled when President Johnson unexpectedly announced he wouldn't seek reelection, and many were encouraged by Robert Kennedy's entry into the 1968 presidential race. But when Kennedy was assassinated in June 1968, the Democrats lost an important (if recently converted) critic of the war. Scheer, who was skeptical of Kennedy's transformation, was at the Ambassador Hotel in Los Angeles when Kennedy delivered his victory speech following the California primary. After conducting what turned out to be Kennedy's final interview, Scheer arrived in the ballroom just moments before shots rang out in the kitchen.

Once again, the nation recoiled in horror. Even Tom Hayden grieved, despite having called Kennedy "a little fascist" in a private conversation a few days before. With his Cuban fatigue hat in hand, Hayden wept at Kennedy's casket in Saint Patrick's Cathedral. "With King and Kennedy dead," SDS leader Todd Gitlin wrote later of the New Left, "a promise of redemption not only passed out of American politics, it passed out of ourselves."

Even before the 1968 assassinations, however, violence had become a New Left preoccupation. According to Gitlin, thoughts of violence "organized the movement's fantasy life." As the Democratic national convention approached, some of those fantasies began to look plausible. In Chicago, one of the last bastions of old-school Democratic machine politics, young radicals could confront the party of war under the bright lights of the national media. That summer, movement leaders lined up permits and recruited antiwar activists, but many had misgivings about the violent overtones in these internal discussions. "In my recruiting trips around the country," antiwar leader Dave Dellinger wrote later, "the two questions I was always asked were: (1) Is there any chance that the police won't create a bloodbath? (2) Are you sure that Tom [Hayden] and Rennie [Davis] don't want one?" At some conferences during the spring, a majority of activists preferred to continue organizing in their communities, but Hayden and other movement leaders reserved the right to call an action in Chicago.

That confrontational spirit informed Hayden's *Ramparts* articles earlier that summer. His June 15 essay, "Two, Three, Many Columbias," echoed Che's famous slogan about Vietnam and celebrated the occupation of several buildings at Columbia University, where protestors objected to the university's war-related research as well as its plans to build a gym in Harlem. The occupation lasted for five days and led to the arrest of seven hundred protestors, including Hayden. In his article, Hayden depicted that action as a refutation of the older generation's teaching about social change.

> American educators are fond of telling their students that barricades are part of the romantic past, that social change today can only come about through the processes of negotiation. But the students at Columbia discovered that barricades are only the beginning of what they call "bringing the war home."

One *Ramparts* reader, seventeen-year-old Maurice Isserman, eagerly ingested Hayden's article as he prepared for his freshman year at Reed College. Later, as a professional historian of the period, he reflected on its impact.

> "Two, Three, Many Columbias" was a primer for a politics that valued the gut instinct of young radicals over experience, continuity, and historical perspective and, sadly,

proved to be one of the most influential pieces Hayden
would write in the 1960s.

Isserman lamented that influence insofar as Hayden's piece encouraged readers to "bring the war home" in the most literal ways.
One of the Columbia protestors, Ted Gold, would do so by joining Weatherman and preparing bombs in the basement of a
Greenwich Village townhouse. When one of those bombs ex-
ploded in April 1970, it killed him and two others. In Isserman's
view, Hayden's article was symptomatic of the left's failure to communicate across generations. By then in his late twenties, Hayden
saw little to admire in his predecessors, and he did little to restrain
his even more youthful and radical SDS successors. It was notable,
Isserman thought, that Hayden omitted the article from an anthology of his writings published in 2008.

Hayden's piece in the July 13 issue of *Ramparts* also prescribed
the peace movement's proper relationship to the Vietcong.

The peace movement should catch up with the worldwide
feeling that the Vietcong are the heroes of this war. This is
the only position which is radically educational because it
poses the possibility that Americans should sometimes support communist-led revolutions.

As he wrote these articles, Hayden was organizing the Peace
and Freedom Party and planning to disrupt the Democratic convention at Chicago's International Amphitheater. He later presented that disruption as a form of personal and national discovery.
For him, it was a matter of "finding out how far you were willing
to go for your beliefs, and finding out how far the American government was willing to go in suspending the better part of its tradition to stop you. You wouldn't know without entering the
amphitheatre." The theatrical allusion is telling. The events in Chicago wouldn't be guided by logical argumentation, or even the
usual political logic of reciprocity. Instead, Chicago would be a

dramatic conflict. Like Greek tragedy, it would reveal character and make the truth visible and irrefutable. That truth, once revealed, would presumably point Americans to the proper course of action in Vietnam.

The *Ramparts* staff didn't want to miss that showdown. As early as January, Peter Collier had tipped off Hunter Thompson to the mayhem planned for Chicago. In a letter to his editor at Ballantine Books, Thompson cited Collier's " 'certain knowledge' that all manner of hell is going to break loose in terms of critical protests, demonstrations. *Ramparts* has numerous connections with SDS and other radical types, and Collier says they're going to freak out the convention." *Ramparts* planned to convert its connections with the protestors into first-rate coverage. Low on funds and in the middle of a move to new offices near Fisherman's Wharf, Hinckle made some executive decisions. He would transport a staff of ten to Chicago, install them in the luxurious Ambassador Hotel, and cover the convention and demonstrations from there.

Hinckle also decided to produce the *Ramparts Wall Poster*, which would cover the convention and offer schedules, maps, and previews of that day's activities. The concept was born when assistant managing editor Fred Gardner asked Hinckle for a week off during August. Hayden had asked Gardner to produce a daily leaflet for the demonstrators in Chicago. Hinckle immediately endorsed the idea but put it on a grander scale. "Yeah, Freddy, you can do it, we'll do a wall poster," Hinckle said. "One side will be news from the street, the other side will be news from the convention." "The idea sprang fully formed from his head," Gardner said later. "It was the most brilliant thing I ever saw a publisher do."

The *Ramparts Wall Poster* was a single full-folio sheet (36" × 24") whose title and format recalled the publications produced by Mao's Red Guards during the Cultural Revolution. Its motto ("Up Against the Wall") punned on the popular revolutionary slogan drawn from a LeRoi Jones lyric, "Black People!" ("All the stores will open if you say the magic words. The magic words are: Up against the wall mother fucker this is a stick up!") For its newsroom, the *Wall Poster* took the second floor of a YMCA building near Division Street. Contributors included Hayden, Adam Hochschild, Paul Krassner, Carl Oglesby, and Richard Rothstein, who later became the national education correspondent for the *New York Times*.

Gardner worked feverishly to plan and produce the *Wall Poster*. As he was finalizing the third issue, he received a call from Hinckle. "Stop the presses!" Hinckle bellowed. He had the biggest story of the year: Lyndon Johnson had decided to run for reelection after all. "Warren had it from somebody he'd met at the bar in the Pump Room, the fancy restaurant at the Ambassador," Gardner recalled. "He was writing it up and wanted to run it as our lead story. I said I'd come get it, thinking it sounded very far-fetched and that I could talk him out of it when the time came."

As Gardner was about to enter the Ambassador Hotel, he saw a chocolate-brown Rolls Royce pull up. A man in a chocolate-brown suit with brown pumps and white spats emerged from it. It was Colonel Sanders, the Kentucky Fried Chicken icon, who proceeded to hand out dimes to the shoeshine boys on his way into the hotel. "I stopped and stared," Gardner said later. "I didn't know that there really was such a person. I thought it was a corporate logo. I wondered if I was having my first-ever 'bad trip.' Maybe what the so-called speed people had given me contained some really strong hallucinogens." In fact, Harlan Sanders was part of the Kentucky delegation.

After reviewing the LBJ scoop, Gardner decided against publishing it. That decision, he recalled, led to a showdown over editorial control.

> That evening Hinckle got wind of the fact that we weren't planning to run his LBJ-to-run story. He came over to the *Wall Poster* office with a friend named Herb Williamson. "You're drunk, Warren," [I said]. "You'd be embarrassed if this thing ran. Go back to the hotel and get some sleep."

But Hinckle insisted, and a shoving match between Gardner and Williamson ensued. In the end, Hinckle ran the story in two parts; Gardner returned to the Bay Area and resigned from *Ramparts*. Hinckle's second headline, "LBJ's Takeover Plot," ran in 185-point type, and the poster was included in a September issue of the magazine. He later suspected that his scoop had thwarted President Johnson's plan.

SDS leader Todd Gitlin also wrote for the *Ramparts Wall Poster*. By that time, he was familiar with Chicago as well as several *Ramparts* writers; Adam Hochschild had been a classmate at Harvard, and Gitlin met *Ramparts* editor Paul Jacobs while attending a Berkeley antiwar event in 1966. In Gitlin's view, *Ramparts* was enjoyable, creative, and made the New Left accessible to the reading public. It wasn't a movement magazine, he later remarked, but it "filtered a New Left sensibility—not analysis—though a modernist filter." He was impressed by the magazine's professional look and felt it was "a place where grown-up journalism met the movement." For him, that blend produced an interesting tension between sound investigative reporting and "devil-may-care wildness."

Gitlin was on the scene when the Democratic convention began. As expected, Chicago was bedlam. Thousands of demonstrators took to the streets, and a small minority of them (some of them yelling "Kill the pigs" and "Your wife sucks cock") taunted the police. Other chants reported by the *Ramparts* staff included, "Pig, pig, fascist pig," "Pigs eat shit, pigs eat shit," "Ho, Ho, Ho Chi Minh," and "Two, four, six, eight, organize to smash the state!" Officers cleared Lincoln Park with tear gas and clubs, which led to street warfare for the next three days and nights. The National Guard was called in Tuesday night and took up positions on Michigan Avenue.

The clashes were broadcast nationally and provided an alarming backdrop for the maneuvers inside the convention. The key debate concerned the party's peace plank. Congressman Phil

Burton urged withdrawal from Vietnam, and Senator Edmund Muskie of Maine countered that opponents of the war wanted peace at any price. Other speakers followed in the same vein, and the peace plank was defeated. Reporting for *Harper's* magazine, Norman Mailer observed that the debate echoed the measured rhetoric of Secretary of State Dean Rusk. According to Mailer, Rusk was "always a model of sanity on every detail but one: he had a delusion that the war was not bottomless in its lunacy."

But the real story in Chicago had little to do with floor debates. As cameras rolled, Chicago police flayed provocateurs, peaceful protestors, and observers alike. Gitlin struggled to understand what he saw around him on the streets of Chicago. Two decades later, he reflected on the ethics of his coverage.

> One day the *Wall Poster* sent me to cover a [National Mobilization Committee to End the War in Vietnam] meeting, where I heard Tom Hayden speak, in chillingly cavalier tones, about street actions which would run the risk of getting people killed. . . . I stared at a typewriter in the *Wall Poster* office for hours before deciding to use the quotes. Then, a day or two later, I was buying a disguise for Hayden to help him stay "underground" while the cops were looking for him, and setting up his network TV interview, false beard and all.

Other reporters grappled with the same decision. *Village Voice* correspondent Paul Cowan, who also contributed to the *Ramparts Wall Poster*, witnessed young people throwing rocks and slabs of sidewalks at the police. After filing a story about that provocation, he asked his editor to kill it. "The police riot seemed to me a far greater evil than the fact that some kids had wanted to provoke it," Cowan wrote later. "I didn't want my story to dilute that impression."

Gitlin's work on the *Ramparts Wall Poster* was unpaid and, in his view, underappreciated. For one issue, Hinkle completely re-arranged the front page. "Tear Gas in the Pump Room!" the new headline blared, referring to the famous restaurant in the Ambassador Hotel, where Hinckle and his colleagues were embedded. "We were furious," Gitlin said. "Many of us quit." Part of his anger was connected to the staff's extravagant lodging, which removed them from the story at hand.

> We were crashing on floors, and they were staying at luxury hotels. They were watching the streets from some hotel tower aerie. I found it tremendously offensive. Not just the spending, but their presumption. They presumed to know stuff they didn't know. . . . What did they know about Chicago? It would be different if Studs Terkel disagreed.

Scheer, at least, was sympathetic. He later told *Time* magazine, "There we were, all staying at the Ambassador Hotel in Chicago, while the movement kids were getting their skulls cracked."

In Chicago, the *Ramparts* contingent included Pete Hamill and *New York Times* reporters Sidney Zion and Sidney Schanberg, who contributed to the magazine's coverage. The special relationship between *Ramparts* and the *New York Times*, much of it arranged by Marc Stone, had proven to be mutually beneficial. Stone frequently offered exclusives to the *Times* on the theory that its coverage could make or break a *Ramparts* story. "It was really a dirty technique in a sense," Stone said in 1969. "But, on the other hand, with the kind of stories that I've been handling, if you make *The Times*, you're made. If you don't make *The Times*, you've got a tough fight. Any time I can get a good break in *The Times*, *The Times* can have an exclusive."

Another member of the extended *Ramparts* family in Chicago was Hunter Thompson, who found himself scampering from agitated cops on Michigan Avenue. Two police officers posted outside the front doors of his hotel blocked his retreat. "I finally just ran between the truncheons, screaming, 'I live here, goddamnit! I'm paying fifty dollars a day!'" The experience rattled even a seasoned reporter who thrived on action. "I went from a state of Cold Shock on Monday, to Fear on Tuesday, then Rage, and finally Hysteria—which lasted for nearly a month," he later wrote.

For Thompson, Chicago was transformative. Having built his reputation covering fringe groups like the Hell's Angels and student radicals, he began to target what he saw as the corruption and violence of mainstream American politics. "I went to the Democratic convention as a journalist and returned a raving beast," he later told a fellow journalist. He took away another lesson from Chicago as well; a few years later, he created his own wall posters while running for sheriff in Aspen, Colorado.

For all the drama in Chicago, and all the talent Hinckle had assembled to report on it, the magazine's coverage was unremarkable. Certainly the presence of so many newspaper and television reporters made it difficult for a monthly magazine to stand out. *Harper's* solved that problem by sending novelist Norman Mailer to cover both party conventions, and *Esquire* dispatched William Burroughs and Jean Genet to Chicago.

But part of *Ramparts'* problem, Sol Stern later thought, was its reluctance to cover the whole story. "We didn't tell the truth about the conspiracy to riot," he recalled. Stern traced that failure to the magazine's close connections to the protestors, most notably Tom Hayden, who in September 1967 asked Stern to join him on a Czechoslovakian cruise with North Vietnamese officials and members of the National Liberation Front of South Vietnam (NLF). According to Stern, Hayden's speech there went well beyond that of the mainstream U.S. peace movement.

> Hayden wasn't interested in ending the war so much as making an alliance with the other side. At one of the final plenary sessions, he gave a long speech summarizing the conference's accomplishments and emphasizing our need

to work together for the common objective: a Vietnam liberated and unified by the Communists.

In his speech, Hayden invoked the climactic episode from
1960 film *Spartacus*, in which Roman slaves protect the protag-
onist by rising to declare that they are Spartacus. That cinematic
allusion, Stern maintained, "was perfectly consistent with the
New Left's tendency to enact the revolution as theater. But Hayden was also deadly serious about his 'We are all Vietcong now'
announcement."

Forty years later, Stern called Hayden's speech a turning point
in the history of American radicalism. "It wasn't just that Hayden
was rooting for the other side—abolitionist William Lloyd Garrison had done the same during the Mexican War—but that he was
proposing to sabotage the American war effort by all means necessary," Stern wrote. His point is complicated by the nature of that
effort, which violated the very international laws American jurists
and diplomats had pressed for after World War II. But Stern's claim
was more visceral; by flouting the norms of patriotism and pressing
an internationalist perspective, Hayden risked alienating Americans who opposed the war precisely because it violated their patri-
otic ideals.

Hayden's plans to confront the Chicago police, Stern maintained, were well known to the *Ramparts* staff, which was "determined to be there for the combat."

We saw ourselves as both journalistic observers and participants, and we had no problem with the conflict of interest. . . . But our plans for a journalistic bombshell
fizzled. . . . We didn't dare touch the one big story that was
ours exclusively: how a relatively small group of American
radicals had made common cause with the enemy and was
leading the left toward self-destruction and nihilism.

This was Gitlin's dilemma writ large. For Stern, the conflict wasn't restricted to the decision to tell or withhold the story about street provocation; it also concerned the extent to which some of the provocateurs were collaborating with the Vietcong to thwart American efforts abroad.

That moral quandary wasn't receiving serious attention back at the Ambassador. "It was champagne and strawberries," Stern said. "We ran up enormous bills while the magazine was on the brink of bankruptcy." But according to Hinckle, the hotel bill was another casualty of Chicago. When it arrived in a thick stack of itemized charges, Hinckle reviewed them with business manager Bob Kaldenbach. Noticing one that appeared to be for the services of a prostitute, Hinckle told Kaldenbach to ask the hotel about it. By doing so, Hinckle later claimed, they beat the entire bill. That maneuver fit a pattern. "When Warren had the money, he was generous," Fred Gardner commented later. "When he didn't, he would screw you."

After the convention, Hinckle and the other staffers repaired to the Algonquin Hotel to put the next issue together and continue the movable feast. Eventually Hinckle would also stick the Algonquin with a large unpaid bill. Joe Ippolito's father, a New York City cabdriver, later stopped by the Algonquin and asked whether any *Ramparts* people were there. The doorman replied with a thumbs-down and the raspberry.

Stern later lamented Hinckle's tendency to "piss away the money," but others found it harder to tease out that habit from the magazine's success. According to Gene Marine, "It made a difference that we stayed at the Algonquin. I got a different reception than if the call-back number was at a friend's apartment." Marine also recalled attending several New York parties where "Norman Mailer was at the top of the food chain and a bunch of guys you never heard of from *Mademoiselle* were at the bottom." At one such party, a New York writer asked him about a reported $22,000 bill from the Algonquin. "Maybe . . . for this month," Marine replied. "The guy looked impressed," he noted later. For Marine, that kind of goof was consistent with the magazine's send-up of the JFK conspiracy literature. For a while, at least, *Ramparts* was selling the mainstream media's values back to it.

As the nation watched the Democrats implode in Chicago, Eldridge Cleaver was on the campaign trail.

In March 1968, a group of mostly white leftists—including *Ramparts* regulars Robert Scheer, Bob Avakian, Tom Hayden, and Michael Lerner—met in the Bay Area to boost the fledgling Peace and Freedom Party (PFP). The immediate goal was to collect enough signatures to place the party's candidates on the ballot for the fall election. Given the prowar leanings of the two major parties, a third party seemed to be the only practical option for many antiwar activists.

A month before that meeting, the party's founders approached Cleaver about an alliance with the Black Panthers. Many were working with him on the Free Huey campaign, which had become a powerful organizing tool. The campaign included a large rally at the Oakland Auditorium in February, the same month the PFP proposed an alliance. Coinciding with Newton's birthday, the event also marked Stokely Carmichael's new status as prime minister of the Black Panther Party. The speeches that night were smoking hot. SNCC leader H. Rap Brown told the crowd, "Huey Newton is our only living revolutionary in this country today. He has paid his dues. He has paid his dues. How many white folks did you kill today?" SNCC leader James Forman promised massive retaliation if any black leaders were assassinated: "For my assassination—and I'm low man on the totem pole—I want 30 police stations blown up, one southern governor, two mayors, and 500 cops, dead. . . . And if Huey Newton is not set free and dies, the sky is the limit!"

By adopting the Panthers' ten-point program, the PFP cemented that alliance. In August, just before the debacle in Chicago, the new party held its convention in Ann Arbor. Cleaver received the presidential nomination over comedian and activist Dick

Gregory. At age thirty-three, Cleaver was ineligible for the office, but he chose Jerry Rubin as his running mate and began his campaign. The PFP also ran Newton for Congress in Cohelan's district, and Seale and Kathleen Cleaver ran for state assembly.

Still shaken by the Oakland shootout and Hutton's death, Cleaver spoke out angrily that fall on a wide range of issues—so angrily, in fact, that a fellow Panther began calling him "El-Rage." While addressing a group of San Francisco lawyers, Cleaver said, "We need lawyers who have a gun in one hand a law book in the other, so if he goes to court and the shit doesn't come out right, he can pull out his gun and start shooting." After a polite ovation, one lawyer asked Cleaver, "What can we whites do to help the black man's cause?" Cleaver responded, "Kill some white people!"

In a June 1969 piece for *Ramparts*, Kathleen Cleaver reflected on her husband's campaign following his release from state prison. "It was after Vacaville that he began cursing in his speeches," she wrote, "cutting through a lot of intellectual bullshit to talk in the simplest terms about the basic reality confronting people." But Cleaver's appearances also included a good deal of clowning. He called for "pussy power" at a "Pre-Erection Day" event in Berkeley, threatened to beat Governor Reagan to death with a marshmallow, and led a group of five thousand Berkeley students in an improvised cheer of "Fuck Ronald Reagan."

The conflict between Cleaver and Reagan was intensified by an offer Cleaver received from UC Berkeley's Committee for Participant Education, a program that grew out of the Free Speech Movement. When the committee asked Cleaver to teach a class called Social Analysis 139X, Reagan and Max Rafferty, the conservative superintendent of public instruction in California and author of *What They Are Doing to Your Children*, criticized the offer. In her *Ramparts* piece the following year, Kathleen Cleaver concluded, "Reagan, Rafferty, and the state legislature couldn't wait to idiotically condemn the most socially acceptable endeavor in which Eldridge had ever participated."

But her husband's response, which ran in the October 26 issue, was even more direct. Addressing Reagan as "Mickey Mouse," Cleaver asked, "Who in the fuck do you think you are, telling me that I can't talk, telling the students and faculty members that they cannot have me deliver ten lectures?" California's elected leaders, Cleaver continued, "can kiss my black nigger ass." He finished the piece by targeting Reagan.

> You are not a man. You are a punk. Since you have insulted me by calling me a racist, I would like to have the opportunity to balance the books. All I ask is a sporting chance. Therefore, Mickey Mouse, I challenge you to a duel, to the death, and you can choose the weapons. And if you can't relate to that, right on. Walk, chicken, with your ass picked clean.

Reagan reportedly complied by naming his choice of weapons: words of more than four letters each.

Cleaver's quixotic campaign for president didn't appeal to the masses. In the general election, Cleaver received 36,623 votes, while Alabama governor and segregationist George Wallace received 9.9 million. An incarcerated Newton pulled 7 percent of the vote in Cohelan's congressional district compared to Scheer's 45 percent two years before. In the next election cycle, Scheer ran for U.S. Senate on the PFP ticket and was trounced. A generation later, Scheer told third-party presidential candidate Ralph Nader, "I ran as an independent candidate once for the Senate in California with the Peace and Freedom Party, a disastrous event in which I marginalized myself even beyond my normal place."

Meanwhile, the wheels of justice were turning in Newton's case. In September 1968, an Oakland jury found Newton guilty of voluntary manslaughter in the Frey killing. His defense counsel, Charles Garry, dismissed the outcome as "chickenshit verdicts." The Oakland police shared that view. Displeased that Newton wasn't convicted of homicide, two drunken officers fired shotgun rounds into Black Panther Party headquarters that night. Newton received a sentence of two to fifteen years, but attorney Fay Stender later argued that the trial judge had failed to instruct the jury that it could deliver a ruling for involuntary manslaughter. The ruling was reversed, and two years later Newton walked out of the Alameda County jail to the enthusiastic applause of ten thousand supporters.

Ironically, Newton's release delivered Ed Keating another setback. After his ouster from *Ramparts*, Keating helped Charles Garry during Newton's trial and wrote a book about it for Ramparts Press. There he dismissed the prosecution's case as "a flimsy fabric, resting on only a few declared 'facts.' " He also maintained that McKinney, or perhaps a third man mentioned by one of the witnesses, might have killed Frey. But Newton wouldn't have testified to that effect, Keating claimed, because he was "a revolutionary who could never bring himself either to inform on a black brother or cooperate in the prosecution of a brother by an oppressive white power structure. Newton was prepared to face the gas chamber rather than betray these standards." Neither argument cut much ice, but the book's main problem was its timing. When it appeared in 1971, *Free Huey!* had already been scooped by Stender's successful appeal.

The same day Newton was sentenced in 1968, the California District Court of Appeals again revoked Cleaver's parole for the April shootout with the Oakland police. He was given sixty days to turn himself in to the authorities at San Quentin. That week, Scheer wrote a letter to the *New York Review of Books* soliciting funds for Cleaver's defense.

> Everyone who is familiar with Cleaver's work in the Bay Area understands how his tact, diligence and integrity helped to create the sane setting in which black people and white people could work in a cooperative effort held together on the basis of mutual respect.

Scheer's advocacy had crossed into bald propaganda. If he could connect Cleaver's behavior that year to tact, sanity, and mutual respect, anything was possible.

On November 22, the fifth anniversary of President Kennedy's assassination, Cleaver spoke at California Hall on Polk Street in San Francisco. In his remarks, he reflected on the controversy his political activity had created since his release less than two years earlier.

> I've had more trouble out of parole officers and the Department of Corrections simply because I've been relating to the Movement than I had when I was committing robberies, rapes, and other things that I didn't get caught for. That's the truth. If I was on the carpet for having committed a robbery, well, there would be a few people uptight about that. But it seemed to be localized. . . . There's something more dangerous about attacking the pigs of the power structure verbally than there is in walking into the Bank of America with a gun and attacking it forthrightly.

Cleaver then recounted his latest dealings with the San Francisco–based bank.

> My wife told me this evening that she received a phone call from the Bank of America saying that they were going to repossess our car because we were three months behind in our payments. That's not true, but I wished I had never paid a penny for it. I wished that I could have just walked onto that lot and said, "Stick 'em up, motherfucker! I'm taking this."

Fantasies of grand theft auto were only the beginning. Two days earlier, eight Panthers had been arrested for robbing a San Francisco gas station. Cleaver repudiated such nickel-and-dime operations and repeated the Panthers' call for freedom for all incarcerated black men and women.

> Turn them all over to the Black Panther Party. Give them to us. . . . We have a program for them that will keep them all active—twenty-four hours a day. And I don't mean eight big strong men in a conspicuous truck robbing a jive gas station for $75. When I sit down to conspire to commit robbery, it's going to be the Bank of America, or Chase Manhattan Bank, or Brinks.

Cleaver then considered "this system that is the enemy of the people" and its leaders, including Ronald Reagan, Jesse Unruh, and "Mussolini Alioto," Cleaver's nickname for San Francisco mayor Joseph Alioto. "When you see [Alioto] will you swear that he doesn't frighten you, or that he doesn't look like Al Capone?" Cleaver asked rhetorically. "Alioto reminds me of convicts that I know in Folsom Prison. And this is not a contradiction."

Working toward a crescendo, Cleaver turned his attention to the modern state's monopoly on sanctioned violence.

> When I speak up for convicts, I don't say that every convict is going to come out here and join the Peace and Freedom Party. I'm not saying that. Or that he would be nice to people out here. . . . I know a cat who tattooed across his forehead, "Born to Kill." He needs to be released also. Because whereas Lyndon B. Johnson doesn't have any tattoos on his head, he has blood dripping from his fingers. LBJ has killed more people than any other man who has ever been in any prison in the United States of America from the beginning of it to the end. He has murdered. And people like prison officials, policemen, mayors, chiefs of police—they endorse it. They even call for escalation, meaning: kill more people.

The December issue of *Ramparts* ran excerpts of the address and featured Cleaver on the cover. Meanwhile, the magazine's book division hastily assembled a volume for Random House, *Eldridge Cleaver: Post-Prison Writings and Speeches*, and gave Cleaver's "A Letter from Jail" a juicier title: "The Courage to Kill: Meeting the Panthers." In the book's introduction, Scheer recounted an episode with Cleaver three days before he was required to turn himself in. After dining in Chinatown, they were preparing to cross Columbus Avenue to order a cappuccino at Tosca Cafe. A patrol car pulled up, tires squealing. "The doors sprang open," Scheer wrote, "and two cops jumped out and headed toward Cleaver, hands on holsters, shouting, 'What did you call us?' " Their faces, Scheer wrote, were "flushed pink and uncomprehending," and for the first time, the word pig struck him as "terribly precise." Within moments, two more patrol cars arrived with red lights flashing. After a brief encounter, the officers withdrew, but not before offering what Scheer called an illogical admonishment. "Don't ask for police assistance the next time unless it is really required," one of them told Scheer.

As Cleaver's deadline approached, the monk Keating once likened to him was embarking on an exciting voyage. Thomas Merton, who rarely left his hermitage in Kentucky, received permission to attend a conference on monastic renewal in Bangkok. Even before Keating's departure from *Ramparts*, Merton had lost touch with the magazine, which had to pass muster with his superiors at the monastery. "Best wishes for *Ramparts*: keep in there fighting," he wrote Keating back in 1966. "I don't often see it, which means that you must be a bit on the warm side and are not getting through."

Before departing for Asia, Merton lingered on the West Coast, visiting the Center for the Study of Democratic Institutions and staying with Lawrence Ferlinghetti. At the San Francisco airport, he paid excess baggage for all the books he had picked up at City

Lights. He traveled to India, Ceylon, and Tibet, where he visited with the Dalai Lama, before returning to Bangkok to present his paper. After that presentation, he returned to his cottage for a nap. Some colleagues thought they heard a shout from his room. When they checked on him, he lay dead on the floor, an electric fan across his chest. He had electrocuted himself while stepping out of the shower.

Back in the Bay Area, Cleaver was also contemplating a trip abroad. The afternoon before his scheduled trip to San Quentin, he addressed a chanting crowd of demonstrators from his front porch. While a Panther who resembled him continued to speak, Cleaver slipped through the house, climbed the back fence, and met a waiting car, where two members of the San Francisco Mime Troupe made him up to look like a sick old man. With $15,000 in cash, courtesy of his royalty check for *Soul on Ice*, he flew to New York in disguise, caught a connecting flight to Montreal, boarded a freighter to Cuba, and arrived in Havana on Christmas morning. The Cubans offered him a uniform, pistol, and AK–47 machine gun before escorting him to a penthouse stocked with food, rum, and cigars. A cook, maid, and two security guards attended to him there.

Cleaver's flight meant forfeiting the $50,000 bail bond that Keating, Paul Jacobs, Hinckle, and two others had posted on his behalf. Kathleen Cleaver later justified that forfeiture in the pages of *Ramparts*.

> Eldridge Cleaver's debts have been paid with his blood, with his suffering, with his work, with his life. . . . Must Eldridge also pay the salaries of his tormentors, his would-be murderers, his enemies? What's left is the mother of Eldridge Cleaver's child, more fuel for the fire that has set this country aflame, and of this country I say with Robert Williams, "Let it burn, let it burn."

According to Kathleen, fundraising efforts paid back those who posted her husband's bail. But her vision of a nation in flames was the more memorable image.

By the time Cleaver landed in Cuba, his interview with *Playboy* magazine was in broad circulation. In that exchange, Cleaver clarified the context for his earlier remarks about violence. In doing so, he described the civil war that Merton had warned white liberals about five years earlier.

> I've said that war will come only if these basic demands [by the Black Panther Party] are not met. Not just a race war, which in itself would destroy this country, but a guerrilla resistance movement that will amount to a second Civil War, with thousands of white John Browns fighting on the side of the blacks, plunging America into the depths of its most desperate nightmare on the way to realizing the American Dream.

Heady shit, as the CIA might say. But by the time Cleaver's clarification appeared, *Ramparts* had bigger problems than an editor in exile.

8

THE WAR'S DESOLATION

As 1968 drew to a close, the left was unraveling. Months earlier, some demonstrators left Chicago feeling triumphant, even giddy. They had survived a showdown with the Establishment, revealed its ugliness, and assumed that the rest of America would join their movement. Millions had witnessed the protests and crackdowns on television, but most failed to appreciate the achievement. "To our innocent eyes," Todd Gitlin wrote, "it defied common sense that people could watch even the sliver of the onslaught that got onto television and side with the cops—which in fact was precisely what the polls showed."

In November, Richard Nixon defeated Humphrey in the presidential election, the Vietnam War ground on, and the New Left was forced to confront a stubborn reality. It had exposed the weakness of American liberalism but hadn't replaced it with anything stronger. Moreover, its attacks had alienated mainstream America and made a successful new coalition unlikely. "New Left radicalism was a vine that had grown up around liberalism," Gitlin wrote later. "They had sprung from the same energy and soil of possibility, and although by now the two represented different cultures, different styles, different ideologies, like it or not they were going to stand or fall together." Falling separately was a third possibility, and by the end of 1968, that seemed to be a likely outcome.

If the left was on the ropes, *Ramparts* was on the respirator. Soon after the Chicago extravaganza, and with the magazine's accumulated debt approaching $5 million, the creditors began hovering, and new money was more difficult to generate, especially given *Ramparts'* position on Israel and connection to the Black Panthers. "I couldn't find anyone else to con," Hinckle said later. His last best hope for a savior was Stanley Weiss, a rich businessman and investor living in Mexico City. Hinckle discovered him through Gerry Feigen, a longtime Gossage partner, *Ramparts* consulting editor, and San Francisco proctologist. "Just making money is no way for a grown man to behave," Feigen told Weiss after treating him. "You've got to be willing to stick your finger into an electric light socket."

Weiss offered to invest $50,000 while he contemplated a larger stake. After a dozen well-marinated meetings with Hinckle, Weiss said he was prepared to invest $500,000. The complicated transaction would give him half ownership of the magazine, which some employees found disconcerting given his status as a newcomer. But Hinckle saw few options: "We sorely needed an angel, and here was one right from central casting—fun loving, lean without a lean look, liberal and libertine, well-tanned, rich, and above all highly desirable in that he desired us." Moreover, Hinckle reassured his colleagues, Weiss didn't seem like the type to hang around the office looking at galley proofs.

As the final arrangements drew closer, Weiss summoned the magazine's key players to Mexico in February 1968. Annoyed that Weiss had purchased coach tickets for their flight, they assumed they were bound for Weiss's home. Upon their arrival, however, they learned that they would convene at the Cuernavaca home of author and psychoanalyst Erich Fromm. When the puzzled *Ramparts* crew assembled around Fromm's seminar table, he lectured them for the next day and a half on his latest theory, a synthesis of Freud and Marx. Slowly they put it together: Fromm was Weiss's shrink, and this meeting would determine his investment.

Noting his audience's restlessness, Fromm confided to an associate during a break that he had misgivings about his guests. Scheer overheard the exchange from an adjacent bathroom, where he was coping with a case of *turista*. Emerging from the bathroom, Scheer startled his host. When the group reassembled, Fromm leveled the charge of eavesdropping. As Fred Mitchell noted later, Scheer called him on it:

> "You think that I was eavesdropping! Listen, I've got diar-rhea from the trip down here, and I was caught in the toilet when you started talking to [your associate]. I didn't want to be there, but I couldn't get out quickly enough! And then when I knew that you were talking about what to do with us, then I wanted to make some noise and get out in a hurry, and that's why I broke in on you. But . . . !"
>
> Fromm tried to flag him down, but Scheer continued:
>
> "I was too busy trying to get my pants on and get out! And I'd have made it sooner except that the toilet leaks, and I had my hand in the back, jiggling that little valve thing . . ." and as he said this, he held up his right hand and began to show us all how he'd rolled back his sleeve to keep it dry.

"It took about fifteen minutes to restore peace to the table," Mitchell recalled. In the end, Weiss kept his money. "It is not every day half-a-million dollars goes down the toilet," Hinckle noted later.

When that investment fell through, the *Ramparts* enterprise was effectively over. The official announcement didn't come until January 1969, when the board of directors put *Ramparts* into bankruptcy. Hinckle told reporters at the Fisherman's Wharf office, "The magazine is bankrupt; the phones are out; there's no booze in the closet; we're dead." He resigned as editor and president of the corporation, but Fred Mitchell wasn't finished yet. With $500,000 already invested in *Ramparts*, he told the press, "Even if I have to put out a four-page mimeograph, I'll do that." There was, how-ever, no plan in place to continue the magazine. "The whole staff could leave," Mitchell said, "or we could elect the copyboy treas-urer and carry on. It could go a lot of different directions."

In the meantime, Hinckle and *New York Times* legal reporter Sidney Zion began lining up the money for their new venture, *Scanlan's*. The stock prospectus listed "The Late Howard Gossage" as the company's chief executive officer. Diagnosed with leukemia in February 1968, Gossage had tried to pack as much living as he could into the final eighteen months of his life. "The way Gossage went about dying changed many things," Hinckle recalled, "including my own relationship with *Ramparts*. When a man like that tells you he has only six months to go and asks you to help him save the world in that time, you don't say you're too busy." If Gossage's adventures distracted Hinckle from *Ramparts*, it was also true that his death compounded the effect of Hinckle's departure. Though he never drew a salary from *Ramparts*, Gossage gave it early credibility in San Francisco, helped bridge the generation gap there, and engineered some of its most notable publicity coups.

Scanlan's appeared in 1970 and got off to a quick start. By publishing Hunter Thompson's "The Kentucky Derby Is Decadent and Depraved" with Ralph Steadman's distinctive artwork, Hinckle helped create Gonzo journalism, and the magazine's circulation zoomed to 150,000. Thompson thought he smelled a franchise. He told Hinckle that he and Steadman could travel the country together producing pieces from high-profile American events. Together, Thompson wrote Hinckle, he and Steadman would "shit on *everything.*"

But when *Scanlan's* ran a memo purportedly from Vice President Spiro Agnew about a top-secret plan to cancel the 1972 election, Hinckle picked a fight that reached the Oval Office. In his memoir, *Blind Ambition*, former White House counsel John Dean recalled his first order from President Nixon. "I'm still trying to find the water fountains in this place," Dean complained to one Nixon advisor. "The President wants me to turn the IRS loose on a shit-ass magazine called *Scanlan's Monthly* (sic)." Nixon had already directed Attorney General John Mitchell to begin an FBI investigation of the magazine; now the Mounties impounded the December 1970 issue at the Montreal printing press. The

Montreal papers reported that Washington had ordered the seizure, but Hinckle later noted that the problem was "financial as well as political." *Scanlan's* went down in flames after eight issues.

As *Ramparts* wound down its operations, Scheer invited staffers to his Berkeley home for drinks. There he reflected on the magazine's contribution and considered the prospects for a new publication at some point. But David Horowitz interrupted to argue for reviving *Ramparts*. His memoir describes the scene.

> The magazine was too important to be allowed to die, I said with passion. It had captured a wide audience and secured national newsstand distribution—something that no other radical magazine had been able to achieve. Moreover, there was a way to save it.

Horowitz had learned from business manager Bob Kaldenbach that *Ramparts* could file for Chapter 11 bankruptcy, pay a fraction of its debt, and remain in business. Scheer embraced the plan, and Kaldenbach was named corporate president to help the magazine navigate the bankruptcy proceedings. Scheer raised $180,000 from Stanley Sheinbaum, who had married film studio heiress Betty Warner, and two other investors.

In his own way, Scheer tried to keep costs down. Lowell Bergman, who was editing an alternative weekly in San Diego, recalled that he agreed to sell *Ramparts* an article for $80 during this time. But when the check never arrived, Bergman, who was broke, finally hitchhiked the five hundred miles to San Francisco to inquire about his money. There he befriended the *Ramparts* bookkeeper, Betty Van Patter, and Scheer took him to Enrico's, the renowned North Beach bistro. Over lunch, Scheer explained that money was tight. Bergman never received his check.

Compared to Hinckle's circus, the new regime was highly streamlined. The monthly budget was slashed from $200,000 to almost a quarter of that figure, and the staff dropped from fifty to nineteen, only six of whom were writers and editors. After a brief hiatus, *Ramparts* resumed publishing in April 1969. The masthead listed Mitchell as publisher, Scheer as editor, and Collier as executive editor. David Kolodney, a former philosophy student who had worked on the Scheer campaign in 1966, became managing editor.

The revived magazine came out firing. Susan Sontag contributed "Some Thoughts on the Right Way (for us) to Love the Cuban Revolution," in which she maintained that Cuba was "astonishingly free of repression and bureaucratization." Although she warned against stereotypes and easy generalizations, she concluded that Cuba was, on balance, a salutary counterpoint to America's "too white, death-ridden culture." The cover story was the Oakland 7 case, which was finally going to trial. Erlich's article with Terence Cannon, a co-defendant, was accompanied by a photo of the group outside the Alameda County courthouse. Taken by a rock photographer, the picture resembled a promotion for the upcoming act at the Fillmore Auditorium. But that issue's cover photograph was the capper. It showed a young, redheaded American boy—Stermer's son, in fact—holding a Vietcong flag. The caption read, "Alienation is when your country is at war and you want the other side to win."

The staff's alienation had another source as well. Business as usual under Hinckle now produced festering resentment directed at Scheer. Part of the problem was Scheer's manner. "I was a hardass and very busy," Scheer admitted later. One colleague recalled Scheer rebuking him for moving to the music at a jazz club. "We don't do that," Scheer said imperiously. On another occasion, he repeatedly refused to run a piece Adam Hochschild had written about Cuba. "Adam, I don't think you're getting my point," Scheer said before igniting the article with his lighter.

But it was Scheer's handling of the next Sontag piece that brought the staff's complaints to the surface. At eighteen thousand words, her article on Sweden came in long and late, forcing the editors to cut other pieces at the last second. "The final straw,"

Horowitz wrote later, "was the discovery that Scheer had promised Sontag a $1,500 fee, which amounted to our entire editorial budget. In the past such extravagance was readily overlooked, but now circumstances were so tight that we were fearful of not being able to pay our own modest wages."

The staff called a "crisis meeting" to air grievances. When Scheer angrily dismissed the complaints as an attack on his authority, Kolodney lost his temper. He detailed the strains Scheer had caused and criticized his arrogance in denying them. "You disgust me," Kolodney concluded before leaving the meeting. After an awkward silence, the meeting adjourned. "Well, I guess it's over," Collier told Horowitz, who still had hopes for the magazine.

The tension carried over to the August issue, which featured the showdown in Berkeley over People's Park. In April, Berkeley activists had claimed a university-owned parking lot south of campus and turned it into a park. Frank Bardacke argued in a widely distributed leaflet called "Who Owns the Park?" that they could expropriate the land under the doctrine of users' rights. "When the University comes with its land title we will tell them: 'Your land title is covered with blood. We won't touch it. Your people ripped off the land from the Indians a long time ago. If you want it back now, you will have to fight for it again.' "

At the same time, Tom Hayden was casting Berkeley as a "liberated zone" that could serve as a revolutionary model for the rest of America. In this scheme, the expropriation and development of People's Park would unite the radicals and hippies in a common effort. Hundreds of residents answered the call and began landscaping the lot, and a local pastor consecrated the new park in an elaborate ceremony on May 11, 1969.

Like Clark Kerr, Berkeley chancellor Roger Heyns was caught between youthful protestors and a conservative governor prepared to challenge them. Heyns produced various scenarios under which the park's development could proceed, but no one was willing to take legal responsibility for the project. On May 15, 1969, a crew of workers moved in, bulldozed the park's perimeter, and erected a chain-link fence around it. Meanwhile, the police sealed off eight city blocks, and a helicopter circled overhead. Demonstrators gathered on campus and marched toward the park to recapture it. When police halted their progress, some marchers began breaking windows on Telegraph Avenue. The Alameda County sheriff's department, whose tactical squad became known as the Blue Meanies after the army of music-haters in the Beatles' film, *Yellow Submarine*, responded with tear gas and birdshot; later they switched to buckshot. Enraged protestors yanked an officer from a burning car and nearly killed him, but he pulled his pistol and escaped. In the end, the Blue Meanies shot 110 people. One of them, student James Rector, died four days later.

Berkeley protests were commonplace, but the violence was unprecedented. Moreover, the political stakes seemed lower than usual. Previous demonstrations had targeted systemic civil rights violations, speech restrictions, and a controversial war. Stripped of its emotional trappings, People's Park was essentially a routine land-use conflict. But if the issue was largely symbolic, the battle was joined. Five days later, the National Guard interrupted a midday memorial on campus for Rector. Sealing thousands of students, visitors, and campus employees in an enclosed area, they bombarded them with tear gas from helicopters. On May 22, Scheer was arrested along with 481 others and spent the night at the Santa Rita Prison Farm, not far from the university-run Livermore lab. He was treated roughly, and his *Ramparts* article on the experience referred to his captors as pigs. That piece was converted into a spoken-word album, "A Night at Santa Rita," with bassist Ron Carter and James Spaulding on flute.

Governor Reagan later defended the police actions against campus protestors. "If it takes a bloodbath, let's get it over with," he told the California Council of Growers in April 1970. "No more appeasement."

Standing on Telegraph Avenue, Scheer and Horowitz had witnessed "Bloody Thursday" together, but Horowitz's mind was on the magazine and its future. As work crews fenced off the park, he urged Scheer to reconsider the staff's grievances. He also noted that fellow staffers wanted to support Scheer; in fact, Horowitz said, they were helping Scheer write the article about police repression that would appear under his byline. According to Horowitz, Scheer responded, "*You* can't write." Evidently, Scheer regarded Horowitz's comment as a criticism of his writing ability.

"This little bullet fixed my resolve," Horowitz later remarked. He drew up a list of demands that he knew Scheer would find unacceptable. The staff voted 17–2 to support them, with Scheer and Stermer in the minority. Horowitz also sought allies on the board of directors, who passed his proposal by a single vote after five East Coast directors failed to attend the meeting. One of the new guidelines required Scheer to receive approval before granting an interview; when Scheer did otherwise, Horowitz directed Kaldenbach to fire Scheer.

Horowitz tried to keep Stermer on board, but the art director was loyal to Scheer, whom he regarded as the magazine's backbone. In his view, Scheer had produced the best ideas and kept the magazine honest, even in the face of Hinckle's sensationalism. Stermer was also skeptical of the new egalitarianism. "That was the time when people started thinking collectives were the way to do it," Stermer recalled. "And there was this movement to turn *Ramparts* into a collective. . . . They may not have given a damn about me, but they needed what happened to the manuscript after it left the typewriter, and they didn't know how to do that."

Horowitz asked for a meeting with Stermer. "He came into the art department," Stermer said, "closed the door and said, Look, this collectivization thing doesn't need to affect you." He offered Stermer complete control over the art department as well as a job title so that his name wouldn't be listed last on the alphabetically ordered masthead. "It was that obvious," Stermer said. He decided to make his displeasure known.

So I opened the door, and I yelled, *David Horowitz just made me a separate and unequal offer to all the rest of you! I get to be a dictator of my own department and you all have to take a vote to go to lunch or something. How do you like that?* Then I turned to David and said, David, I quit.

The last of the triumvirate was gone.

The next week, Stermer read his letter of resignation at a board meeting. A secretary interrupted the meeting to report a telephone call for him. "It was my wife, Carol, saying, 'Don't come home, now or ever.' . . . So that evening I was both jobless and homeless." He repaired to Andre's and reflected on his situation: "Jesus fucking Christ, I'm broke, I've got to pony up child support and alimony, I'm going to freelance and I don't even have a portfolio." Decades later, Stermer called it "a perfect end to the sixties."

Months later, Ralph Schoenman, Horowitz's former colleague in London, wrote to Scheer at the magazine. Schoenman noted that he, too, had built an institution only to have "others do what anthropologists tell us they will do." The meaning was clear, Horowitz wrote later: *Kill the father*. The note annoyed Horowitz, but when he reflected on his dealings with Schoenman and Scheer, he felt "the satisfaction of having stood up to the two of them and beat them both."

The *Ramparts* coup enacted a process common to many New Left organizations. Suspicious of hierarchy, members regularly challenged their own leaders. That reflex was especially strong in 1969, which Collier later described as a time of "elemental cell division" on the left. Certainly *Ramparts* staffers no longer shared, if they ever did, Mitford's view that Hink/Scheer (and Stermer) *were* the magazine. Horowitz's comment on Telegraph Avenue suggested that they saw themselves as worker bees while Scheer and others took the headlines. When he and Collier toppled Scheer, Horowitz presented the parricide as a triumph for the forces of progress.

"After the victory," Horowitz noted, "we set out to institute the revolution we had promised." A board of editors, listed alphabetically on the masthead, replaced Scheer. Salaries for all staffers were leveled to $500 per month. (Scheer's annual salary had been $25,000.) The antihierarchical orientation arose from the movement, but according to Collier, it also reflected a labor market reality. "No one would do the shit work otherwise," he recalled.

Although their authority wasn't formalized, Horowitz and Collier became the decision makers. "Collier and I had engineered the change of power, and carried it through," Horowitz wrote. "Everybody recognized this fact, and acted out of that recognition." Everybody, that is, but the radical collective employed in the mailroom. When Horowitz and Collier tried to cut their budget, which exceeded the editorial one, the mailroom staff resisted. Because all decisions had to be made collectively, the move to trim costs turned into a protracted group deliberation that devolved into a set of nasty personal charges and countercharges.

The coup by Collier and Horowitz had another unforeseen side effect. Hinckle's spendthrift ways had cost the magazine plenty, but his promotional flair had raised its profile not only in the mainstream media, but also in the community of prospective funders. When he and Horowitz took over, Collier predicted that the treasure hunt would slacken, if only because they had no plans to match Hink/Scheer's extensive travel. Horowitz and Collier chose instead to continue cutting costs, at first by moving the office to a Victorian on Union Street and later by switching to newsprint. But the Hinckle regime understood something that eluded Horowitz and Collier. Fresh capital was the key to survival, and "no matter how radical their self-understanding," Horowitz realized later, "potential funders still wanted to be associated with glamour and success." In contrast, Collier and Horowitz stressed fiscal responsibility, political sobriety, and personal sacrifice. As Horowitz learned, "this was not the kind of message that got anyone excited."

"Unable to raise new funds," Horowitz recalled, "we began to develop scams that were borderline criminal, but which the reigning rhetoric of the Left encouraged us to think of as a kind of civil disobedience." One such rhetorician was Abbie Hoffman, whose *Steal This Book* was excerpted in *Ramparts* under the title "America on Zero Dollars a Day." Adapting Hoffman's revolutionary ethic to its own institutional needs, the magazine put half its staff on unemployment. When their benefits expired, they were "rehired," and the other half of the staff was formally laid off to collect benefits. Like Hinckle, the new editors also ran printing jobs when they knew they couldn't pay the bill.

But even when the magazine resorted to these measures, it remained in the red. Once again, Kaldenbach offered an idea; they could dissolve the corporation and sell the *Ramparts* name to a new one. The magazine's principal stockholders, who realized their investments were worthless, approved the plan only because they wanted the magazine to survive. The only other option, it seemed, was shutting the doors for good.

Despite the internal turmoil, Ho/Coll continued to attract a long roster of talented writers, including Noam Chomsky, Alexander Cockburn, Jonathan Kozol, Seymour Hersh, and Kurt Vonnegut. Angela Davis interviewed Huey Newton in prison, and two *New Left Review* editors, Tariq Ali and Robin Blackburn, interviewed John Lennon for the July 1971 issue. Ali's final question was "How do you think we can destroy the capitalist system here in Britain, John?" Lennon replied:

> I think only by making the workers aware of the really unhappy position they are in, breaking the dream they are surrounded by. . . . The idea is not to comfort people, not to make them feel better, but to make them feel worse, to constantly put before them the degradations and humiliations they go through to get what they call a living wage.

Although the interview originally ran in a British publication, Lennon's answer matched the temper of *Ramparts* under Horowitz and Collier. For all its bombshells, the magazine under Hink/ Scheer was resolutely impish, and that playfulness was often missing during the Ho/Coll years. The more severe tone was matched by a downgraded look—mostly newsprint with a glossy insert, and none of Stermer's whimsy.

The editorial content reflected new or growing concerns among progressives and radicals. Collier wrote about Native Americans and the short-lived takeover of Alcatraz, the abandoned island penitentiary in the San Francisco Bay. The magazine also ran a number of important pieces about the environment. During the Hink/Scheer years, Gene Marine had spun his articles about the despoliation of the American wetlands into a book, *America the Raped*. Under Ho/Coll, Paul Ehrlich warned of uncontrolled population growth, sociologist Harvey Molotch covered the massive oil spills in the Santa Barbara Channel, and Barry Weisberg challenged the rapid development accompanying oil exploration in Alaska. The May 1970 issue, which coincided with the second annual Earth Day, was dedicated to ecology and included pieces by Marine, James Ridgeway, and Murray Bookchin, the former CIO organizer turned social ecologist.

Food safety, a key topic for progressives since the time of Upton Sinclair, was another *Ramparts* staple. Again, Marine parlayed a story about "food pollution" into a book. Peter Collier asked Daniel Zwerdling, a young freelancer from Ann Arbor, to contribute a story on food additives. Zwerdling knew nothing about the topic, but he learned that the FDA hadn't conducted any studies on the effects of such additives. "*Ramparts* was far ahead of its time on the food stories," Zwerdling noted in 2008. "*The Washington Post* is running the same story on antibiotics in the meat industry now." But Zwerdling reserved his main accolade for the magazine's treatment of younger writers. "*Ramparts* took risks on young, unknown writers and let them have a voice in the magazine." In 1980, Zwerdling landed at NPR, where he filed investigative and documentary reports for its major news shows and eventually hosted *Weekend All Things Considered*.

The sociology of sports was another prominent *Ramparts* theme. Harry Edwards, who orchestrated the black power salute at the 1968 Olympic Games, wrote about racism in sports. Jack Scott, who had earned a Ph.D. in sociology from Berkeley, wrote about steroid abuse, profiled Edwards for *Ramparts* in 1968, and then served as athletic director at Oberlin College, where he hired Tommie Smith, the Olympic sprinter who raised a gloved fist on the victory stand in Mexico City. The Ramparts book division complemented the magazine's sports coverage by producing Dave Meggysey's *Out of Their League*, an exposé of professional football based on the left-wing linebacker's years with the St. Louis Cardinals. When Hunter Thompson received threats during his run for sheriff in Aspen, Meggysey helped convert the journalist's home into the fortified compound of legend.

Ramparts under Ho/Coll also ran more coverage of women's issues. Sociologist Marlene Dixon outlined various forms of gender inequality and maintained that women "must learn the meaning of rage, the violence that liberates the human spirit." Dixon also cited feminist Roxanne Dunbar: "We are damaged and we have the right to hate and have contempt and to kill and to scream." Other material—including articles on the Pill, childbirth, women in prison, an interview with Anaïs Nin, and an excerpt from a Simone de Beauvoir book—was less inflammatory but extended far beyond the discussion of women's issues during the Hink/Scheer years.

In September 1971, Susan Griffin's cover story examined the politics of rape, which the editors subtitled "the All-American crime." The article circulated widely through rape crisis centers that were popping up around the country. Two years later, Griffin wrote "Confessions of a Single Mother," which described the challenges faced by divorced or never married mothers. Griffin, a SLATE alumna, was by then a freelancer, but she had already served as a *Ramparts* proofreader and contributor to the *Sunday Ramparts*. She also helped form one of the first women's consciousness-raising groups with Anne Weills, Denise Hinckle, Elissa Horowitz, and other women associated with the magazine.

Griffin thought the *Ramparts* workplace was sexist and cited a common office practice as an example. When the staff worked overtime to put the magazine to bed, they frequently took time off to eat dinner at Vanessi's or Enrico's. The male editors charged their meals to expense accounts, but lower-paid female staffers had to buy their own meals. That practice was modified when Griffin and others spoke out against it, but eventually the meals were downgraded to sandwiches. During this time, she also became aware of—and conflicted about—reports that Black Panther Party members were beating their wives. She worked with Eldridge Cleaver on *Soul on Ice*, and though Cleaver didn't thank her in the book, he said he might visit her home some night to do that, a comment she understood as an implied threat of rape.

The magazine under Horowitz and Collier strengthened its national reporting by hiring Andrew Kopkind and James Ridgeway to staff a DC bureau in December 1970. As a *New Republic* staff writer and Washington correspondent for the *New Statesman*, Kopkind had covered Scheer's 1966 congressional campaign. Ridgeway had also written for the *New Republic* and profiled *Ramparts* for the *New York Times Magazine* in April 1969, just as *Ramparts* resumed publishing. Together, Kopkind and Ridgeway produced a section called "Hard Times" that ran in the front of the magazine.

The DC bureau briefly included a young Brit Hume, who was then a protégé of muckraking Pulitzer Prize–winning columnist Jack Anderson. Both became CIA surveillance targets after Anderson quoted Pentagon documents about Nixon's Pakistan policy. Hume's debut at *Ramparts* came in February 1973, when he described the new cabinet as "Richard Nixon's final revenge on the Washington press corps" and lambasted Congress for its failure to challenge Nixon's claims of executive privilege. Neither Anderson nor Hume was a leftist, and one *Ramparts* editor said that dealing with Hume "was like working with someone from a totally different generation." Another staff member, Elliot Kanter, recalled Hume's visit to the magazine's office, then located on University

Avenue in Berkeley. "He seemed a bit bemused by the set-up in Berkeley," Kanter said. After a short stint with *Ramparts*, Hume jumped ship to ABC News.

With a few notable exceptions, the magazine stopped producing the exposés that had roiled the mainstream media during the Hink/Scheer years. Seymour Hersh contributed several investigative pieces on defense-related issues, but despite the magazine's monthly publicity efforts, the *New York Times* picked up only one *Ramparts* story during the Ho/Coll years, an exposé of the National Security Agency's extensive intelligence-gathering techniques. Published in August 1972, the article noted that the NSA had cracked the Soviet codes. By publishing the piece, *Ramparts* alerted the Soviet Union to this purported fact and risked prosecution under the Espionage Act of 1918. After checking with one of Daniel Ellsberg's lawyers, the editors learned that prosecution was unlikely, in part because the government would have to reveal even more classified material to secure a conviction.

In the end, it was simpler and cheaper to run opinion and analysis, including the work of an exiled Eldridge Cleaver. In Algeria, he also passed his novella, *The Black Moochie*, to Scheer, and *Ramparts* published excerpts. Scheer's introduction described it as "notes for an autobiography, novel or whatever, on his experiences growing up in Los Angeles." In one passage, Cleaver reflected on his schooling.

> Mrs. Brick was my teacher and she looked like Betty Grable. All the cats were in love with her. We'd rub up against her and try to peep under her dress. We'd dream about her at night. She had a fine ass and big tits. She dressed sexy. I used to get a hard-on just looking at her. She knew that I wanted to fuck her, to suck her tits.

This was perhaps as far from Keating's original intention as *Ramparts* had traveled. One letter to the editors claimed that Cleaver wrote "with a poignancy and feeling unmatched by any other living American writer." Another concluded that *Ramparts* "must hate our black people and want to arouse the White Citizens Councils and the white backlash to the boiling point of refusing blacks all rights inherent in the Constitution."

Hayden's was another clear voice during the Ho/Coll years. The editors turned over the July 1970 issue to excerpts from *The Trial*, his account of the conspiracy proceedings that followed the Chicago protests, and paid him the entire editorial budget of $1,500. According to Horowitz, Hayden said he needed the money to buy gas masks for the Black Panthers. In that issue, Hayden noted that in early 1968, he and his colleagues had "planned a protest at the Democratic convention, which we believed might be militant and chaotic, possibly even violent in some ways, but nevertheless legal and permissible." But the events in Chicago, he wrote, would lead future historians to "locate the late Sixties as the time when America's famous democratic pragmatism began hardening into an inflexible fascist core."

Hayden's account of the Chicago trial reflected his positions leading up to the convention. He and his co-defendants placed Che's portrait and an NLF flag on their defense table to indicate that it was "a 'liberated zone' right in front of the jury's eyes." He also commented on the proper way to understand the Black Panthers.

If we consider the Panthers as embryonic Vietcong in the U.S., if we assume that a Vietnamese situation is developing here, it becomes logical to adopt and improve the strategy of the anti-Vietnam war movement and direct it against the aggression at home. First *this would mean recognizing that Bobby Seale and other Panthers should not even be tried in the courts of the present U.S. government.* But the most enlightened approach that a white could adopt toward the "facts" would be to dismiss them as irrelevant, as an internal matter of the black colony. . . . All we need to know is that the

Panthers, like the NLF, rely on popular support, not coercion, for their success.

This shaky compound of assumption, logic, and fantasy wasn't unique to Hayden, and Horowitz and Collier drew a stark conclusion from it: "The system cannot be revitalized; it must be overthrown. As humanely as possible, but by any means necessary."

With its echoes of Malcolm X, that statement summarized the magazine's revolutionary line that year. Although the May 1970 issue was the ecology special, the cover photograph depicted incendiary protests at UC Santa Barbara that spring. A bomb blast in the faculty club had killed a custodian, and protestors razed the local branch of the Bank of America. The cover photograph showed the bank in flames, and the caption quoted the lead editorial: "The students who burned the Bank of America in Santa Barbara may have done more towards saving the environment than all the Teach-ins put together." Inside, the editors dismissed the national program of environmental teach-ins that accompanied Earth Day as "a con." In the final analysis, they argued, capitalism was the real culprit: "We must, in short, junk the business system and its way of life, and create revolutionary new institutions to embody new goals—human and environmental."

The May cover was too much even for some of the magazine's longtime supporters. Marc Stone, who had become *Ramparts'* publisher after Fred Mitchell stepped down in December 1969, began to distance himself from the magazine. The Bank of America cover was a concern, but he was also frustrated by his inability to influence the magazine's general direction, and his son Peter began to take on many of his duties. Philanthropist Edgar Lockwood, who had helped raise $200,000 to keep the magazine alive the year before, also objected to the cover. He wrote a long letter to the magazine resigning from the editorial board.

Striving to catch and hold the public eye, you have opened our minds to the obscenities of power, to the economic self-interest of powerful groups that control the seats of decision-making. At other times, you have blurred issues by inaccuracies and half-truths in order to take advantage of immediate opportunities to make a point.

Lockwood maintained that encouraging bombings and burnings helps "raise a further false issue for the radical right, the superpatriots of the working class and their political representatives to exploit." Lockwood also challenged the editors' conclusion that the system must be overthrown.

That statement in my view is irresponsible and can only lead to dangerous escalation of your already inflated rhetoric. I don't know what you mean by it, and I suspect you don't either, but there are innocent young people who will read in it a sanctification for their wild flailing and bitterness.

Ramparts had covered a good deal of wild flailing in previous issues, not all of it performed by innocent young people. Two notable examples were the Altamont rock concert, where Hell's Angels stomped and stabbed one man to death in front of the stage, and the notorious Manson murders in Los Angeles. Many observers thought these grisly events marked the unofficial end of the utopian counterculture of the 1960s, but Horowitz's utopian goal of scrapping capitalism persisted.

The editors ran Lockwood's letter in the October 1970 issue along with a rebuttal. They defended their editorial, which "characterized the burning of the Bank of America's Isla Vista branch as a justified gesture of rage against the continuing rape of that community and the interminable murder in Southeast Asia." They also charged Lockwood with an inconsistency. By his own account, Lockwood had helped revive the magazine not because he always shared its politics, but because he believed in the free exchange of ideas. By withdrawing his support, the editors argued, Lockwood was effectively stifling that exchange. The implication was that Lockwood's liberalism required him to finance their antiliberal cause.

As for portraying revolution as a real political alternative, the editors stood by their earlier claim.

> It is indeed *revolutionary* politics that has turned out to be realistic and practical even in the short-run. This was the gist of our editorial, as well as Hayden's analysis: to project *reform* within the present system and within the present framework of political options as a real political alternative to the present rush towards destruction—*that* is the height of irresponsibility.

They argued that Wilson, Roosevelt, Truman, and Kennedy had left the country with "a legacy of racism and domestic imperialism that may yet lead to open racial warfare." By way of conclusion, they cited no less an authority than the founder of the Black Panthers: "In the last analysis, as Huey Newton would say, the spirit of the people is greater than the Man's technology."

The same revolutionary spirit informed the living arrangements of some *Ramparts* contributors. Many were already living in groups, largely for convenience and economy. Sol Stern, for example, lived with fellow writers and their girlfriends in a collective they called the Fisherman Family. One of its members, Michael Lydon, produced a 1970 *Ramparts* special report on the Rolling Stones' U.S. tour the year before. Another member was Craig Pyes, who later shared a Pulitzer Prize for a series of *New York Times* stories on Al Qaeda. In a send-up of Weatherman, whose name was drawn from Bob Dylan's "Subterranean Homesick Blues," the Fisherman Family printed t-shirts with a fist clutching a fish; the caption read, "You don't need a fisherman to know which way the fish smells."

Other collectives took themselves more seriously. One notable example was a Berkeley commune begun in 1970 called the Red

Family. After Hayden and Scheer arranged a loan from Stanley Sheinbaum, the collective acquired three adjoining properties south of campus. By that time, Hayden wrote later, he and Scheer were on "improving terms after a short period of painful distance." Now divorced from Weills, Scheer had moved his retired mother out to Berkeley and wanted to remain close to his son Christopher. He therefore declined offers to leave the Bay Area and began mixing book projects and teaching with freelance work for *Esquire*, *Playboy*, and *New Times*, a New York slick founded in 1973.

In his memoir, Hayden described such collectives as "one response to the pressures of constant street demonstrations and police harassment." Some Berkeley communes, he explained, held classes in karate and self-defense, taught medical aid for injured demonstrators, and "developed methods for harboring underground fugitives." They typically "practiced the 'free relationships' between men and women advocated by Simone de Beauvoir" and were especially supportive of women who had grown weary of "mass rallies where macho rhetoric filled the air."

Militancy was the dominant mood of the commune. According to Horowitz, whose home life was more conventional, the Red Family's headquarters were festooned with shotguns and portraits of North Korean dictator Kim Il Sung, Ho Chi Minh, Huey Newton, and Geronimo. One SNCC member also recalled seeing "guns all over the place" while visiting Hayden at the commune. Though less specific about the interior decoration, Hayden later described the Red Family as a vanguard of the revolutionary trends converging around them. Its members resisted imperialism and supported the Black Panthers, whose run-ins with law enforcement were frequent and sometimes lethal. In 1969 alone, 348 Panthers were arrested for various crimes; from late 1967 through 1969, their clashes with police had left nine officers and ten Panthers dead.

According to Scheer, the Red Family focused on three issues: rent control, community control of the police, and war crimes. For the last of these, the collective established a tribunal. Orville Schell, who later became dean of Berkeley's journalism school, took the testimony. The Red Family also started a child-care center, Blue Fairyland, which was attended by Christopher Scheer and Jane Fonda's daughter Vanessa. According to Scheer, an attractive single mother with a child at Blue Fairyland turned out to be an informant.

But within the Red Family, Hayden wrote, "the struggle to shed male chauvinism, in both personal relationships and movement work, was the most consuming." While the women formed consciousness-raising groups, the men "went to morbid meetings in which we explored why males were oppressive and given to appalling 'ego trips.'" The discussions took the form of self-criticism, in which any form of self-justification drew suspicion. "I found these meetings to be torture sessions," Hayden recalled. He later noted that his personality and role in the antiwar movement made him "particularly ill suited for becoming a 'new man.'"

That mismatch wasn't lost on his housemates. In 1971, Hayden returned to Berkeley after a speaking engagement on the East Coast. When he entered the house, he found his fellow communards sitting solemnly in a circle. They accused him of male chauvinism, and he tried to defend himself. "There were no open minds," he wrote later, "just collective will." Expelled from the Red Family, Hayden moved to Santa Monica, where he continued his activism and married Jane Fonda in 1973.

The post-*Ramparts* period wasn't especially happy for Scheer, either. Still angry about the ouster his recruits had engineered, he endured what he later called a "crazy, bitter time." In 1970, he joined a delegation headed by Cleaver that visited Saigon, Peking, and Pyongyang. Four years later, he was still living collectively with Weills and six other people. In 1976, the same year he interviewed Jimmy Carter for *Playboy*, he signed on with the *Los Angeles Times* as a national correspondent. Although his views would evolve over the next three decades, many friendships from his commune days endured.

• • •

As Nixon served his first term, the left continued to founder. The Democrats maintained control of Congress, but when they finally selected an antiwar presidential candidate in 1972, Nixon demolished him—despite the best efforts of *Ramparts*, which ran a controversial cover that month. A color photograph depicted slaughtered Vietnamese men, women, and children from the My Lai massacre. In the middle of that photograph, *Ramparts* added a picket sign: "Re-elect the President." In the aftermath of Senator George McGovern's loss, Theodore Roszak later wrote, "the liberal wing of American politics found its position in the national mainstream steadily undermined, as, one by one, the old Democratic Party constituencies drifted into the conservative camp."

The magazine's fortunes also suffered. Ideologically, the shift from Hink/Scheer to Ho/Coll was one of degree. Scheer, too, had criticized liberalism, protested alongside Hayden, and reached out to the Black Panthers. But Hinckle and Stermer were rebels, not leftists, and they tempered Scheer's radical tendencies. Moreover, Scheer himself had run for office on the belief that electoral politics remained relevant. Forged in the violence and despair of 1968, the magazine's new line rejected anything short of revolution and explicitly conceded the symbols of patriotism to the right wing. Together, those gestures struck many seasoned observers as political suicide.

Another reason for *Ramparts*' difficulties was the corporate media's response to its success, which encouraged competitors. The first television news magazine, *60 Minutes*, began airing in 1968, and its blend of hard-hitting exposés and lighter cultural coverage was soon turning a profit. Mainstream newspapers were picking up their game, too. Peter Stone, who worked for *Ramparts* on the business side before launching his own career as a political reporter, later suggested that the magazine's work emboldened the *New York Times* to take more risks with its own reporting. In 1969, when the *Times* ran the so-called Pentagon Papers—classified documents about the war leaked to it by defense analyst Daniel Ellsberg—it was claiming part of *Ramparts'* territory.

Technology and finance were also changing the media land-scape. Berkeley journalism professor Lowell Bergman, who started his career as a typesetter, noted that the falling costs of offset print-ing combined with generous credit from printers helped new magazines and newspapers find their audiences. For a while, at least, *Ramparts* made the most of that opportunity. "*Ramparts* made the big leap to credibility because the stories held up," Bergman said. But even the successful upstarts faced a slew of new competi-tors fighting for the same readers. *Ramparts* and *Crawdaddy!* begat *New Times* and *Rolling Stone*, which begat *SunDance* and *Mother Jones*, and so on. In the early 1970s, David Weir, who co-founded the Center for Investigative Reporting with Bergman in 1977, counted thirteen alternative publications in San Francisco alone.

For a magazine that saw itself as politically sophisticated, *Ram-parts* ran many pieces that were coalition-destroying devices. Lib-erals in particular remained high-value targets. In his introduction to a November 1970 piece on the Berkeley police force, for exam-ple, Hayden called Berkeley "a mini-Vietnam in which the ma-nipulative skills of University of California administrators Clark Kerr, Charles Hitch, and Roger Heyns have failed to keep control of the 'youth problem.' " By that time, Governor Reagan and Pres-ident Nixon were probably worthier adversaries than university administrators, and even after Berkeley's most explosive confronta-tions, many residents didn't recognize their city in Hayden's de-scription. Most of the violence directed at Berkeley demonstrators had come from the sheriff's department, and the city's police force was notably more progressive than its Oakland counterpart. But Hayden blurred that difference.

Their education and training has only made Berkeley po-licemen more sophisticated oppressors. They are not into spontaneous police brutality; their specialty is full-scale counter-insurgency. Brutality is only a tactic within a larger strategy to remove cultural and political radicalism from Berkeley.

Ramparts editors didn't spare their revolutionary allies, either. Horowitz frequently corrected the ideological errors of contributors and other radical organizations. In one of his pieces for *Ramparts*, Horowitz criticized what he called SDS's "hand-me-down Marxism." "David thought he was Marx to Hayden's Lenin," *Ramparts* contributor Derek Shearer recalled. Part of Horowitz's worldview was based on the experience of his parents in the Communist Party. He once asked Frank Bardacke, "Don't you realize, Frank, that Party members are the best people with the worst politics?"

Horowitz also reproached Weatherman, which emerged from the radical wing of SDS, for being irresponsible and unpolitical. In Horowitz's analysis, the group made three political errors: underestimating the enemy's strength, overestimating the forces they hoped to catalyze, and calling for a war against the American state. Horowitz ended the article by quoting Vladimir Lenin on "serious politics" and John Lennon on movement tactics. "Let's own up now," the rock star exhorted, "and see who's who, who is doing something about what, and who is making music and who is laying down bullshit."

Finally, Horowitz had a bone to pick with the Black Panthers. After reading a piece in the Panther newspaper about the conflict over Chenpao Island, which the Chinese and Soviets both claimed, Horowitz decided to discuss the article's pro–China bias with the Panthers directly. But when he arrived at the Panthers' headquarters on Shattuck Avenue, his first visit there, he learned that Bob Avakian had copied the article almost word for word out of the *Peking Review*.

Political fragmentation, media competition, and revolutionary zeal all made *Ramparts'* survival more difficult, but Peter Collier later remarked that the magazine's demise was a foregone conclusion. In his view, *Ramparts* peaked between early 1967 and Hinckle's departure at the end of 1968. During that period, the magazine embodied youthful enthusiasm: "It was like a movie where Mickey Rooney jumps up and says, 'Hey kids, let's put on a play!' " But by the time Collier and Horowitz took over the editorial duties, the magazine's moment had passed. "Everything else was epilogue," said Collier. When the United States signed a peace treaty with Vietnam in January 1973, the issue that had catapulted the magazine into the spotlight disappeared. Instead, the Watergate scandal was dominating the news, and the *Washington Post's* coverage left little room for a low-budget Berkeley monthly to maneuver.

Despite these difficulties, the *Ramparts* staff felt a frantic desire to keep the magazine going, and raising the ideological stakes seemed the best way to accomplish that. In that sense, Collier recalled, "There was something to Newton's phrase, 'The sky's the limit.' " In his view, the magazine's anti-Americanism during his tenure "went from high jinks to something more hardened." After Nixon's reelection in 1972, the editors began to cast *Ramparts* as "the disloyal opposition." They also ran Soledad inmate Bob Cratchit's articles guiding readers on effective ways to shoplift, cheat on their taxes, and otherwise evade or flout the law. Eventually Cratchit recanted in a letter to the editors, noting that "ripping off is neither therapeutic nor good politics." Nevertheless, *Ramparts* continued to sell his guides in pamphlet form.

Instead of striking back, Collier recalled, many Americans waited for the prodigals to return to the fold. "The country was strong enough and generous enough and forgiving enough to absorb all our treason," he maintained. At the time, however, such humility was no part of the magazine's project. "*Ramparts* started broad and anarchic, with lots of different perspectives," Lowell Bergman said later. "But as with many organizations, the leadership slowly took control. They thought they knew better, and Horowitz thought he knew everything." Soon the young editor's worldview would be shaken to its core.

9

TWILIGHT'S LAST GLEAMING

By 1973, Horowitz and Collier were beginning to look beyond *Ramparts*. At Collier's suggestion, they hatched a plan to write a bestselling saga of the Rockefeller family. Over the years, they had met Abby and Marion Rockefeller and thought a book about young radicals in America's ruling families would have popular appeal. Marion was a Berkeley resident, and when Horowitz visited her home, she produced a diagram of her family's empire, labeling its center "The Disease." Horowitz and Collier signed a contract with Holt, Rinehart and Winston and received a $50,000 advance.

To free up time to pursue these projects, Horowitz and Collier recruited a new editorial team for the magazine. Horowitz approached Bo Burlingham, a senior editor at an alternative weekly in Boston. Burlingham had been president of the SDS chapter at Princeton and eventually joined Weatherman. When Horowitz contacted him, he and a dozen other Weatherman members were under indictment in Detroit for conspiring to violate the Federal Firearms and Explosives Act. But Burlingham had admired *Ramparts* for years and decided to accept Horowitz's offer.

Burlingham moved to Berkeley, where Horowitz and Collier had relocated the office to University Avenue. Burlingham wasn't thrilled with his new home. "Berkeley was like being in a straitjacket," he said later. "It was stuck in 1969. There were all these people with ideas that were totally wrong." He was already distancing himself from his Weatherman experience, which discouraged independent thinking and included group criticism sessions called Weather fries. "We had been through Weatherman," he recalled later. "We'd already seen the dark side. Weatherman was a cult. It was like I had gotten stupid when I was in it." As a new father, too, Burlingham was more attuned to his family responsibilities and less interested in ideological posturing.

Despite his disenchantment with Berkeley, Burlingham settled into the job of managing editor and brought several new faces to the magazine. They included *Boston Globe* writer Tom Oliphant, who reviewed the 1972 presidential campaign, and Craig Unger, a Boston freelancer who decades later would examine the link between the Bush and Saud families. Another Burlingham recruit was Derek Shearer, a Yale graduate who contributed "Poor Derek's Almanac," a regular feature. Shearer's parents wrote the popular Walter Scott celebrity column for *Parade* magazine, and their family home in Los Angeles served as a salon for young liberals, including Yale law student Bill Clinton. Clinton's friend Strobe Talbott was then courting Brooke Shearer, Derek's younger sister.

Shearer's boyhood friend, David Obst, also joined forces with the magazine during Burlingham's tenure. By that time, Obst had become a veritable Forrest Gump of the New Left. He was on hand at the 1968 Democratic convention in Chicago, helped Daniel Ellsberg protect the Pentagon Papers, and witnessed the People's Park demonstrations in Berkeley while pursuing his graduate studies there. Having started an alternative news service, he also had extensive media contacts. His most notable success was helping Seymour Hersh launch his 1969 story about the My Lai massacre, in which the 20th Infantry's Charlie Company killed hundreds of Vietnamese civilians, including many women and children. That story sparked international outrage and further diminished domestic support for the war.

After accepting his new position at *Ramparts*, Burlingham picked up Obst in Washington, DC, and the two drove across the country together. Obst's memoir described his first impressions back in the Bay Area.

> I arrived in Berkeley and showed up at the *Ramparts* offices.
> I was ready to help lead the vanguard of the revolution that

was going to change the world. Only one small problem: When I turned around to look at our followers, nobody was there . . . the Movement was over.

Burlingham soon drew the same conclusion about the magazine. "It's dying," he thought. "It's not there."

Obst later wrote that he should have listened to I. F. Stone, who told him in 1971, "I've seen snot-nosed kids like you guys come and go. You're not going to change much." There were three reasons for that, Stone explained. First, their adversaries wouldn't go quietly. Second, the younger generation was obsessed with violence. "Too much TV," Stone speculated. Third, that violence was alienating mainstream Americans. "Listen," Stone continued, "the Soviet Union's leaders are the same wooden Indians as we have here, and the Chinese peasant is just as exploited as he ever was, but Marx and Mao at least had a vision. They had a program, one they could get people to risk everything to follow. What do you kids have?"

Obst's sojourn with *Ramparts* was short-lived, but while crashing on Burlingham's floor in Berkeley, another project swam into his ken. *Washington Post* reporter Carl Bernstein called to see whether Obst would serve as literary agent for a book he was writing with his colleague, Bob Woodward. The success of *All the President's Men* brought Obst other quality projects, including John Dean's *Blind Ambition*. Eventually he returned to Southern California, where he wrote and produced films. In 1984, Orwell's year of the toad, Obst hit pay dirt with *Revenge of the Nerds*.

Burlingham's road was a little rockier. As managing editor at *Ramparts*, he discovered that Horowitz and Collier weren't ready to cede editorial control of the magazine. One of Burlingham's recruits, Min Yee, wrote a cover story challenging the leftist notion that U.S. prisoners were revolutionary leaders in waiting. That concept was buoyed by the success of *Soledad Brother: The Prison Letters of George Jackson*, which appeared in 1970. Earlier that year, a plan to spring Jackson from prison shocked mainstream

America. Jackson's seventeen-year-old brother Jonathan commandeered a Marin County courtroom and passed weapons to three San Quentin inmates participating in a trial there. After abducting the judge, district attorney, and three jurors, Jackson tried to escape in a van. He died in the ensuing shootout along with two of the prisoners and Judge Harold Haley, who was killed when a sawed-off shotgun taped to his head discharged. The Panthers had helped plan the abduction, but Newton withdrew his support when success seemed unlikely. Using weapons registered to Angela Davis, Jonathan Jackson decided to execute his part of the plan anyway. Later that month, Weatherman bombed the Marin County courthouse in retaliation for his death.

Horowitz was "furious" about Yee's story, Burlingham said later. "At the time, Horowitz was kowtowing to Newton. He made us run something from *Revolutionary Suicide*, which was a piece of shit." But some critics took Newton's 1973 autobiography more seriously. In the *New York Times Book Review*, veteran journalist Murray Kempton faulted the book but suggested that Newton came "not as an avenger but as healer." Referring to Newton's seminars with psychoanalyst Erik Erikson at Yale University, Kempton finished his piece with a flourish.

> Here is the only visible American who has managed to arrive at a Platonic conception of himself. And here is the first contemporary personage for whom there will be a diagnosis by Erik Erikson. And just what do you suppose the analyst of Luther and Gandhi—those other curious mixtures of prophetic presumption and mother wit—will make of Huey P. Newton?

Without endorsing Newton's literary efforts, Kempton surrounded the author with distinguished company.

In August 1973, Burlingham traveled to Detroit for his conspiracy trial, but the prosecutors unexpectedly dropped the charges. For the first time in years, Burlingham felt free to chart a new course for himself and his family. He returned to Berkeley, but he was already planning his exit from *Ramparts*, especially since Horowitz and Collier were recruiting yet another editorial team to guide the magazine. By the end of the year, Burlingham was back in Boston.

Horowitz and Collier's new succession plan for the magazine included an editorial team of Adam Hochschild, Paul Jacobs, and Richard Parker. Hochshild and Jacobs were Hink/Scheer alumni, and Parker, who had recently completed a Ph.D. in economics at Oxford University, was Stanley Sheinbaum's colleague at the Center for the Study of Democratic Institutions. Parker was involved with the center's magazine, which had a large circulation, and he had also founded an alternative weekly in Santa Barbara.

Sheinbaum approached Parker about working at *Ramparts*. "You're going to be an editor, and you're going to fix it," he said. "I'll give you $50,000, and you'll fix it." The center's founder, Robert Maynard Hutchins, endorsed the idea. "Santa Barbara is a good place to retire at any age," Hutchins told Parker. "You're too young to retire." Sheinbaum introduced Parker to Paul Jacobs, who also received a proposal from Adam Hochschild that included $25,000 for good measure. Carol and Ping Ferry, who were associated with the Hutchins Center, pledged $100,000. Sheinbaum then brokered a deal with Collier and Horowitz.

When the new editorial trio arrived in fall 1973, they planned to continue the magazine's move toward broader cultural material, including more pieces on literature, music, and sports. But mostly they wanted to change the magazine's didactic tone. Part of that problem, Parker thought, was related to the magazine's location in Berkeley, which was beholden to a misshapen student politics. In San Francisco's more cosmopolitan setting, the left was a developed culture, not just a set of ideas.

The trio encountered immediate resistance from the incumbent editors, led by David Kolodney, who still felt responsible for the magazine's content. Because the magazine was organized as a staff trust, important decisions were made collectively. "We showed up, and there was a staff in place," Parker recalled. "Nobody was clear about what was going on." Horowitz was still on the seven-person editorial board, but he rarely appeared in the office. The other six editors, including the recently recruited trio, slogged through long, ostensibly democratic meetings. That arrangement led to conflicts, some less predictable than others. In the aftermath of the OPEC price hikes of 1973, for example, the incumbent editors wanted to run an energy piece by Parker as the cover story. Parker resisted, believing that another story in that issue was stronger. He found himself shouting at his colleagues not to run his piece as the cover story, a rare event in the annals of journalism.

Shortly after that argument, the new editorial team decided to withdraw. Neither Sheinbaum nor the Ferrys had put their money in the *Ramparts* kitty, and Sheinbaum's money followed the trio. At the time, however, they had no specific plan for using it.

Later that fall, a series of news bombshells hit the Bay Area. In November 1973, an unknown revolutionary group called the Symbionese Liberation Army murdered Oakland school superintendent Marcus Foster. Foster, the first black superintendent in Oakland's history, was shot eight times with cyanide-laced bullets as he left a school board meeting. An SLA communiqué issued the following day took responsibility for the attack, which also injured Foster's deputy. The communiqué denounced an Oakland school board proposal for student identification cards as "the newest extension of police surveillance . . . patterned after fascist Amerikan tactics of genocide murder and imprisonment practiced by Amerikan-financed puppet governments in Vietnam, the Phillipines, Chile, and South Africa." It ended with a revolutionary flourish: "Death to the fascist insect that preys upon the life of the people."

In a *Ramparts* cover story attributed to the editors, Horowitz criticized the SLA, which had grown out of a black prison organization. "In 'executing' Marcus Foster and in making no effort to justify that execution by any doctrine of specific guilt, the SLA assumes the power of life and death over everyone," Horowitz wrote. "It has killed a defenseless individual whose guilt is not only not proved, but is mainly a fantasy of his executioners." But some Berkeley revolutionaries were displeased with Horowitz's editorial. According to Horowitz, Stew Albert argued that it gave "a green light to the police to murder the SLA."

Three months after the Foster murder, the SLA struck again when they kidnapped media heiress Patty Hearst from her Berkeley apartment. Days later, the first of several audiotape messages from Hearst arrived at KPFA. In the first recording, Hearst told her parents she was safe. Meanwhile, her captors tried to arrange the release of jailed SLA members in return for Hearst. After that effort failed, the SLA demanded that the Hearst family distribute $70 worth of food to each needy California household. Hearst's father donated $6 million for food that was distributed in the Bay Area, but the SLA refused to release his daughter, claiming that the donation was inadequate.

As the kidnapping story unfolded, William Knowland, publisher of the *Oakland Tribune*, began to fear for his safety. He had already offered a $100,000 reward for information leading to a conviction in the Foster murder. Now he watched as his San Francisco counterpart tried to ransom his daughter from a group of violent fanatics. Soon after the Hearst kidnapping, Governor Ronald Reagan helped Knowland celebrate the *Oakland Tribune's* 100th anniversary. Two days after that, Knowland committed suicide at his summer home on the Russian River. Knowland wasn't the only one who was fearful. "Looking back," Horowitz wrote later, "I realize that this was the first time in my life I had been afraid of the Left."

Two months after the kidnapping, a fifth audiotape was released. Hearst denounced her parents, supported the revolution, and adopted Tania as her nom de guerre. Shortly after that, the SLA robbed a bank in San Francisco's Sunset district. Hearst wielded an assault rifle during the heist, which left two customers dead. When the police tracked the SLA to a house in Los Angeles, a shootout ensued, and the house went up in flames. None of the six occupants survived the standoff, but Hearst and two others watched the incident on television from their Anaheim hotel room. In April 1975, the SLA robbed another bank in the Sacramento area, killing a customer. Hearst was captured five months later.

The trial of Patty Hearst revealed that a *Ramparts* contributor had played a significant role in the SLA saga. Hearst testified that she met Jack Scott in an East Bay apartment after the Los Angeles shootout, and that he and his family drove her east in August 1974. Scott then drove her to Las Vegas, where he left her. Despite this connection, *Ramparts* missed a major story that played out in its own backyard. Two days after Hearst was captured, *Rolling Stone* published a detailed account that many observers regarded as its best investigative reporting. "It was the scoop of the 70s," publisher Jann Wenner said later. Freelance journalists Howard Kohn and David Weir never considered sending it to *Ramparts*, even though Jack Scott was one of their sources. "*Ramparts* was struggling and in disarray," Weir recalled. Scott later admitted to harboring Hearst, but no criminal charges were ever filed against him. When her 1981 book linked Scott to terrorist groups, he sued her for libel and settled for $30,000.

During Hearst's trial, her high-priced lawyers argued that she had been brainwashed and shouldn't be held responsible for the San Francisco bank robbery that left two innocent people dead. She was sentenced to seven years and served twenty-one months before President Carter commuted her sentence. Later, President Clinton pardoned her. For many, the upshot of the Patty Hearst saga was as dispiriting as it was disturbing. The SLA's crimes were shocking, law enforcement showed how far it would go to preserve its monopoly on sanctioned violence, and the courts reinforced the perception that the rich lived in a separate legal universe. Although Horowitz condemned Foster's murder, the magazine's calls for revolution had helped create space for the mayhem.

Much to Horowitz's relief, Newton also condemned the SLA after the Foster murder—perhaps because the SLA sympathized with Cleaver, who had become Newton's bitter rival. Partly because of that feud, which left several Panthers dead, Horowitz hadn't met Newton. But a new channel opened up when Horowitz met producer Bert Schneider while raising money for the magazine. Schneider's success in television (*The Monkees*) and film (*Easy Rider* and *Five Easy Pieces*) had turned him into a Hollywood player. After much courting on Horowitz's part, Schneider visited San Francisco and made an unexpected request. Would Horowitz remove Cleaver's name from the magazine's masthead? Horowitz resisted Schneider's suggestion but agreed to meet with Newton in Oakland.

Horowitz visited Newton's Lake Merritt penthouse and later toured the Black Panther Party's health clinic, newspaper office, and school site. Newton encouraged Horowitz's suggestions and quickly accepted several of them. "Having Huey's ear made me feel politically powerful in a new way," Horowitz wrote later. "I was tired of pouring energy into grand abstractions like 'the revolution,' and longed to see my efforts lead to practical results." But few of his *Ramparts* colleagues joined those efforts. Collier backed away, as did Bob Kaldenbach, whose wife issued an ultimatum after he reviewed the books for Jimmy's Lamp Post, a bar and restaurant that Newton wished to have transferred to the party. "From then on," Horowitz wrote later, "I was on my own."

Marty Kenner, a New York stockbroker, was Horowitz's main contact with Newton. Kenner had already arranged an event for the Black Panthers at composer Leonard Bernstein's New York home. That event became the centerpiece of Tom Wolfe's *Radical Chic*, which featured the incongruities of cultural elites making common cause with Newton's "brothers off the block." Kenner was also helping the Panthers open a school in Oakland, and

Horowitz pitched in with the fundraising. He started a nonprofit organization called the Educational Opportunities Corporation (EOC) and raised $100,000 in donations for the Oakland Community Learning Center. Located at 63rd Avenue and East 14th Street, the school enrolled some 150 children and quickly became the party's signal institution in the community.

As Horowitz became more involved with the school, Kenner bowed out. As he did, he warned Horowitz about Elaine Brown, a rising figure in the Black Panther Party. According to Kenner, she had accused him of being an agent and threatened to kill him before Newton intervened. Despite the warnings, Horowitz continued to work with Newton. He also spent more time in Los Angeles, where he stayed with Schneider and his girlfriend, Candice Bergen, in their Benedict Canyon home. Through Schneider, Horowitz met Jack Nicholson, Jane Fonda, and other Hollywood stars, and the magazine's coverage reflected those new connections. In September 1971, *Ramparts* interviewed Nicholson about his directorial debut, *Drive, He Said.* The film included a depiction of campus radicalism, but Nicholson distanced himself and his film from revolutionary action. "I know people are trying to do good things, but I don't see a lot of success in the attempts," he told *Ramparts.*

Meanwhile, Horowitz continued to raise money for the Panthers. When Saul Landau brought out *Fidel,* his 1974 documentary about Castro, he screened it to a full house at San Francisco's Surf Theater and announced that he would donate that night's proceeds to the Black Panther legal defense fund. After the screening, Horowitz said nothing about the film but instead asked Landau, "So is this all you're going to do for the Panthers?" "Horowitz had his head so far up Huey Newton's ass he couldn't see anything," Landau said later.

By that time, Newton's behavior had become especially erratic and dangerous. Drinking heavily and abusing cocaine, he banished Seale from the Black Panthers after a petty quarrel. Shortly after pistol-whipping his tailor, Newton was arrested for shooting a teenage prostitute in the jaw; she died three months later. He was charged with murder and fled to Cuba, leaving Elaine Brown in charge of the organization.

The Black Panther Party's finances were in disarray, and Brown asked Horowitz to recommend a bookkeeper. He suggested Betty Van Patter, whom Horowitz had brought over to the EOC from *Ramparts*. Horowitz told Brown that Van Patter was "able and politically willing," but that she could be "overly scrupulous." Van Patter had complained, for example, when *Ramparts* put half its staff on unemployment to artificially lower the payroll. The move struck her as immoral, but Horowitz and Kaldenbach maintained it was necessary to keep the magazine alive.

Brown hired Van Patter, and over the next two months, Horowitz received two telephone calls from his former *Ramparts* colleague. In the first, Van Patter told him that Brown was running for city council and wanted her to manage the campaign. In the second call, Van Patter was upset. She wanted Horowitz to help her contact Brown, but he hadn't seen the Panther leader for over a month.

On December 17, 1974, Horowitz received a call from Betty's daughter, Tamara Baltar, a former office worker at *Ramparts*. She was worried about her mother, who hadn't been seen for three days. When Baltar called her mother's workplace, she learned that Van Patter was no longer an employee there. Horowitz discovered that Brown had fired her after an argument the week before. When he finally reached Brown, she became agitated and criticized Van Patter. "She went around sticking her nose into everything, asking everybody questions," Brown told Horowitz. "She knew all our little secrets. You told me she could be trusted. Do you know who she worked for before she came to us? The firm has offices in Hong Kong and the Philippines. She was probably working for the CIA."

A few days later, two police officers appeared at Horowitz's home. They suspected that the Panthers had killed Van Patter, who was last seen at a bar on University Avenue in Berkeley. She left by herself after a black man she seemed to know entered the bar and handed her a note. Hoping to aid the investigation, Horowitz later contacted one of the officers. It was an unusual move for him. "In my radical cosmos," Horowiz wrote later, "the police had always been the enemy." But Horowitz thought there might still be time to save Van Patter's life.

The following month, the police pulled Van Patter's corpse out of the bay near Foster City. They identified her using dental records and estimated that her body had been in the water for two weeks. Her skull had been smashed with a blunt object. Tamara's brother suspected the Panthers, but when Horowitz seconded that suspicion, Tamara rejected it. "The Panthers are good people," she said.

Horowitz later maintained that few of his left-wing colleagues wanted to investigate Van Patter's death. When Collier contacted local reporters about the story, one Pulitzer Prize–winning anchorwoman told him she wouldn't touch it unless black reporters did so first. Collier also contacted the police, who received him coolly. "You guys have been cutting our balls off for the last ten years," one officer told him. "You destroy the police and then you expect them to solve the murders of your friends."

A year after Van Patter's death, Horowitz received a call from a Panther contact who had relocated to another state. In a series of conversations, Horowitz learned more about Van Patter's murder as well as the party's other violent practices and criminal operations. Horowitz later said he was horrified and withdrew from political activity. He wasn't the only one who was lying low. Bobby Seale disappeared from public view for more than a year. According to Horowitz, "Seale had been whipped—literally—and then personally sodomized by Newton with such violence that he had to have his anus surgically repaired by a Pacific Heights doctor who was a political supporter of the Panthers."

In 1978, former *Newsweek* writer and *Ramparts* contributor Kate Coleman wrote an investigative piece on the Panthers for *New Times*. The piece was co-authored by *Chronicle* crime reporter Paul Avery and sponsored by the Center for Investigative Reporting (CIR) in Berkeley. Using Horowitz as a source, Coleman described the Panthers' criminal activities and connected the party to Van Patter's murder, which remained unsolved. Coleman learned that Van Patter was last seen alive at the Lamp Post, the Panther bar to which she had been summoned. Tamara Baltar, who by that time was working for CIR, typed the piece, but she also thought CIR was conducting "a witch hunt of the Black Panther Party" and eventually quit. Later, Baltar and her family asked private detective Hal Lipset to investigate. He also concluded that the Panthers were responsible but warned that it would be dangerous for Baltar to go public with the accusation.

Horowitz later wrote that Van Patter's murder affected him profoundly. As the 1970s wound down, he began questioning and then repudiating his earlier political views. Eventually he signed up for a different revolution, this one led by Ronald Reagan, and he and Collier became vocal critics of the Black Panthers and the New Left.

In her 1992 book, *A Taste of Power*, Elaine Brown dismissed rumors that the Panthers harmed Van Patter, who she said "was having trouble finding work because of her arrest record." Through Van Patter's connection to *Ramparts*, Brown also linked her to Cleaver, Newton's rival, and faulted Van Patter for her financial queries.

> Immediately Betty began asking Norma, and every other Panther with whom she had contact, about the sources of our cash, or the exact nature of this or that expenditure. Her job was to order and balance our books and records, not to investigate them. I ordered her to cease her interrogations. She continued. I knew that I had made a mistake in hiring her.

The party's illicit activities were Brown's chief concern. "Under the various definitions of U.S. criminal and tax codes, there was no question that many of our money transactions could be ruled illegal," she noted. But she claimed that Van Patter's record, not the party's racketeering, was the real problem.

> Moreover, I had learned after hiring her that Betty's arrest record was a prison record—on charges related to drug trafficking. Her prison record would weaken our position in any appearance we might have to make before a government body inquiring into our finances. Given her actions and her record, she was not, to say the least, an asset. I fired Betty without notice.

But Van Patter had no prison record, for drug trafficking or anything else. She had once been arrested for obstruction of justice—specifically, for lying to Berkeley police about harboring a burglary suspect—and received six months probation, which was later expunged. (Brown was forced to make changes to the paperback edition.) That left Van Patter's questions about the party's finances as the only credible grounds for her dismissal.

Five years after Brown's book appeared, Horowitz addressed Van Patter's murder in his memoir, *Radical Son*. On the twenty-fifth anniversary of Van Patter's death, he also raised the issue more pointedly in a Salon.com article, "Who Killed Betty Van Patter?" The next year, Elaine Brown responded to Horowitz's charges in the *Nation*. She noted that no arrests had been made in the Van Patter case, and that the continuing interest in the murder demonstrated a racial double standard. "White people always want me to tell them about *fucking Betty Van Patter*," she said, "but not one person has ever called to ask me who I think killed George Jackson."

An even more remarkable response to Horowitz's efforts came from Representative Barbara Lee, the former Ron Dellums aide who replaced him in Congress in 1998. Describing Horowitz as "one of my most vocal detractors," Lee addressed some of his claims in her 2008 book, *Renegade for Peace and Justice*. In Lee's version, Betty Van Tanner [*sic*] disappeared with a large sum of money from the Black Panther treasury six weeks before the police discovered her body. "Horowitz suspected that Party members had murdered her and stolen the money," Lee claimed. "This kind of tactic had been seen before and was known to have been used by the government's anti-Panther COINTELPRO group."

In fact, COINTELPRO had been disbanded more than two years earlier, and it was much more likely that Van Patter had discovered evidence of wrongdoing, not vanished with missing money. But in one brief passage, Lee managed to suggest that Van Patter had brought about her own demise, and that the government had tried to frame the Panthers for it. She didn't explain how the two incongruent suggestions added up, and her misquotation of Van Patter's last name did little to establish her expertise on the matter. When alerted to Lee's version of Van Patter's demise, Bo Burlingham found it despicable. "Betty was a sweet person trying to make the world a better place to live," he said. Other *Ramparts* veterans agree. It was inconceivable that Van Patter had done anything illicit, and it was unlikely that anyone but the Panthers was to blame for her murder.

For her former colleagues, Van Patter's death was both a trauma and a permanent reminder of the party's thuggishness. Many also believed that Horowitz was partly to blame for her murder. Both Burlingham and Christopher Hitchens, who wrote for *Ramparts* under the name Matthew Blaire, maintained that Horowitz felt guilty, and rightly so, for recommending Van Patter to the Panthers in the first place. They and others regarded Horowitz's subsequent outspokenness as a form of belated atonement. Many questioned Horowitz's conversion story and especially the way Van Patter's murder authorized a series of right-wing positions supported by overheated personal attacks.

As the Van Patter murder story played itself out, Eldridge Cleaver returned from exile. After surrendering at the American embassy in Paris, he flew first class to New York accompanied by two FBI agents. By that time, former Attorney General John Mitchell was in prison himself for his role in the Watergate scandal. Unable to make the $100,000 bail, Cleaver served nine months in the Alameda County jail. After his bail was posted, he announced that he had become a Christian and met with Billy Graham in Los Angeles. In the end, he received probation for an assault charge in connection with the April 1968 shootout.

Some years later, a story circulated that a former Black Panther asked Cleaver, "Hey, Eldridge, what's all this shit, now you're a big conservative and you're into all this religion and everything. What the hell is that all about?" Cleaver lit a joint and said, "Look, brother, we've *seen* all the revolution we're gonna see."

Van Patter's death coincided with *Ramparts'* final demise. Earlier that year, the staff had returned to San Francisco, setting up office on Hyde Street one door up from the Buena Vista Cafe. But circulation was declining, authors were impatient with the low rates and slow payments, and suppliers were less willing to work on credit. The staff responded by cutting corners: combined issues, shrinking page counts, more newsprint, and exchange ads with other magazines. "We were trying to dress for work," editorial board member Elliot Kanter recalled.

The month after Van Patter's body was discovered, *Ramparts* missed an issue. The following month, the editors claimed in an open letter, "The worst seems to be over." The May/June issue ran articles by James Fenton and Gabriel García Márquez, but in July, the staff published a four-page open letter that described the magazine's "necessary viewpoint" and asked readers to choose one of three options: renew their annual subscriptions ($8); renew and receive an autographed book by Daniel Ellsberg, Joseph Heller, Denise Levertov, or Kurt Vonnegut ($25); or sign up for a lifetime subscription and receive all four signed books ($150).

When that approach failed, the August/September issue made an even more direct appeal. The nine-person staff ran a signed, full-page announcement opposite the table of contents and under the headline "A Matter of Life or Death." It explained that *Ramparts* needed $60,000, or about $1 per reader, to survive. "Whatever you can do," the staff wrote, "we ask you to do it now." It wasn't enough. After producing the August/September issue, the staff moved the office files to a rental house, still hoping to revive the magazine. "Then fade to black," Kanter recalled.

Ramparts' eventful life came to a quiet end, but its influence was still reverberating through American public life.

10

FULL GLORY REFLECTED

When *Ramparts* closed its doors for good in 1975, its circulation had dipped below sixty thousand, a fraction of its peak. By itself, however, the low circulation didn't break the magazine. In fact, *Ramparts* lost more money at its peak than it did at its trough. Moreover, many political magazines had found ways to survive at that lower altitude. The more urgent challenge was *Ramparts'* shrinking media niche. Toward the end of its life, it was competing not only with established outlets, but also with upstarts created at least partly in its own image.

One such publication was *New Times*, the biweekly New York slick founded in 1973 by Time-Life veteran George A. Hirsch. Like *Ramparts*, *New Times* ran investigative pieces and found a large readership. Its circulation reached 350,000, but the magazine couldn't attract and retain advertisers. Contributor Daniel Zwerdling recalled that the publisher's market research indicated that muckraking had peaked, and when *New Times* folded in 1978, the organization started a running magazine. In its eulogy, *Time* magazine maintained that the demise of *New Times* reflected the "unlettered self-absorption" that characterized the 1970s. Hirsch's comment reinforced that theory: "Where did [the readers] go? Well, where did all the people go who didn't vote last week?" Editor Jonathan Z. Larsen also questioned the public's appetite for hard-hitting political stories. "We bore readers the bad news, and they slew the messenger."

Another *Ramparts* competitor sprang from its own loins. By 1975, the devil-may-care wildness in the *Ramparts* DNA was alive and well at *Rolling Stone*. After *Scanlan's* went under, *Rolling Stone* publisher Jann Wenner recruited Hunter Thompson and ran the articles that culminated in Thompson's bestselling book, *Fear and Loathing in Las Vegas* (1971). In the wake of that book's success, Thompson set up the magazine's national affairs desk in Washington. That move led to another successful book, *Fear and Loathing: On the Campaign Trail, '72.*

Thompson yielded to no one in his hatred for President Nixon, whom he described as "a nightmare of bullshit, intrigue, and suspicion." But like most *Rolling Stone* writers, Thompson gave radical politics a wide berth. His favorite presidential candidates were mainstream Democrats: Robert Kennedy, George McGovern, and Jimmy Carter. "We were discouraged by New Left and presidential politics," Wenner recalled. "We were relatively apolitical until the Chicago convention. We did some leftist stories, but we also denounced Abbie Hoffmann and Jerry Rubin in a cover story. You can't just do doctrinaire politics." At one point, Ralph Gleason suggested that Wenner survey *Rolling Stone* readers in the military for their views on drugs and music. "It was the sort of thing *Ramparts* could have and should have done," Wenner said later.

Under Bo Burlingham, *Ramparts* had implicitly acknowledged *Rolling Stone*'s success by running more music stories and album reviews. Although *Ramparts* couldn't compete with Wenner and Gleason on their own turf, some *Rolling Stone* writers credited *Ramparts* for what it made possible. "The Bay Area publications could be divided roughly into two camps at that time," David Weir recalled. "The music, hippie, pot, and back-to-the-land magazines were one direction," Weir said. "The other direction was political. *Ramparts* was the godfather of that movement. It set the standard and attracted the talent."

Wenner later described the relationship between *Rolling Stone* and *Ramparts* as one of "overlapping trajectories." During his time at the *Sunday Ramparts*, Wenner picked up layout ideas from Stermer and learned the importance of wit and showmanship from

Hinckle. But there were important differences, too. "I was very clear about the importance of rock music and the middle-class Baby Boomers," Wenner recalled. "That became a dominant fact of the culture." Their business approaches were also different. "*Ramparts* didn't have a business plan. That was the fun of it, and it was wonderful to watch," Wenner said. "But we had more seriousness of purpose around the desire to survive."

Two years after Ralph Gleason died of a heart attack in 1975, Wenner moved *Rolling Stone* to New York. Hunter Thompson was unhappy about the move and what he saw as the related change in the magazine's personality. "The fun factor had gone out of *Rolling Stone*," he said later. "It was an outlaw magazine in California. In New York, it was an establishment magazine. It became like an insurance office, with people communicating cubicle to cubicle."

When his own magazine work faltered in the 1980s, Thompson returned to newspaper journalism. A young William Randolph Hearst III recruited him and Hinckle to write columns for the *San Francisco Examiner*. While skewering Reagan and his followers, Thompson came to resemble an earlier *Examiner* columnist, Ambrose Bierce, who perfected the art of journalistic invective while collecting a check from Will Hearst's grandfather. Later, Hearst worked with Wenner on *Outside* magazine, and a group of *Examiner* writers launched Salon.com in 1995. That publication became an important outlet for David Horowitz's later work.

Shortly after *Ramparts* went under, another direct descendant hit the newsstands. Setting up shop over a McDonald's franchise in San Francisco, *Ramparts* alumni Adam Hochschild, Paul Jacobs, and Richard Parker hired Tamara Baltar as office manager and spent eighteen months developing their own magazine, *New Dimensions*. They tested their concept in December 1975 and were preparing to launch when they learned that a local newsletter had already copyrighted their title. They invested in a bottle of vodka and began brainstorming. Having rejected "Big Bill Haywood," they settled on "Mother Jones" after the Progressive Era icon, but they had no time to test the new title before publishing the first issue in February 1976.

Mother Jones inherited the *Ramparts* mailing list and hired Stermer to design its earliest covers. But from the outset, the new magazine assumed a postrevolutionary posture. The first cover story, by Bo Burlingham, explored the new directions taken by 1960s activists. "We find ourselves in the trough of the post-Vietnam wave," Burlingham wrote. "The issues which moved the Movement belong to another era, as we focus our attention on the pocketbook crises of the 1970s." The war was over, the student movement had crested, and *Mother Jones* writers had no plans to ride shotgun with the Panthers or chauffeur heiresses after their crime sprees. What was needed, the editors thought, was purposeful engagement and durability. Consistently touting environmental protection, women's rights, and later the Sandinistas in Nicaragua, *Mother Jones* understood itself as an extension of grassroots American progressivism, more La Follette than Marx.

If *Rolling Stone* inherited *Ramparts'* wildness, *Mother Jones* carried on its muckraking. It did so by turning its sights on what Hochschild later called "the great unelected power wielders of our time—multinational corporations." The magazine broke major stories on the Ford Pinto's exploding gas tank and the health risks posed by the Dalkon Shield IUD. But much like Ralph Nader's consumer advocacy, that kind of investigative journalism was swamped by a powerful shift to the right behind the leadership of Ronald Reagan. "We were, perhaps, a bit too naive about the remarkable staying power of the American political and corporate system," Hochschild admitted later.

In addition to monitoring corporate malfeasance, *Mother Jones* took its own business practices more seriously than *Ramparts* ever did. Its advisors included direct mail and circulation experts, and it developed good relations with suppliers and printers. Richard Parker came to respect his vendors, many of whom were small-town midwestern Republicans. "They were stand-up guys,"

Parker recalled. *Ramparts* had a long history of burning its printers, a practice he detested. As he reflected on that period, Parker recalled a *Scanlan's* piece he had written for which he was never paid. "When you call Hinckle," he directed me, "tell him he owes me $1,000."

Because Parker wanted *Mother Jones* to be self-sufficient, advertising revenue was crucial. He sold a three-month package to cigarette giant R.J. Reynolds, which could no longer advertise its product on television. Hochschild opposed the move on moral grounds, but Parker thought the magazine's solvency was a more important consideration. Besides, the median age of *Mother Jones* readers was thirty-one—old enough to understand the consequences of smoking. Parker prevailed, but when the ads ran, the editors also published investigative pieces about smoking and the tobacco industry, and R.J. Reynolds pulled out.

By that time, Hochschild and Parker had forced out Jacobs, reportedly for failing to give the magazine sufficient attention. Jacobs died in 1978, the same year Parker left the magazine. Parker later compared that departure to a divorce. "Adam stayed to raise the kids," he added. When advertising and subscription revenues couldn't cover the magazine's costs, *Mother Jones* looked increasingly to donations from Hochschild and others to survive.

Like *Ramparts*, *Mother Jones* provided an outlet for a new generation of writers and social critics, including Barbara Ehrenreich, Todd Gitlin, Molly Ivins, Eric Schlosser, and Bill McKibben. Also like its precursor, *Mother Jones* has served as a launching pad for other ventures. When Michael Moore was fired after a short stint as editor, he filed a lawsuit for unfair termination, settled with the magazine's insurance company, and reportedly put that money toward the production of *Roger and Me*, the first of several successful documentary films. In 1998, former *Mother Jones* publisher Don Hazen founded AlterNet, a popular online syndication service based in San Francisco.

Another magazine, the Berkeley-based *Tikkun*, grew less directly out of *Ramparts*. Launched in 1986 and edited by Michael

Lerner, it has focused on Israel and Palestine, Jewish culture, and the intersection of religion and politics in the United States. The work of activist Rabbi Abraham Heschel, a *Ramparts* contributor, has also been a focal point for *Tikkun* from its earliest days. Lerner's work received special attention when Hillary Clinton popularized "the politics of meaning," the title of his 1997 book.

Given this genealogy, *Ramparts* must be considered the origin of the Bay Area's current media presence in contemporary politics and current affairs. That presence now includes popular weblogs such as Daily Kos, which, like *Ramparts*, burst unexpectedly onto the national scene. Although the two operations aren't genetically linked, the historical parallels are striking. Like *Ramparts* during the Hink/Scheer years, Daily Kos achieved prominence by opposing a misbegotten war and targeting its supporters, including incumbent Democrats. Bolstered by netroots support, Ned Lamont's 2006 primary campaign against Senator Joe Lieberman in Connecticut was an uncanny replay of Scheer's congressional bid forty years earlier.

Important differences also separate the two outfits and their historical moments. Although Daily Kos stakes out its political positions aggressively, those positions are typically liberal, not radical. The blog's readership burgeoned during the Iraq War, but the community has never supported "the other side" in that conflict. Unlike *Ramparts*, Kos Media is run frugally and profitably, and while Hink/Scheer flourished by declining to defend any political ground, Democratic leaders court Daily Kos founder Markos Moulitsas Zuniga and other key bloggers for their fundraising and communicative power. But the blog's clout lies in its independence and willingness to challenge the political and media establishments on any issue. In this, it resembles its Bay Area forebear.

Ramparts' media influence hasn't been restricted to the Bay Area, of course. Its impact was international, and the British left in particular read it with interest. Alexander Cockburn, who wrote for the *New Left Review* and contributed to *Ramparts* in the early 1970s, recalled that he and his friends were especially struck by the magazine's look. "For the European left," Cockburn said, "the high production values were a source of envy and wonder." For that very reason, however, the magazine didn't seem sufficiently radical. "It didn't feel like the smoldering cinders of incipient revolution," Cockburn recalled. The magazine's tone, too, was too popular for their taste. " 'Rigor' was a very important word at the time, unfortunately," he said. And while Cockburn and his colleagues were well aware of *Ramparts'* CIA stories, they were more concerned with European and Third World issues. For these reasons, *Ramparts'* journalistic influence was mostly a domestic matter.

Much like Allen Ginsberg's effect on American poetry, *Ramparts* loosened the breath of American political journalism. With few exceptions, muckraking was virtually dormant when *Ramparts* ran its first whistleblower pieces. At the *Nation*, Carey McWilliams had converted a journal of opinion into a forum for investigative reporting, but even when its stories were potential blockbusters, they rarely received mainstream coverage. One anecdote illustrates that magazine's plight. When the *Nation* described preparations for the invasion of Cuba months before the Bay of Pigs, the *New York Times* picked up the story and thereby earned a private rebuke from President Kennedy. The newspaper's coverage, Kennedy complained to editor Turner Catledge, had amounted to a premature disclosure of security information. When Catledge noted that the story had already appeared in the *Nation*, Kennedy replied, "But it was not news until it appeared in the *Times*." *Ramparts* also needed the *New York Times* to convert its stories into news, but it did so more regularly—and more spectacularly—than its senior counterpart.

In addition to running controversial content, *Ramparts* helped create a new politics of style by fusing radicalism and a supercharged celebrity culture. Again, the *Nation* provides a counterpoint. Its old-school approach rarely made media stars of the figures it covered, and according to *Village Voice* writer Jack Newfield, a trip to the *Nation's* office in Greenwich Village during this time "was like walking into the 1930s." In contrast, *Ramparts* rep-resented what Todd Gitlin called "a New Left sensibility goes Pop" that helped produce "a glamour of rebellion, a rebellion of glamour." A decade earlier, radicals had been blacklisted, and a re-cently conscripted Elvis Presley made old-fashioned news by sim-ply reporting for duty. In the media world *Ramparts* helped create, John Lennon or Jane Fonda could make headlines with their polit-ical opinions and augment their celebrity by voicing them. Younger audiences regarded this process as the natural order of things.

Ramparts also affected American public life more broadly. It vigorously promoted civil rights, challenged the U.S. line in Viet-nam, and played a critical role in the black power movement by of-fering Eldridge Cleaver a professional home. Cleaver used that opportunity to establish political connections among the New Left and quickly became the Black Panther Party's most important recruit. Kathleen Cleaver credited Keating's efforts on Cleaver's behalf for that development. "Without that, the Black Panthers wouldn't be the Black Panthers we know today," Cleaver said. "I wouldn't have joined if it had been only Huey and Bobby. I know I wouldn't have crossed the country to do it." Historian Peniel E. Joseph concurred: "In less than two years, the Black Panthers would reflect Cleaver's vision as much as, if not more than, Newton's."

But *Ramparts* didn't just give Cleaver a job. The magazine also helped transform a handful of armed militants into internationally respected revolutionaries. In her recent study of media responses to the Black Panthers, Jane Rhodes charted the party's move from distributing hand-lettered mimeographed flyers to fielding con-tract offers from major publishers. The *Ramparts* editors, she con-cluded, were "a major force in this process." In addition to making Cleaver an international literary celebrity, the *Ramparts* staff con-ceived Bobby Seale's *Seize the Time*, which was excerpted in the magazine, reviewed in the *New York Times*, and widely regarded as the Panthers' definitive story. Seale's book supplemented *Soul on*

Ice, the magazine's extensive coverage of the Panthers, Scheer's collection of Cleaver's writings, and Marine's book on the Black Panthers to establish the party as a revolutionary icon. In producing that body of work and creating an audience for it, *Ramparts* left an indelible mark on the Black Power movement.

Ramparts also opened a new chapter in the history of the CIA. Before the Michigan State story, the CIA rarely received negative press, much less strict oversight. When *Ramparts* described its operations in Vietnam, the CIA responded by spying on the magazine's staff. When *Ramparts* ran the NSA story, it exposed two decades of secret CIA work. But when the CIA's illegal domestic surveillance was made public, the game was up. Author Tim Weiner described the CIA's operations after the Michigan State story.

> This exercise in extralegal snooping [of *Ramparts*] grew into a much larger effort: prying into the unruly world of the underground press. And that grew into Operation MHCHAOS, the biggest domestic spying caper in the CIA's history, aimed in essence against Vietnam War protesters. The exposure of MHCHAOS during and after Watergate remains a low point in the agency's history.

For the first time, Congress created intelligence oversight committees. The Senate version, headed by Frank Church, was especially effective at bringing a generation of CIA and FBI malfeasance to the surface. In an impressive understatement, CIA director George H. W. Bush wrote to President Ford, "This is a turbulent and troublesome period of the Agency."

The Church Committee hearings led to legislation, most notably the Foreign Intelligence Surveillance Act of 1978. That law created the first procedure for authorizing CIA domestic surveillance, which the agency had previously performed unchecked. Dick Cheney, at that time President Ford's chief of staff, watched the hearings and drew his own conclusions. A quarter century later, Vice President Cheney and his legal staff ignored FISA procedures for domestic wiretaps, which they considered an encroachment on executive power. As a result, the Bush administration's actions in the global war on terror resurrected constitutional issues that many had regarded as settled law.

When I decided to learn more about *Ramparts* and its history, President George W. Bush's second term was half over. The invasions of Iraq and Afghanistan had already claimed thousands of American lives and pulverized Iraqi society. Each year, the occupations of those countries cost American taxpayers roughly $150 billion over and above the $500 billion we were already spending on the military. In addition to weakening the economy and postponing urgent work on other national priorities, the occupation of Iraq helped the Democrats take control of the House and Senate in 2006. Nancy Pelosi, an ally of San Francisco Democrat Phil Burton, became the first female Speaker of the House.

Meanwhile, the corporate media was in bad odor. Four years earlier, most mainstream reporters and pundits had accepted one or more of the Bush administration's justifications for the Iraq invasion. In particular, they credited Secretary of State Colin Powell's speech before the UN Security Council in February 2003. But while listening to Secretary Powell at the time, I was struck by the rhetorical weakness of his presentation. He seemed to include marginal or unsupported scraps of information to make the case feel weighty, and he relied heavily on adjectives and adverbs, not nouns and verbs, to carry the argument. Anyone who has graded student papers would recognize both strategies. Nevertheless, the corporate media considered Powell's presentation an unqualified success.

Many mainstream journalists later admitted that they failed to challenge the administration's claims about Iraq, but most maintained that no one had called it correctly. What they meant, of course, was that nobody in their world got it right. The woods were full of well-informed critics pointing out the obvious weaknesses of the administration's case. When the corporate media marginalized these critics, they found new ways to air their views. The wonders of the Internet, developed an hour's drive south of Pelosi's district, provided fresh pastures for these critics and millions of online readers.

Meanwhile, my *Ramparts* research was shading my understanding of the Bush administration, the debates over Iraq, and the media coverage of both. A Mark Twain quip came frequently to mind: "History doesn't repeat itself, but it rhymes."

In 2007, I began conducting the interviews for this book. In Southern California, I met David Horowitz for lunch in Calabasas, an upscale suburb not far from Malibu. As we chatted on the patio of an Italian restaurant, Horowitz discreetly checked his Black-Berry for a message from his wife. He asked me if I was from "a political family." Not really, I replied, sensing that my tribe's cocktail-hour shouting matches didn't rise to that standard. He seemed to relax. I was exactly the sort of person he wanted to reach, he said. I gathered he meant that I was younger and not obviously in the grip of a theory.

Horowitz listed his deviations from right-wing orthodoxy, as if to establish ideological common ground with me. He didn't overlook what he regarded as his own culpability at *Ramparts*. "We celebrated a lot of bad people," he admitted. "But I wanted to make the revolution." His critique of the left was more pointed, especially on the fate of Betty Van Patter. He recalled that Adam Hochschild had tried to run Kate Coleman's story on the Black Panthers in *Mother Jones*, but that the younger staff members objected. "This is what I hate about the left," he said. "It's incapable of telling the truth. Especially about itself." Hochschild remembered that incident differently. He would have gladly run Kate Coleman's first piece, he said, which was never offered to *Mother Jones*. The magazine passed on another Coleman piece in the 1990s, but Hochschild was no longer an editor and never saw the manuscript. Horowitz eventually ran that piece in his own magazine.

In Horowitz's view, the New Left started with three

magazines—*Ramparts, Studies on the Left,* and *New Politics*—with a major assist from the *Village Voice.* But even within that group, Horowitz said, *Ramparts* distinguished itself. It was stylistically innovative, broke good stories, and brought the left into mainstream American journalism. His years at *Ramparts* were also a critical part of his professional development. "It wasn't all Marxese," he said of the magazine's content. "I was a Marxese writer. *Ramparts* taught lefties how to write, to do journalistic stuff." The magazine didn't reflect the counterculture's values, he said, but "it was an incubus, the camel's nose under the tent. It showed that you could sell radical ideas the way other ideas are sold. That's a very, very significant development." So significant, in fact, that Horowitz began to see its effects everywhere. "The *Ramparts* culture is now the literary culture," he maintained. He felt locked out of that community, noting that his books were rarely reviewed in major periodicals. As we parted, he commented in passing on his aggressive public persona. "I work on the knife's edge," he said. "I learned that on the left."

Robert Scheer was harder to catch. I tried two email addresses but received no reply. I also had two telephone numbers for him, courtesy of a mutual friend. Next to the home number, my friend wrote, "Never answers." Next to the cell number, he added, "Always grumpy." But in 2008, I attended the *Los Angeles Times* Festival of Books, which was originally developed in part by Scheer's wife, newspaper executive Narda Zacchino. Scheer was part of panel that filled a large lecture hall on the UCLA campus. In addition to offering his political analysis, he delighted the audience by noting that he was the same age as GOP presidential candidate John McCain, and that he had lost his keys three times that morning.

My best chance for face time with Scheer lay in staking out his book-signing tent. When I introduced myself, it was obvious that he had never seen my emails. He offered two more email addresses and asked whether I was willing to wait while he finished signing books. He bantered easily with his fans and seemed to be enjoying the moment. One older woman said he was becoming more handsome as he aged. He did look tan and fit, the result of a daily regimen of swimming and walking, and he had long ago quit drinking. He smiled and shook his head in bemusement. As the line shortened, he looked up at his minder, a younger woman who had escorted him to the lecture hall and book-signing tent. "You look very familiar," he said. "Have we ever lived together?" It was an expert blend of counterculture flirtation and a senior moment.

Scheer and I chatted for an hour before agreeing to visit again in the Bay Area. But weeks later, the second interview still wasn't scheduled. Scheer was promoting his new book, and his dance card was full. By chance, however, I met a fundraiser for the Center for Investigative Reporting who was staying at his house in south Berkeley. When I dropped her off there, she invited me in. Scheer and Narda were trying to schedule the rest of their day. We chatted about the book business—Narda also had a new book out—and the conversation turned to *Ramparts*. The women excused themselves, and Scheer and I proceeded to talk for seven straight hours. During that time, his son Christopher appeared, and Narda occasionally supplied Scheer with a snack or cup of tea. Otherwise it was an unscheduled and uninterrupted verbal marathon. At 9:30, the four of us repaired to a neighborhood restaurant for a tasty Sicilian meal and two more hours of talk.

My dominant impression of that day, aside from Scheer's prodigious verbal energy, was the open and spontaneous quality of his home life. With Narda, the mother of his other two grown sons, the former latchkey kid and communard had assembled a lively household. At several points in our gabfest, I offered him respite. No, he said, let's keep talking. He seemed to draw energy from the exchange and from the friends and family streaming in and out of the house. Later that week, I attended a dinner hosted by Scheer and Narda at Chez Panisse, the center of north Berkeley's Gourmet Ghetto. Its founder, Alice Waters, had been a volunteer in Scheer's 1966 campaign. Christopher Scheer and his eight-year-old son were there, as were Anne Weills and her husband, a former Red Family member. Anne and Narda greeted each other with a

hug; they had long since become close friends. Daniel Ellsberg attended, as did a dozen or so Bay Area media folk. I began to sense
the warmth and resilience of this community, which forty years
earlier had struck so many as dangerously un-American.

Warren Hinckle was even harder to pin down than Scheer.
Leaving a message on his answering machine was like stuffing a
note in a bottle, flinging it off the Golden Gate Bridge, and waiting patiently for a reply. Some Bay Area journalists laughed when I
mentioned my difficulty. Just go by Gino & Carlo in North Beach,
they said, or the Double Play in the Mission. One day I did stop by
Gino & Carlo, an old-school bar formerly frequented by Charles
McCabe, the legendary *Chronicle* columnist of my youth. Hinckle
wasn't there, but a college basketball betting pool posted on the
wall had Carol Doda's name penciled into one of the slots. When
my half-hearted stakeout failed, a writer at a San Francisco alternative weekly said he could have six North Beach bartenders call
him as soon as Hinckle walked into their workplaces. Then he
would call me.

In the end, that wasn't necessary. While attending Book Expo
America in Los Angeles, I strolled by a booth and happened to
mention my *Ramparts* project. I learned that Hinckle, who had a
new book out on Hunter Thompson, was holding court at a
nearby booth. I made a beeline there, but Hinckle had already departed for the convention center bar. "Maybe you could watch
him for a while," one of the marketing people said. When I arrived, Hinckle was easy to spot; he was the only person with an eye
patch. Resting comfortably against the bar, his entire body seemed
perfectly adapted to that posture. His drink, change, cell phone,
and other personal items were spread out before him.

When I introduced myself and mentioned a mutual friend, he
said that he wasn't especially interested in rehashing the *Ramparts*
story for posterity, but that he was happy to help a friend of a
friend. He also seemed open to a decent conversation if one was
forthcoming. We finished our drinks, and I offered to buy another
round. "Make it a double," he told the bartender, "since I know

you're busy." It was true; a labor strike had just gone into effect, and a lone bartender was covering the house.

For the next hour, Hinckle was helpful, engaging, and good company in every way. His barroom bonhomie seemed practiced but utterly authentic, not a set of manners so much as a way of life. After going over the *Ramparts* stories and legends, I asked why he thought the magazine had been so successful during his tenure. "Probably because the rest of the press was so shitty," he replied. He offered this judgment gently. The corporate media's shortcomings disturbed him no more than the Church's had fifty years earlier. But his answer was remarkable for another reason. In a rare departure from interviewing custom, he had declined an obvious opportunity to burnish his own legend, even a little bit. Could it be that Hinckle really didn't give a damn? As I considered this possibility, he excused himself, picked up his cell phone, and placed a call to celebrity editor Judith Regan.

AFTER *RAMPARTS*

Michael Ansara runs a call service business, raises funds for nonprofits, and serves on the planning committee for the Massachusetts Poetry Festival. In 1997, he pled guilty to conspiracy in a contribution swap scheme to support Teamster president Ron Carey's reelection bid.

Bob Avakian is chairman of the Revolutionary Communist Party, USA, which he has led since its inception in 1975. His memoir, *From Ike to Mao and Beyond: My Journey from Mainstream America to Revolutionary Communist*, was published in 2005.

Tamara Baltar worked at *Mother Jones*, the Center for Investigative Reporting, Kaiser Hospital, and the University of California, Berkeley. She lives in western Massachusetts.

Larry Bensky received a George Polk Award in 1987 for his Pacifica Radio coverage of the Iran-Contra hearings. He retired as host of KPFA's "Sunday Salon" in 2007 and continues to serve as a national affairs correspondent.

Bo Burlingham freelanced for *Esquire, Harper's, Boston Magazine*, and *Mother Jones* before joining *Inc.* as a senior editor in 1983. He served as executive editor for seven years and is now an editor-at-large.

Eldridge Cleaver endorsed Ronald Reagan for president, was baptized into the Mormon church, and ran unsuccessfully for office in California. In 1992, he was convicted of cocaine possession and burglary; two years later, he entered recovery for a crack addiction. He died of prostate cancer in 1998.

Peter Collier was the founding publisher of Encounter Books, which he ran until 2005. In 2006, he became vice president and chief operating officer of the David Horowitz Freedom Center.

Donald Duncan appeared in David Zeiger's documentary, *Sir! No Sir!* (2005), which focuses on the antiwar activities of those who served in Vietnam.

Reese Erlich is a freelance writer and broadcast journalist whose books include *Target Iraq*, co-authored with Norman Solomon.

Fred Gardner wrote *The Unlawful Concert* in 1970 and later served as public information officer for San Francisco district attorney Terence Hallinan.

Maxwell Geismar died in 1979. His memoir, *Reluctant Radical*, appeared in 2001.

Todd Gitlin is a professor of journalism and sociology at Columbia University and a contributing writer to *Mother Jones*. His many books include *The Sixties: Years of Hope, Days of Rage*.

Howard Gossage died of leukemia in 1969. *The Book of Gossage*, which includes essays and recollections of him, appeared in 1995.

John Howard Griffin wrote *The Church and the Black Man* (1969) and *A Time to Be Human* (1977). He died of diabetes in 1980.

Susan Griffin is a Berkeley-based poet, essayist, playwright, and screenwriter. She co-wrote the 1990 documentary, *Berkeley in the Sixties*.

Tom Hayden served in the California state legislature from 1982 to 2000 and is currently a visiting professor of sociology at Pitzer College. City Lights published an anthology of his work, *Writings for a Democratic Society*, in 2008.

Marianne Hinckle founded a San Francisco printing company in 1981.

Warren Hinckle edited Francis Ford Coppola's *City* magazine, wrote a column for the *San Francisco Examiner*, and received the H.L. Mencken

Award for his work there in 1988. He is editor and publisher of *Argonaut 360* in San Francisco.

Adam Hochschild is a lecturer at the Graduate School of Journalism at the University of California, Berkeley. His books include the award-winning *King Leopold's Ghost* (1998) and *Bury the Chains* (2005). He is a longtime board member of the Foundation for National Progress, which publishes *Mother Jones*.

David Horowitz is president of the David Horowitz Freedom Center, editor of FrontPageMag.com, and founder of Discover the Networks. His most recent book is *Indoctrination U: The Left's War Against Academic Freedom*.

Brit Hume left ABC News in 1996 to join the Fox News Channel, where he served as managing editor, host of "Special Report with Brit Hume," and a panelist on "Fox News Sunday."

Joe Ippolito has an accounting practice in San Jose.

Elliot Kanter is a librarian at the University of California, San Diego.

Edward Keating and **Helen Keating** divorced in 1971. She co-founded the Palo Alto Peace Center and was a realtor until her death in 1986. He wrote and consulted until his death in 2003.

Andrew Kopkind joined the staff of the *Nation* in 1982. Along with his partner, he co-hosted a radio program on gay issues in Boston. He died in 1994.

Paul Krassner published the *Realist* until 1974, relaunched it as a newsletter in 1985, and put out its final issue in 2001. His most recent book (*Who's to Say What's Obscene?*) is scheduled for publication by City Lights in July 2009.

Michael Lerner is the editor of *Tikkun* and the rabbi of Beyt Tikkun Synagogue in San Francisco. His books include *The Politics of Meaning* and *The Left Hand of God*.

Henry Luce sank into obscurity.

Gene Marine wrote for *Playboy*, *TV Guide*, and other publications. He lives in Berkeley.

Frederick Mitchell founded Scrimshaw Press with his wife Margaretta. He died in 1996.

Jessica Mitford wrote her second memoir, *A Fine Old Conflict*, in 1977. She died in 1996. Six years later, J. K. Rowling, author of the Harry Potter series, cited Mitford as her biggest literary influence.

David Obst lives in Santa Barbara. His memoir, *Too Good to Be Forgotten: Changing America in the '60s and '70s*, was published in 1998.

Richard Parker lectures on public policy at Harvard University and is a member of the *Nation*'s editorial board. His books include *John Kenneth Galbraith: His Life, His Politics, His Economics* (2005).

Martin Peretz is editor-in-chief of the *New Republic*.

James Ridgeway was the Washington correspondent for the *Village Voice* until 2006, when he joined the staff of *Mother Jones*.

Robert Scheer wrote a weekly column for the *Los Angeles Times* from 1993 to 2005. He writes an op-ed column for the *San Francisco Chronicle*, edits Truthdig.com, teaches communications at the University of Southern California, and appears on "Left, Right, & Center," a weekly public radio program.

Derek Shearer is a professor of diplomacy and world affairs at Occidental College in Los Angeles. He served as ambassador to Finland from 1994 to 1997.

Stanley Sheinbaum is the founding publisher of *New Perspectives Quarterly*. He was president of the Los Angeles Police Commission after the Rodney King incident and Los Angeles riots and served as a regent of the University of California from 1977 to 1989.

Dugald Stermer is a distinguished professor of illustration at the California College of the Arts in San Francisco. He serves on the San Francisco Arts Commission and the board of the Delancey Street Foundation.

Sol Stern is a senior fellow at the Manhattan Institute and contributing editor to *City Journal*.

Judy Stone was an editor and film critic for thirty years at the *San Francisco Chronicle*. Her third book, *Not Quite a Memoir: Of Films, Books, the World*, appeared in 2006.

Marc Stone retired from public relations work in 1977 and moved to Palo Alto, where he died in 1988.

Peter Stone is a staff writer for the *National Journal*. His first book, *Heist: Superlobbyist Jack Abramoff, His Republican Allies, and the Buying of Washington*, was published in 2006.

Hunter S. Thompson worked on book projects and contributed irregularly to *Rolling Stone* until 2004. The following year, he committed suicide at his Colorado home.

William Turner has written books on the FBI, the Robert Kennedy assassination, the secret war against Castro, and other topics. His memoir, *Rearview Mirror: Looking Back at the FBI, CIA, and Other Tails*, appeared in 2001 with a foreword by Oliver Stone.

Jann Wenner is the publisher of *Rolling Stone* and owner of *Men's Journal* and *Us Weekly*.

Maurice Zeitlin is a distinguished professor of sociology at UCLA.

ACKNOWLEDGMENTS

Many colleagues and friends deserve special recognition for helping this book finds its way. Gene Marine started me thinking about the project at an event sponsored by the California Studies Center at the University of California, Berkeley. After that talk, Jeff Lustig, Dick Walker, Chuck Wollenberg, and other members of the California Studies Association helped me off to a fair start. Patrick Dillon, Mark Dowie, Reese Erlich, Mark Ettlin, Elaine Katzenberger, and Derek Shearer offered encouragement and good advice at the outset. Will Lippincott helped me shape the proposal, and Ellen Adler, publisher of The New Press, supported the project early and often. Ellen, Adam Hochschild, and Chuck Wollenberg commented helpfully on the complete manuscript. I'm also grateful to Jyothi Natarajan and Maury Botton of The New Press for their expert project management.

Steve Keating and Bo Burlingham shared their *Ramparts* collections (and recollections) with me, thereby saving me many trips to the Cal library. Steve also passed along an unpublished manuscript by his mother about the magazine and her family. Likewise, Margaretta Mitchell provided excerpts from an unpublished manuscript by her late husband Fred. By doing so, they made unique contributions to our understanding of *Ramparts*. Robert Scheer lent me his early publications as well as David Horowitz's *Student*, Fred Gardner lent me his issues of the *Ramparts Wall Poster*, and Tamara Baltar passed along some rare publications from the *Ramparts* period. Guy Stilson and Gregory Stilson graciously permitted me to reproduce the magazine's images in this book. For other images, I'm indebted to Steve Keating, Warren Hinckle, Katie Edwards and the Jessica Mitford estate, Dugald Stermer and Bob Seidemann, Michael Millman, Margaretta Mitchell, Jann Wenner, Jeffrey Blankfort, David Hiser, and Tamara Baltar.

Huge kudos to Melissa Edeburn and Michael Sexton. Melissa commented helpfully on the manuscript and coordinated the photo research and permissions work. Michael prepared the photographs for production and took the author photograph.

I'm especially grateful to everyone who fielded my questions about the magazine's life and times. A list of interviewees can be found elsewhere in this book, but I was struck by the openness and generosity of those exchanges. Only three persons, citing various reasons, declined to speak with me. Originally trained as a medievalist, I'm still adjusting to the amazing notion of consulting my subjects directly.

I learned a great deal from those who wrote about *Ramparts* before me, especially Warren Hinckle, James Ridgeway, Adam Hochschild, Peter Collier, and David Horowitz. I also benefited from *Time* magazine's many pieces on *Ramparts* and its decision to make them freely available online.

My work at PoliPointPress, where I serve as editorial director, introduced me to several *Ramparts* alumni and fired my interest in the project. I thank my publisher, Scott Jordan, for his support both at work and on this project. By hiring me to lecture on California culture at San Francisco State University, Professor Saul Steier indirectly aided this project. I'm grateful to him and to my students for sharpening my sense of *Ramparts*' time and place.

Beth Tudor was a constant source of support and understanding as I undertook this project. For favors large and small, I also thank Rhoda Dunn, Rory Feehan, Stephanie M. Lee, Cherilyn Parsons, and Robert Shaffer.

My family has helped me in myriad ways. I'm especially grateful to my parents, Doug and Gladys Richardson; to my siblings, Rod Richardson, Scott Richardson, and Eve Wehler; and to my daughters, Ashley and Mary Richardson. The experience we've shared is what matters most.

NOTES

1. The Dawn's Early Light

11 "The next day, he called on": O'Brien 2005, 697.

12 "Mr. President": SLATE Newsletter, Mar. 17, 1962, http://archive
.slatearchives.org/gs/HASH26a3.dir/doc.xml?page=3.

14 "the top priority of the United States Government": Quoted in
Weiner 2007, 184.

14 "wanted to keep the commies from stacking the meeting": Jacobs
1995, 81–82.

14 "political baptism that transformed fear into determination": *Berkeley in the Sixties* (1990).

15 "couldn't hit a loud foul": Jacobs 1995, 97.

15 "I'm for Castro because Castro is for the black man": Horowitz
1997, 110.

15 "To provide security for his street rallies": Pearson 1994, 45.

16 "How stupid can you get?": Rarick 2005, 89.

17 "Would you rather be temporarily deranged": Quoted in Lee and
Shlain 1985, 37.

18 "Soon after that, the LSD was flowing freely": Lee and Shlain 1985,
119–20.

2. When Our Cause It Is Just

20 "Helen noted later": Helen Keating's quotes are from an unpublished manuscript provided by her son, Steve Keating. They appear
with his permission.

23 "There might even be a swinging nun there": Hinckle 1974, 37.

23 "When you unsnap your brassiere": "Voice from the Sewer," *Time*,
Aug. 17, 1959.

23 "In his memoir, Hinckle encapsulated that spirit": Hinckle 1974,
119.

24 "Whether a homicide would be reported at all": Hinckle 1974,
30–31.

25 "I came to accept the Church": Hinckle 1974, 2–5.

25 "If he were president": Hinckle 1974, 40.

27 "From now on, it's no more Mr. Nice Guy": Hinckle 1974, 50–51.

28 "I listened to John talk": Letter to Merton, Nov. 15, 1963. Quotes from Keating's correspondence appear with the permission of Steve Keating.

29 "According to Hinckle, the distribution list that day": Hinckle 1974, 66.

30 "You have done well to speak out": Letter to Keating, Apr. 7, 1964. Quotes from Merton's correspondence appear with the permission of the Merton Legacy Trust.

30 "We went into the press conference with that kind of story": Ridgeway 1969.

31 "Gossage was the Socrates of San Francisco": Hinckle 1974, 106.

32 "My own feeling on the new line": Letter to Keating, Nov. 25, 1964.

33 "Hinckle reminded him": Hinckle 1974, 89–92.

34 "But when the first message": Hinckle 1974, 183–84.

34 "Oh, dear": http://www.peterysussman.com/decca-reaction/response-to-the-nation-review/; Sussman 2006, xii–xiii.

34 "According to Hinckle, British Communists": Hinckle 1974, 104.

34 "Announcing that the magazine": Hinckle 1974, 96.

35 "They almost certainly knew": I'm grateful to Adam Hochschild, private communication, for this formulation.

36 "It's like a well": Fred Mitchell, unpublished manuscript. Quotes appear with the permission of Margaretta Mitchell.

37 "It's a dangerous thing": *University Daily Kansan*, May 12, 1967.

38 "When it was all over": Quoted in Hinckle 1974, 124.

39 "My image was surly": Hamill 1996.

40 "I was pretty intransigent about what I did": Hamill 1996.

3. The Perilous Fight

43 "One historian described it": Jacobs 2004, 154.

44 "Scheer lived with his mother": Scheer 1988, xiv–xvi.

46 "In the case of Cuba": Zeitlin and Scheer 1963, 9.

46 "The revolutionaries have tried": Zeitlin and Scheer 1963, 218.

48 "The idea that Communist or Viet Minh rule": Scheer 1965, 78.

48 "When he mentioned Scheer's intellect": Hinckle 1974, 103.

49 "Within an hour of their arrival": Mackenzie 1997, 16.

50 "Duncan soon joined the *Ramparts* staff": Quoted in Mackenzie 1997, 17.

51 "You mean you *really* stayed outside": Hinckle 1974, 101.

52 "They're going to cut me up": Hinckle 1974, 185.

54 "He raced through each 18-hour day": Hochschild 1975.

57 "It's a shame we can't nail this jackal": Turner 2001, xi.

57 "He told Turner that right-wing organizations": Turner 2001, 78–90.

58 "Paranoia is a little like dog shit": Hinckle 1974, 197.

61 "Describing his candidate's effect": Lang 1967, 49.

61 "If it was unreasonable to call out those discrepancies": Lang 1967, 42.

61 "He later noted that it led to": Lang 1967, 50.

61 "Breaking with Democratic tradition": Lang 1967, xii–xiii.

62 "Scheer called Cohelan": Quoted in Lang 1967, 175–79.

62 "They implied that this crew": Evans and Novak, *Washington Post*, Feb. 7, 1966.

63 "The typical primary voter": Quoted in Lang 1967, 178.

63 "Reflecting on the effort shortly after the primary": Lang 1967, 117.

64 "Instead of meeting with Chávez": Cannon 2003, 159.

65 "Unless Governor Brown can find some potent issues": McWilliams 1966.

66 "By this time, Hinckle had begun publishing a spinoff newspaper": *Sunday Ramparts,* Oct. 2, 1966.

66 "When staff writer Bill Turner asked Hinckle and Scheer": Turner 2001, 60.

4. When Freemen Shall Stand

68 "I fell in with a group of young blacks": Cleaver 2006, 40.

68 "When she visited him in San Quentin": Cleaver 2006, xiii.

69 "Bev is really the only person he can communicate with": Letter to Merton, Aug. 26, 1965.

70 "Inspired in part by Robert Williams's *Negroes with Guns*": Pearson 1994, 109–11.

71 "The first day Eldridge came in the office": Collier and Horowitz 1989, 261.

71 "Cleaver relished the San Francisco scene": Cleaver 2006, xiii.

72 "For years after that, Berkeley radicals": Rorabaugh 1989, 80.

72 "For Cleaver, it was love at first sight": Cleaver 2006, 101–05.

73 "Huey, cool it man": Seale 1970, 127.

73 "Who was that?": Cleaver 2006, 107–10.

73 "According to historian Peniel E. Joseph": Joseph 2006, 177.

76 "According to author Evan Thomas": Thomas 1995, 17.

76 "He would have preferred to fight the Cold War": Thomas 1995, 55.

77 "I was damned if I was going to let the CIA scoop me": Hinckle 1974, 179.

77 "On February 13, 1967, the day before the ads appeared": Wilford 2008, 242.

77 "A surprised Hinckle later wrote": Hinckle 1974, 180.

77 "We were appalled to learn today": Mackenzie 1997, 22.

78 "A few days ago a brief, cryptic report": Mackenzie 1997, 23.

79 "The NSA story, *Time* claimed": "The Silent Service," *Time*, Feb. 24, 1967.

80 "The next day, his task force offered its recommendations": Mackenzie 1997, 24.

80 "Eddie," he said, "you have a spot of blood on your pinafore": Thomas 1995, 330.

81 "According to investigative writer Angus Mackenzie": Mackenzie 1997, 18.

82 "Gossage told him more than once": Hinckle 1974, 181.

82 " 'In fact,' he explained": Hinckle 1974, 183.

82 "Hinckle heard about Keating's move while quaffing cocktails": See Hinckle 1974, 185–95, for his version of these events.

84 "It certainly can be said": *University Daily Kansan*, May 12, 1967.

5. The Havoc of War

87 "Even a half century after its creation": Navasky 2005, 174–76.

87 "His undergraduate experience at Yale": http://www.pbs.org/newshour/gergen/december97/buckley_12-24.html.

88 "In 1980 I found myself seated": *National Review*, Nov. 1, 2005.

88 "The sharp words began": *Firing Line* program taped June 26, 1967. Firing Line Collection, Hoover Institution Archives. Copyright Stanford University.

90 "In the context of the cold war": Erlich 2007, x.

91 "Collier later remarked that his son": Collier and Horowitz 1989, 260.

92 "He was rushed to the veterinarian's": Collier and Horowitz 1989, 260–61.

92 "That fucking monkey should be killed": Thompson 1997, 639.

94 "*Student* sold briskly in paperback": Horowitz 1997, 113.

94 "Like his father, a Communist Party member": Horowitz 1997, 157.

96 "To me, Nasser was Hitler": Ridgeway 1969.

96 "the most carefully selective and skewed history of the conflict": Quoted in *Time*, Dec. 1, 1967.

97 "One frequent visitor, Hochschild later discovered": Hochschild 1986, 93.

97 "I still half expect a smiling man to be there": Hochschild 1986, 13.

98 "Hochschild also admired the literary flair": Hochschild 1975.

98 "Assuming the phones are tapped": Hochschild 1986, 127.

98 "After a slew of CIA front operations were exposed": Hochschild 1986, 127–30.

99 "I was walking down the street in midtown Manhattan": Kuwasi Balagoon et al., *Look for Me in the Whirlwind: The Collective Autobiography of the New York 21* (Random House, 1971), 285. Quoted in Rhodes 2007, 309–10.

101 "When he came to *Ramparts* magazine, he stopped": Garrow 1986, 543 ff.

102 "In his study of King during this time": Garrow 1986, 553.

102 "I picked up an article entitled 'The Children of Vietnam' ": Garrow 1986, 564.

103 "More than anything the Haight": Lee and Shlain 1985, 141–42.

103 "thousands of people, man, all helplessly stoned": Lee and Shlain 1988, 144–45.

104 "Even before the summer of '67": *Rolling Stone*, July 12–26, 2007.

104 "There was madness in any direction, at any hour": Thompson 1971, 67–68.

104 " 'By the end of '66,' he wrote later": Thompson 1979, 155.

105 "Doing your thing doesn't have to include": Roszak 1969, 162.

105 "They quickly draw the conclusion that the status quo": Roszak 1969, 267.

106 "I met [Hinckle] through his magazine": *Paris Review* 156, 2000.

106 "Again . . . it was a good show over there": Thompson 1997, 641.

107 "The hippies grew up in my backyard": Hinckle 1974, 138.

107 "He was not consulted about the Hippie article": Hinckle 1974, 189.

109 "At Gleason's suggestion": Selvin 2004.

109 "What I found objectionable about the hippies": Hinckle 1974, 144–45.

111 "When they returned to their cars, Cleaver told Seale": Seale 1970, 163.

111 "And the next thing I heard was brothers jacking rounds": Seale 1970, 173.

112 "We want a pork chop, off the pig!": Rorabaugh 1989, 81.

6. Bombs Bursting in Air

116 "On this point, *Ramparts* joined": Gitlin 1987, 285.

117 "We blocked traffic and changed the streets": Gitlin 1987, 252.

118 "One of the most horrific experiences of my life": Hinckle 1974, 209.

118 "Hinckle described Jones as a": Hinckle 1974, 219.

118 "Keating suggested that they pluck out the pieces": Hinckle 1974, 225.

120 "I typed up a brief memorandum": Hinckle 1974, 199–200.

122 "Before we toss the Beatles a homosexual kiss": Cleaver 1968, 233.

123 "A blurb from the *Nation* review": Cleaver 1968, 14.

123 "Taken together, the accolades": Cleaver 1968, 4.

123 "In Panther David Hilliard's pithier formulation": Collier and Horowitz 1989, 266.

124 "Beyond dispute is the fact": See Marine 1969 for a detailed account.

125 "When he withdrew his hand": Cleaver 2006, 111.

126 " 'Little by little,' Todd Gitlin later wrote": Gitlin 1987, 271.

126 "If Che could be killed": Gitlin 1987, 249.

127 "This is extremely confidential": Hinckle 1974, 304.

129 "They suffered from that system's": Guevara 2006, 25–26.

130 "What I didn't realize": Horowitz 1997, 174–75.

130 "Soon after that, Hayden moved to Oakland": Hayden 1988, 337.

130 "The romance was a prime example": Horowitz 1997, 196.

7. The Battle's Confusion

132 "With King and Kennedy dead": Gitlin 1987, 310–11.

132 "According to Gitlin, thoughts of violence": Gitlin 1987, 316.

133 "In my recruiting trips across the country": Dellinger 1975, 122.

134 "It was notable, Isserman thought": Isserman 2008. My thanks to Robert Shaffer for bringing this article to my attention.

134 "For him, it was a matter of": Gitlin 1987, 318.

135 "In a letter to his editor at Ballantine Books": Thompson 2000, 15.

138 "According to Mailer, Rusk was": Mailer 1968, 162.

138 "I didn't want my story to dilute that impression": Gitlin 1987, 330.

139 "He later told *Time* magazine": "Manning the Ramparts," *Time*, Feb. 7, 1969.

139 "It was really a dirty technique in a sense": Ridgeway 1969.

140 "I went from a state of Cold Shock on Monday": Thompson 2003, 78–81.

140 "I went to the Democratic convention": Wilkie 1988; quoted in McKeen 2008, 125.

141 "We saw ourselves as both journalistic observers and participants": Stern 2008.

143 "For my assassination": Pearson 1994, 152.

144 "Still shaken by the Oakland shootout": Rorabaugh 1989, 83.

144 "After a polite ovation": Pearson 1994, 170.

145 "Reagan reportedly complied": Rorabaugh 1989, 84.

145 "I ran as an independent candidate": http://www.truthdig.com/report/item/20071105_robert_scheer_debates_ralph_nader/.

145 "His defense counsel, Charles Garry": Keating 1971, 253.

146 "But Newton wouldn't have testified to that effect": Keating 1971, 279–80.

146 "Everyone who is familiar with Cleaver's work": *New York Review of Books,* Nov. 21, 1968.

148 "When I speak up for convicts": Cleaver 2006, 183–91.

149 "Best wishes for *Ramparts*": Letter to Keating, Sept. 8, 1966.

150 "With $15,000 in cash": Cleaver 1978, 142–43.

150 "A cook, maid, and two security guards": Cleaver 2006, 195.

151 "I've said that war will come": Cleaver 2006, 145.

8. The War's Desolation

152 "To our innocent eyes": Gitlin 1987, 335.

152 "New Left radicalism was a vine": Gitlin 1987, 334.

153 "Moreover, Hinckle assured his colleagues": Hinckle 1974, 341.

154 "It is not every day": Hinckle 1974, 353.

154 "The whole staff could leave": "Manning the Ramparts," *Time*, Feb. 7, 1969.

155 "The way Gossage went about dying": Hinckle 1974, 354.

155 "Together, . . . he and Steadman would 'shit on *everything*' ": Thompson 2000, 319.

155 "I'm still trying to find the water fountains": Dean 1976, 34.

156 "The Montreal papers reported": Hinckle 1974, 363.

156 "The magazine was too important": Horowitz 1997, 180.

157 "The final straw": Horowitz 1997, 182. In his memoir, Horowitz evidently confused the two Sontag articles.

159 "Sealing thousands of students": Rorabaugh 1989, 156–64.

159 "If it takes a bloodbath": Cannon 2003, 295.

160 "According to Horowitz, Scheer responded": Horowitz 1997, 183.

161 "Decades later, Stermer called it": Hamill 1996.

161 "The note annoyed Horowitz": Horowitz 1997, 185.

162 "As Horowitz learned": Horowitz 1997, 187.

168 "According to Horowitz, Hayden said he needed": Horowitz 1997, 189.

169 "The cover photo showed the bank in flames": In fact, the caption misquoted the editorial, which read, "The action in Santa Barbara . . . might spark that awakening. If it does, the students who burned the Bank of America will have done more to save the environment than all the Survival Faires and 'Earth Day Teach-Ins' put together."

172 "By that time, Hayden wrote later": Hayden 1988, 421.

172 "In his memoir, Hayden described": Hayden 1988, 420.

172 "According to Horowitz, whose home life": Horowitz 1997, 196.

172 "One SNCC member also recalled": Pearson 1994, 209.

172 "In 1969 alone, 349 Panthers": Pearson 1994, 206.

173 "But within the Red Family": Hayden 1988, 421.

173 "There were no open minds": Hayden 1988, 421–25.

174 "In the aftermath of Senator George McGovern's loss": Roszak 1999, xxix.

176 "But when he arrived at the Panthers' headquarters": Horowitz 1997, 193–94.

9. Twilight's Last Gleaming

178 "Horowitz and Collier signed a contract": Horowitz 1997, 211–12.
180 " 'Listen,' Stone continued": Obst 1998, 218–23.
181 "Here is the only visible American": Kempton 1973.
184 "According to Horowitz, Stew Albert": Horowitz 1997, 237.
184 " 'Looking back,' Horowitz wrote later": Horowitz 1997, 236–77.
186 "Having Huey's ear": Horowitz 1997, 228–29.
188 "She went around sticking her nose into everything": Horowitz 1997, 244–47.
189 "The Panthers are good people": Horowitz 1997, 249–50.
189 "You guys have been cutting our balls off": Horowitz 1997, 259.
189 "According to Horowitz, 'Seale had been whipped' ": Horowitz, "Black Murder Inc.," 1999.
190 "He also concluded that the Panthers": Horowitz 1997, 361–62.
190 "Immediately Betty began asking Norma": Brown 1992, 364.
191 "White people always want me to tell them": Sherman 2000.
192 "Horowitz suspected that Party members had murdered her": Lee 2008, 57.
193 "Hey, Eldridge, what's all this shit": Avakian 2005, 322.

10. Full Glory Reflected

195 "We bore the readers the bad news": "Final Tribute: Time Runs Out for *New Times,*" *Time,* Nov. 27, 1978.
196 "Thompson yielded to no one": Thompson 2000, 42.
197 "The fun factor": Thompson interview, 1980; quoted in McKeen 2008, 247.
198 "We were, perhaps, a bit too naive": Hochschild 2001.
201 "Its old-school approach": Newfield 2003, 115.
202 "Historian Peniel E. Joseph concurred": Joseph 2006, 177–78.
202 " 'The *Ramparts* editors,' she concluded": Rhodes 2007, 234–35.
203 "When *Ramparts* ran the NSA story": Weiner 2007, 270.
203 "This exercise in extralegal snooping": Weiner 2007.
203 "This is a turbulent and troublesome period": Quoted in Weiner 2007, 348.

SOURCES

Interviews

Note: An asterisk indicates a telephone interview. All others were conducted in person.

*Michael Ansara, Sept. 12, 2008
*Tamara Baltar, Oct. 11, 2008
*Frank Bardacke, Sept. 17, 2008
Larry Bensky, Apr. 23, 2007
*Lowell Bergman, Aug. 28, 2008
*Arthur Blaustein, June 8, 2007
Bo Burlingham, June 28, 2008
*Kathleen Cleaver, Sept. 18, 2008
*Alexander Cockburn, Sept. 14, 2008
*Jeff Cohen, May 29, 2007
Peter Collier, Sept. 21, 2007
Anne Dowie, June 27, 2007
Mark Dowie, June 8, 2007
Reese Erlich, Aug. 15, 2007
Fred Gardner, Sept. 26, 2008
Todd Gitlin, June 1, 2007
Susan Griffin, Sept. 2, 2008
*Tom Hayden, May 12, 2007
*Marianne Hinckle, Mar. 31, 2008
Warren Hinckle, May 30, 2008
Christopher Hitchens, May 25, 2007
Adam Hochschild, June 19, 2007
David Horowitz, May 11, 2007
Joe Ippolito, Sept. 25, 2008
*Elliot Kanter, Sept. 22, 2008
Steve Keating, Oct. 7, 2007; Jan. 26, 2008
*Paul Krassner, Sept. 29, 2008
*Saul Landau, Sept. 3, 2008
Jeff Lustig, Jan. 3, 2008

Gene Marine, Sept. 19, 2007; Sept. 23, 2008
Denise McCarthy, Jan. 10, 2008
Margaretta Mitchell, Apr. 17, 2008
★David Obst, Sept. 21, 2007
★Richard Parker, July 29, 2007
★Eve Pell, Apr. 2, 2008
Danny Schechter, June 1, 2007
Robert Scheer, Apr. 26, 2008; June 22, 2008
★Robert Shaffer, July 1, 2008
Derek Shearer, May 10, 2007
Stanley Sheinbaum, May 11, 2007
Dugald Stermer, June 12, 2007
★Sol Stern, March 28, 2008
★Guy Stilson, Oct. 13, 2008
★Judy Stone, June 15, 2008
★Peter Stone, June 15, 2008
★William Turner, Mar. 31, 2008
★Anne Weills, Feb. 12, 2008
★Tuck Weills, Sept. 30, 2008
★David Weir, Aug. 21, 2008
★Jann Wenner, Sept. 19, 2008
★Jon Wiener, Sept. 11, 2008
★Hugh Wilford, Mar. 28, 2008
★Tom Williams, Dec. 11, 2007
Maurice Zeitlin, Apr. 24, 2008
★Daniel Zwerdling, Sept. 19, 2008

References

Avakian, Bob, *From Ike to Mao and Beyond: My Journey from Mainstream America to Revolutionary Communist* (Insight, 2005).
Brown, Elaine, *A Taste of Power: A Black Woman's Story* (Doubleday, 1992).
Cannon, Lou, *Governor Reagan: His Rise to Power* (Public Affairs, 2003).
Cleaver, Eldridge, *Target Zero: A Life in Writing* (Palgrave Macmillan, 2006).
———— *Soul on Fire* (Word Books, 1978).
———— *Eldridge Cleaver: Post-Prison Writings and Speeches,* ed. Robert Scheen (Random House, 1969).
———— *Soul on Ice* (Ramparts Books, 1968; rpt. Delta Books, 1992).

Coleman, Kate, "Souled Out: Eldridge Cleaver Admits He Ambushed Those Cops," *New West*, May 19, 1980; http://colemantruth.net/kate1.pdf.

Coleman, Kate, with Paul Avery, "The Party's Over: How Huey Newton Created a Street Gang at the Center of the Black Panther Party," *New Times*, July 10, 1978; http://colemantruth.net/kate8.pdf.

Collier, Peter, and David Horowitz, *Destructive Generation: Second Thoughts About the Sixties* (Summit Books, 1989).

Dean, John W., *Blind Ambition: The White House Years* (Simon and Schuster, 1976).

Dellinger, Dave, *More Power than We Know: The People's Movement Toward Democracy* (Doubleday, 1975).

Dooley, Thomas A., *Deliver Us from Evil* (Farrar, Straus and Giroux, 1956).

Erlich, Reese, *The Iran Agenda: The Real Story of U.S. Policy and the Middle East Crisis* (PoliPointPress, 2007).

Garrow, David J., *Bearing the Cross: Martin Luther King, Jr., and the Southern Christian Leadership Conference* (William Morrow, 1986).

Gitlin, Todd, *The Sixties: Years of Hope, Days of Rage* (Bantam, 1987; rev. 1993).

Guevara, Ernesto Che, *The Bolivian Diary: Authorized Edition* (Ocean Press, 2006).

Hamill, Pete, "Out There with Dugald Stermer," *San Francisco Focus,* December 1996.

Hayden, Tom, *Reunion: A Memoir* (Random House, 1988).

Hinckle, Warren, *If You Have a Lemon, Make Lemonade: An Essential Memoir of a Lunatic Decade* (Norton, 1974).

Hochschild, Adam, "The First 25 Years," *Mother Jones,* May/June 2001; http://www.motherjones.com/commentary/columns/2001/05/first25.html.

———— *Half the Way Home: A Memoir of Father and Son* (Viking, 1986).

———— "The Rise, Stumble and Fall of *Ramparts* Magazine," *feed/back,* Summer 1975.

Horowitz, David, "Who Killed Betty Van Patter?" Salon.com, Dec. 13, 1999; http://www.salon.com/news/col/horo/1999/12/13/betty/.

———— "Black Murder Inc.," FrontPageMag.com, December 13, 1999; http://frontpagemag.com/Articles/Read.aspx?GUID=47B4C182-0138-42C4-B812-0352B2A95AFC.

———— *Radical Son: A Generational Odyssey* (Free Press, 1997).

———— *Student* (Ballantine, 1962).

Isserman, Maurice, "Will the Left Ever Learn to Communicate Across Generations?" *Chronicle of Higher Education*, June 20, 2008; http://chronicle.com/free/v54/i41/41b00601.htm.

Jacobs, John, *A Rage for Justice: The Passion and Politics of Philip Burton* (University of California Press, 1995).

Jacobs, Seth, *America's Miracle Man in Vietnam: Ngo Dihn Diem, Religion, Race, and U.S. Intervention in Southeast Asia* (Duke University Press, 2004).

Joseph, Peniel E., *Waiting 'Til the Midnight Hour: A Narrative History of Black Power in America* (Henry Holt, 2006).

Keating, Edward, *Free Huey!* (Ramparts Press, 1971).

Kempton, Murray, "Revolutionary Suicide," *New York Times Book Review*, May 20, 1973.

Land, Jeff, *Active Radio: Pacifica's Brash Experiment* (University of Minnesota Press, 1999).

Lang, Serge, *The Scheer Campaign* (W.A. Benjamin, 1967).

Lee, Barbara, *Renegade for Peace and Justice: Congresswoman Barbara Lee Speaks for Me* (Rowman & Littlefield Publishers, 2008).

Lee, Martin A., and Bruce Shlain, *Acid Dreams: A Complete Social History of LSD: The CIA, the Sixties, and Beyond* (Grove Press, 1985).

Mailer, Norman, *Miami and the Siege of Chicago: An Informal History of the Republican and Democratic Conventions of 1968* (D. I. Fine, 1968; rpt. New York Review Books, 2008).

Mackenzie, Angus, *Secrets: The CIA's War at Home* (University of California Press, 1997).

Marine, Gene, *The Black Panthers* (New American Library, 1969).

McKeen, William, *Outlaw Journalist: The Life and Times of Hunter S. Thompson* (W.W. Norton, 2008).

McWilliams, Carey, "How to Succeed with the Backlash," *Nation*, Oct. 31, 1966.

Mitford, Jessica, *Decca: The Letters of Jessica Mitford,* ed. Peter Y. Sussman (Knopf, 2006).

Nasaw, David, *The Chief: The Life of William Randolph Hearst* (Houghton Mifflin, 2000).

Navasky, Victor, *A Matter of Opinion* (Farrar, Straus and Giroux, 2005).

Newfield, Jack, *Somebody's Gotta Tell It: A Journalist's Life on the Lines* (St. Martin's 2003).

Newton, Huey P., *Revolutionary Suicide* (Harcourt Brace Jovanovich, 1973).

O'Brien, Michael, *John F. Kennedy: A Biography* (St. Martin's, 2005).

Obst, David, *Too Good to Be Forgotten: Changing America in the '60s and '70s* (John Wiley & Sons, 1998).

Pearson, Hugh, *The Shadow of the Panther: Huey Newton and the Price of Black Power in America* (Addison–Wesley, 1994).

Rarick, Ethan, *California Rising: The Life and Times of Pat Brown* (University of California Press, 2005).

Rhodes, Jane, *Framing the Black Panthers: The Spectacular Rise of a Black Power Icon* (The New Press, 2007).

Ridgeway, James, "The *Ramparts* Story: . . . Um, Very Interesting," *New York Times Magazine,* April 20, 1969.

Rorabaugh, W. J., *Berkeley at War: The 1960s* (Oxford University Press, 1989).

Roszak, Theodore, *The Making of a Counter Culture: Reflections on the Technocratic Society and Its Youthful Opposition* (Anchor Books, 1969; rpt. University of California Press, 1999).

Scheer, Robert, *Thinking Tuna Fish, Talking Death: Essays on the Pornography of Power* (Farrar, Straus and Giroux, 1988).

——— *America After Nixon: The Age of the Multinationals* (McGraw–Hill, 1974).

——— *How the United States Got Involved in Vietnam* (Center for the Study of Democratic Institutions, 1965).

Seale, Bobby, *Seize the Time* (Random House, 1970).

Selvin, Joel, "Don't Let the Tweed Jackets, Trench Coat and Pipe Fool You—Ralph J. Gleason Was an Apostle of Jazz and Rock with Few Peers," *San Francisco Chronicle,* Dec. 23, 2004.

Sherman, Scott, "David Horowitz's Long March," *Nation,* July 3, 2000; http://www.thenation.com/doc/20000703/sherman/.

Stern, Sol, "From the Danube to Chicago," *City Journal,* Spring 2008; www.city-journal.org/2008/18_2_spring_1968.html.

——— "The Call of the Black Panthers," *New York Times Magazine,* Aug. 6, 1967.

Thomas, Evan, *The Very Best Men: Four Who Dared: The Early Years of the CIA* (Simon & Schuster, 1995).

Thompson, Hunter S., *Kingdom of Fear: Loathsome Secrets of a Star-Crossed Child in the Final Days of the American Century* (Simon & Schuster, 2003).

———— *Fear and Loathing in America: The Brutal Odyssey of an Outlaw Journalist, 1968–76* (Simon and Schuster, 2000).

———— *The Proud Highway: Saga of a Desperate Southern Gentleman,* ed. Douglas Brinkley (Villard/Random House, 1997).

———— *The Great Shark Hunt* (Summit Books, 1979).

———— *Fear and Loathing in Las Vegas: A Savage Journey to the Heart of the American Dream* (Random House, 1971).

Turner, William, *Rearview Mirror: Looking Back at the FBI, CIA, and other Tails* (Penmarin, 2001).

Weiner, Tim, *Legacy of Ashes: The History of the CIA* (Doubleday, 2007).

———— "Operation What?" *New York Times,* Nov. 2, 1997; http://www.nytimes.com/books/97/11/02/reviews/971102.02weinert.html?_r=1.

Wilford, Hugh, *The Mighty Wurlitzer: How the CIA Played America* (Harvard University Press, 2008).

Wilkie, Curtis, "The Gonzo History," *Image,* May 29, 1988.

Wolfe, Tom, *Radical Chic & Mau-Mauing the Flak Catchers* (Farrar, Straus and Giroux, 1970).

———— *The Electric Kool-Aid Acid Test* (Farrar, Straus and Giroux, 1968).

Zeitlin, Maurice, and Robert Scheer, *Cuba: Tragedy in Our Hemisphere* (Grove Press, 1963).

INDEX